Richard Eddy

Universalism in Gloucester

An historical discourse on the one hundredth anniversary of the first sermon of

Rev. John Murray

Richard Eddy

Universalism in Gloucester
An historical discourse on the one hundredth anniversary of the first sermon of Rev. John Murray

ISBN/EAN: 9783337113322

Printed in Europe, USA, Canada, Australia, Japan

Cover: Foto ©Lupo / pixelio.de

More available books at **www.hansebooks.com**

UNIVERSALISM

—IN—

GLOUCESTER, MASS.

AN HISTORICAL DISCOURSE
—ON THE—
One Hundredth Anniversary of the First Sermon of
Rev. John Murray in that Town. Delivered
in the Independent Christian Church,
November 3, 1874,

BY

RICHARD EDDY, D.D., then Pastor of the Church.

WITH ADDRESSES ON THE SAME OCCASION,
NOTES AND APPENDIX.

ILLUSTRATED.

GLOUCESTER, MASS.
PROCTER BROTHERS.
1892.

COPYRIGHTED, 1892, BY RICHARD EDDY, D. D.

STANDARD
PRINTING
COMPANY
PROVIDENCE, R. I.

Introduction.

Delay in the publication of this volume has given opportunity to discover and utilize several important documents which were not available at the time of delivering the Historical Discourse. Except in one particular, explained in foot note 46, the text of the Discourse is unchanged. Added matter is thrown into the Appendix. The author has aimed at accuracy in the presentation of facts, and believes that he has succeeded in giving reliable statements. In what might possibly be disputed, care has been taken to give the original documents or other acknowledged authority.

The illustrations, done in the best Albertype style, add greatly to the value of the book. They are all made from authentic originals, the portrait of Rev. John Murray being from an oil painting made in Portsmouth, N. H., in 1784, the only portrait for which Mr. Murray ever gave a sitting. The original painting is now owned by the Tufts Divinity School, Tufts College. All references in the Discourse to the Life of Murray, are to the edition of 1869.

R. E.

Providence, R. I., May, 1892.

Illustrations.

	PAGE.
Portrait of Rev. John Murray	Frontispiece.
The First Meeting House	9
Portrait of Rev. Thomas Jones	25
The Present Church Edifice	41
Portrait of Rev. Daniel D. Smith	57
Portrait of Rev. Frederic F. Thayer	73
Portrait of Rev. Henry B. Soule	89
Portrait of Rev. Amory D. Mayo	105
Portrait of Rev. W. R. G. Mellen	121
Portrait of Rev. George W. Skinner	137
Portrait of Elmer H. Capen, D. D	153
Portrait of Richard Eddy, D. D	169
Portrait of Rev. Costello Weston	185
Portrait of Rev. William H. Rider	201

CONTENTS.

	PAGE.
I.	
PROGRAMME OF EXERCISES	vi
II.	
HISTORICAL DISCOURSE	9
III.	
EVENING SERVICES: Addresses of Rev. Thomas G. Farnsworth, Rev. Frederic F. Thayer, Rev. Amory D. Mayo, Rev. Joseph P. Atkinson, Benjamin H. Corliss, Esq., Rev. James U. Mitchell, Letters of Rev. W. R. G. Mellen, Rev. E. H. Capen	79

IV.
APPENDIX.

A.	Letter to Rev. Eli Forbes	105
B.	Mr. Murray before the Committee of Safety	107
C.	Action of the First Parish Church	111
D.	Ministerial Helpers	118
E.	The Relly Hymn Book	129
F.	Suit against the First Parish	130
G.	An Appeal to the Impartial Public	133
H.	Answer to "An Appeal"	157
I.	Mr. Murray's Broadside	177
J.	The Charter of Compact	185
K.	Mrs. Judith Murray	189
L.	Mr. Murray's Ordination, Christmas, 1788	191
M.	Agreement to be taxed for support of Mr. Murray	194
N.	The Request from Boston	195
O.	The Act of Incorporation	198
P.	Mr. Murray's Commendation of Mr. Jones	200
Q.	Subscribers to the New Meeting House	202
R.	Laying of the Corner Stone	203
S.	The New Hymn Book	204
T.	Dedication of Children	205
U.	The Church Organization	208
V.	Funeral of Rev. John Murray	215
W.	The Sunday School	221
X.	The Semi-Centennial	222
Y.	Titles of the Organization and Officers of the Church and Society	225
Z.	Addenda	232

V.
INDEX 235

1774   *November Third,*   *1874.*

Centennial Anniversary

OF THE

FIRST PREACHING OF REV. JOHN MURRAY

IN GLOUCESTER.

VOLUNTARY.

INVOCATION AND SCRIPTURE READING.

Rev. WILLIAM HOOPER, of Annisquam.

HYMN.

Written for the occasion by JAMES DAVIS, Esq.

> Dear Father! while we here attend
> This glad memorial of Thy love,
> Thy gracious benediction lend,
> And breathe Thy spirit from above.
>
> We thank Thee for the cheering voice
> That here, a century ago,
> Made heavy laden souls rejoice,
> Thy blessed Gospel truths to know.
>
> How sweet the words of hope it spoke
> Of life through all-abounding grace!
> How broad and strong the faith it woke,
> That ripened into deeds apace!

The harvest sown we gladly reap,
    While in this joyful faith we rest,
And here our festal Sabbaths keep,
    With peace and Christian freedom blest.

May this glad faith — this sacred peace
    To all the sons of men be given,
That wrath, and doubt, and strife may cease,
    And perfect love make perfect heaven.

PRAYER.

Rev. THOMAS G. FARNSWORTH, of Waltham.

HYMN.

Written for the occasion by HENRY C. L. HASKELL.

These same gray headlands faced the tide,
    'Neath later Autumn's glow, —
On these same sands the billows died,
    An hundred years ago, —

When Murray trod this rocky shore
    To point the way above,
And tell the glorious story o'er,
    Of God's far-reaching love.

From seeds of truth by Murray sown,
    'Mid mingled hopes and fears,
A strong and sturdy vine has grown,
    Through all this hundred years.

And we, to-day, our voices raise
    To Heaven's eternal throne, —
Our heartfelt words of prayer and praise
    For many mercies shown.

Lord, keep us in the grand old faith,
    Where'er our paths may be, —
The faith that leads, in life or death,
    To glory and to Thee.

HISTORICAL DISCOURSE.

By Rev. Richard Eddy, Pastor.

HYMN.

Written for the occasion by Miss Sarah G. Duley.

> The years so swiftly gliding,
>   A century's sum have told,
> Since, bringing precious tidings,
>   The shepherd sought this fold;
> Since to the people dwelling
>   Upon this storm-beat shore,
> He came, the good news telling
>   That fear's long night was o'er.
>
> They heard with joy the story
>   Of God's abounding love,
> With glad eyes saw the glory
>   Irradiate from above.
> How bright became death's portal,
>   Robbed of its dreadful fear,
> A path to life immortal,
>   A loving father near.
>
> In childlike faith abiding,
>   He wrought his work below, —
> Dear Lord, in Thee confiding,
>   May we such fervor know.
> O, sainted Murray, resting
>   In heavenly realms, to-day,
> May we, thy worth attesting,
>   Walk steadfast in the way.

BENEDICTION.

HISTORICAL DISCOURSE.

Our fathers trusted in Thee. — PSALMS xxii: 4.
The Lord our God be with us, as He was with our fathers. — 1 KINGS viii: 57.

THE father of history declares at the commencement of his immortal work, that he was prompted to write by his desire to preserve past events from oblivion, and to perpetuate the just renown which belonged to men of departed generations.[1] Not unmindful of these motives, we confess that still higher ones prompt and animate us in meeting here to-day to commemorate the scenes and actors of a former century, and to trace the progress of their work to the present time. Like the Grecian sage, we, too, wish to rescue the past from being forgotten, and to give honor to whom honor is due; but most of all, we would make the occasion one of fresh contemplation of those principles which our fathers cherished with a love stronger than death, that we may bring our tribute of praise to the altar of God, who enabled them to establish here the religion for which they suffered, and the principles of liberty and right in the enjoyment of the dictates of conscience, which they championed for all the religious denominations in the Commonwealth.

[1] Herodotus, Clio, § 1.

A hundred years have now passed since there came to this town, then having a scattered population of little more than forty-five hundred souls, a man who for four years had been busily engaged in preaching in the southern, middle and eastern colonies of the country. He had not placed himself in open, at least not in violent opposition to the then prevalent theological opinions, but wherever he spoke it was soon evident that he entertained more enlarged views of the divine purpose than the people had been accustomed to hear. Still he made no attempt to proselyte, and the thought of organizing a society or church in opposition to the sects then established had probably never entered his mind. Indeed, in many places where he preached, the legitimate inferences from his arguments were not clearly seen either by the preachers or people who flocked to hear him; and it was felt on several occasions, that, like Whitefield, who had immediately preceded him, and to whom in many respects he bore a close resemblance, he differed from other preachers chiefly in the animation of his style, and the fresh and copious power of his illustrations. Nearly all the churches of the land were open to him, and although he seldom visited a place without being involved in disputes with heresy-hunters, or passing through the ordeal of sharp questioning by the resident clergy, it was his policy not to avow himself a believer in universal salvation, in his public discourses, but by dwelling with marked emphasis on the doctrines of the "union of humanity with Christ, freedom from the claims of the law, and the finished salvation which we have in Christ alone"—points of doctrine with which high Calvinists would heartily sympathize — leave his hearers to discover the results to which such doctrines must logically carry them.

In his autobiography Mr. Murray frankly states that this was his early method, and he justified himself by supposing that "the *gradual* dawn of light would eventually prove more beneficial to mankind than the *sudden burst* of meridian day. Thus," he says, "I was contented with proclaiming the truth as it is in Jesus, in scripture language only, leaving to my hearers, deductions, comments and applications."[2] The consequences of this course were disastrous. Many who had gladly heard him became shocked when they learned what his real views were, and declared that he had imposed upon them, and that nothing was too bad to be expected from a man who had practiced such concealments. Some went so far as to say that he had made explicit denial of his belief in the salvation of all men; but it is evident that this charge arose from misapprehension.[3] I think it sufficient for us to say that although he suffered the natural consequences of such a course, he is entitled to the credit of being honest in his convictions that he was not only doing no wrong, but was rendering service to the cause of truth by this indirect way of presenting it.

The event which we celebrate to-day marks an important change in his views of duty in this respect. There was a condition of things in Gloucester which did not exist elsewhere. Universalism was already

[2] Life of Murray, p. 288.

[3] See Life of Murray, pp. 400, 401, where Mrs. Murray shows the distinction which her husband made between Redemption and Salvation, the former being regarded by him as universal, *i. e.* already accomplished for all, and not the latter.

here, some of the most prominent citizens of the town having come to a knowledge and belief of it. As early as the year in which Murray landed in America, if not a twelvemonth or more before, an Englishman by the name of Gregory had visited this place, bringing with him the writings of Rev. James Relly, whose sentiments Murray had espoused before leaving England. This book, read by various members of the Sargent family, and finally loaned to others, arrested attention and became the topic of discussion in domestic and social circles. Its doctrines at first excited wonder, soon were received with great earnestness as the truth, and those who thus received them only needed the impulse of their more public proclamation to bring them forward as a distinct body of Christians.

The occasion for this soon presented itself in an attack made upon Mr. Murray in the public papers of Boston, in which, on the occasion of his second visit to that city in September, 1774, he was accused by Rev. Mr. Croswell of being "a preacher of Relly's doctrine." The admirers of Relly in Gloucester, seeing this accusation, at once sent Mr. Winthrop Sargent as their messenger to Boston,[4] to solicit his presence here.

On the 3d of November, 1774, he came, and remained here nine days. The Deacons and Elders of the First Parish waited upon him, conducted him to the house of their minister, Mr. Chandler, who was then ill, who consented to his occupying the pulpit that evening, and on several subsequent occasions. "Every day and every evening," Mr. Murray says, "was appropriated to the expounding of the Scrip-

[4] October 31st.

tures, in the spacious and well-filled parlor of my new and highly respectable friend; and I had reason to believe that God most graciously crowned my labors in this place, by giving to some brighter views, and inducing others to search the Scriptures for themselves. Every morning commenced, and every day closed, with prayer, and with glad hearts we delighted to hymn the praises of a redeeming God."[5]

On the 14th of December, Mr. Murray again visited Gloucester, and finding that the truth had taken deep root in the hearts of many, concluded to make this his permanent home, although intending to itinerate more or less through a large portion of the country. "Here," he writes in his journal, "my God grants me rest from my toils; here I have a taste of heaven. The new song is sung here, and WORTHY IS THE LAMB constantly dwells upon their tongues."[6]

The Meeting House of the First Parish was open for him again, but only for a brief period, the doors being closed against him sometime during the following month. But meanwhile believers multiplied; a little congregation was collected, who met frequently during the week at each other's houses, and assembled on Sundays in the large parlor of the Sargent mansion, then standing in the rear of the building now owned and occupied by the First National Bank, on the corner of Spring and Duncan streets. Here, with a few interruptions occasioned by his visits to other places, Mr. Murray preached until the following May, when he was urged by Colonels Greene, Varnum and Hitchcock to take the chaplaincy of the

[5] Life of Murray, p. 298.
[6] Life of Murray, p. 312.

Rhode Island Brigade, then in camp at Jamaica Plains, many of the officers of which were his personal friends, as well as in hearty sympathy with his religious sentiments. Intensely patriotic in his feelings towards his adopted country, he accepted the position, and at once entered upon his duties. When Washington, a few weeks later, took command of the Army, the chaplains united in petitioning him for Mr. Murray's removal. Their answer came in the General Orders of September 17th, 1775, as follows:

"The Rev. Mr. John Murray is appointed Chaplain to the Rhode Island Regiments, and is to be respected as such."[7]

His stay in the army, however, was of short duration; his health failed, and severe sickness having brought him low, he was sent back to Gloucester after about eight months' service. Immediately on his recovery, he saw, with great distress, the poverty to which many of the citizens of the town were reduced by the destruction of their ordinary business; and at once made a journey to his friends in Boston, and to the officers of the army, soliciting funds for the relief of the needy. Great success attended his effort, as the following item on the Town Records shows:

"April 3, 1776. *Voted Unanimously*, That this town returns their sincere thanks to the compassionate donors of a sum of money sent by the hands of Mr. John Murray for the relief of our poor, which he lays out in provisions and distributes among them according to their necessities."

Up to this time, although the Meeting House had

[7] Copied from the original Order Book in the State Department at Washington.

been closed against him, and his friends had held religious services in their own houses, as opportunity offered, many of them were still members of the First Parish Church. Mr. Chandler, the former minister, having died, the Church and Parish had invited Rev. Eli Forbes to the pastorate; and on the day after this vote of the town, twenty-four members of the Parish, ten of whom were interested in Mr. Murray's meetings, addressed Mr. Forbes a letter, advising him not to accept the invitation; urging the bad state of the times and the impoverishment of the people as their chief motive in giving this advice, at the same time intimating that his acceptance would destroy the harmony hitherto existing in the parish.[8] It has been said that this was disingenuous on the part of Mr. Murray's friends, since they were then preparing to carry on meetings of their own. But I think that the charge was not well founded. That the town was sadly impoverished the solicitation and acceptance of aid from abroad shows, and is also evident from the agreement with Mr. Forbes, that if, as seemed probable in the then exposed situation of the town, the parish should be broken up, there should be no obligation to pay him any salary.[9] The support of Mr. Murray's meetings, on the other hand, involved little or no expense. The congregation assembled in private residences, and the preacher, having no family dependent on him, refused any compensation. His wants were few, and there was no pecuniary burden imposed in establishing his meetings.

On the settlement of Mr. Forbes, the following

[8] See Appendix A.
[9] History of the Town of Gloucester. By John J. Babson, p. 404.

June, Mr. Murray's friends quietly absented themselves from the Meeting House. And then commenced a long and desperate persecution. A mob collected around the house of Mr. Sargent, determined to ride Mr. Murray out of town; but being dissuaded from this, warned him to leave at once, and threatened violence if he neglected to go. Under the sanction of an old Provincial law, an attempt was made to expel him as a vagrant; but this was frustrated by a deed of gift from one of his friends, which constituted him a freeholder. Letters from abroad were solicited against him, with the view of making him an object both of political and of religious hatred. In these he was accused of being a spy in the employ of the British ministry, of being closeted with tories wherever he went, of having been inimical to the interests of the country, and grossly immoral while in the army, and of being in every respect a bad and dangerous man. Rev. Dr. Stiles wrote a long letter, in which, after misrepresenting Mr. Murray's views of religious doctrines and ceremonies, misstating the facts as to his life before leaving England, and the circumstances of his beginning to preach in America, and insinuating that he was an enemy to the Patriot cause, he avowed his belief that he was "A Romanist in disguise, endeavoring to excite confusion in our churches."[10] Rev. John Cleveland, Pastor of the Second Parish in Ipswich, (now Essex), also entered the lists against Mr. Murray, by publishing a pamphlet of 44 pages, the long title of which commences: "An Attempt to

---

[10] Answer to An Appeal, p. 11.

nip in the bud the unscriptural Doctrine of Universal Salvation." [11]

Of course these attacks, and the insinuations and suspicions of which they were so fruitful, not only increased the rage of Mr. Murray's religious foes, but also roused the wrath of the patriots; and so curses, anathemas, and sometimes stones, followed his steps as he walked our streets. But fearless and undisturbed, he stood at his post, converts multiplied around him, and the affection and zeal of his friends increased as the opposition grew more furious.

On the 27th of the following February he was summoned from a bed of sickness to appear before the Committee of Safety, all the members of which, then present, were his avowed enemies; and was there subjected to a most insulting questioning as to his business here, and his right to remain in the

---

[11] The full title page is: "An Attempt to nip in the Bud the unscriptural Doctrine of Universal Salvation, and some other dangerous Errors connected with it; which a certain Stranger, who calls himself John Murray, has, of late, been endeavoring to spread in the First Parish of Gloucester, to draw away Disciples after him. In a Letter addressed to one of those that are drawn away; if possible to reclaim him and the others. To this End and in Hopes that it may by the Blessing of God serve also to confirm all in some of the most important Doctrines of God's Word, it is made public, in Answer to the Desire of a very respectable Number of Persons of Reputation and Influence in said Parish. To which is subjoined the Dying Testimony for the Truth, and against Error, of their worthy Minister, the Reverend Mr. Samuel Chandler, lately deceased. By John Cleaveland, A. M., Pastor of the Second Church in Ipswich. 2 Cor xi. 3. But I fear lest by any Means, as the Serpent beguiled EVE through his subtilty, so your Minds should be corrupted from the Simplicity that is in CHRIST. Salem MDCCLXXVI."

town.[12] Here he bore himself most manfully, answered all that was charged, and all that was insinuated against him, and declared his firm determination not to be intimidated by any false accusations, nor by threats of violence. The Committee decided that he should leave town, and served a notice on him that he must "depart in five days from the first of March." As he paid no heed to their warning, the matter was brought before a meeting of the town, March 10th, in the records of which is the following minute:

"The question was put whether the town approve of the conduct of the late Committee in desiring Mr. John Murray to depart this town in five days from the 1st of March, 1777. It was voted in the affirmative, by 54 votes for it and only 8 against it."

But he took no notice of this, nor does there seem to have been any further attempt to compel him to leave the place. The following, which came to the notice of the citizens not long after, was sufficient to dispose of the charges against his character and patriotism, and to leave further opposition wholly to his religious enemies:

"CAMP AT MIDDLE-BROOK, May 27th, 1777.

"These may certify, that Mr. John Murray was appointed Chaplain to Col. Varnum's Regiment, by his Excellency General Washington, during the army's lying before Boston. And during his officiating in that capacity his conduct was regulated by the laws of virtue and propriety; his actions were such as to make him respected as an honest man and a good citizen. He lived beloved, and left the army esteemed by all his connections and patrons.

NATHANIEL GREENE, Major General."

[12] See Appendix B.

In September, 1778, Epes Sargent, Winthrop Sargent, Ebenezer Parsons, David Pearce, Catharine Sargent, Judith Sargent, Rebecca Parsons, Hannah Tucker, Rebecca Smith, Judith Stevens, Anne Babson, Nancy Saunders, Lydia Prentiss, Jemima Cook and Jemima Parsons, who had become interested in the movement to establish Universalism, were publicly suspended from the First Parish Church, "until their return from their error in sentiment and practice."[13] Thus cut off from former associates, and formally separated from other Christian believers, our fathers and mothers turned their attention to the creation of an organization for themselves; and on the first of January, 1779, bound themselves together as an "Independent Church of Christ," covenanting and agreeing to walk together in Christian love, and "resolved by God's grace, whether blessed with the public preaching of the Word or not, to meet together to supplicate the divine favour, to praise our redeeming God, to hear his most holy Word, and freely to communicate whatever God shall please to manifest to us for our mutual edification." They also agreed to set apart and receive as their minister, which they considered as being the same as ordaining him, their "friend and Christian brother, John Murray, from a full conviction that the same God that sent the first preachers of Jesus Christ, sent him; and that the same gospel they preached, we have from time received from him." These "Articles of Association" were signed by John Murray, and by all the members of the congregation, — in all, sixty-one persons, — thirty-one men and thirty women.[14]

[13] See Appendix C.
[14] See Appendix G.

What portion of time Mr. Murray gave to the Church, I have no means of knowing, but it is certain that he was often called away to preach in distant places, besides making frequent visits to Boston, Providence, Norwich, and other comparatively near localities. During his absences at this time and for a few succeeding years, other ministers of our faith visited Gloucester. Among these were Moses and Elhanan Winchester, the latter a convert from the Baptists in 1781, a man of learning and of untiring zeal; John Tyler, an Episcopal clergyman, of Norwich, Conn.; Matthew Wright, an eloquent and learned Moravian; Adams Streeter, of Rhode Island, and Noah Parker, of Portsmouth, N. H. Shippie Townsend, a mechanic, of Boston, a writer of several pamphlets in defence of Universalism and also an acceptable lay preacher, was frequently here, and helped on the good work.[15] Thus the number of believers steadily increased, and our fathers soon set about the erection of a House of Worship, which was dedicated on Christmas day, 1780. It was a frame building, thirty-two and a half by forty-eight feet, and stood on the westerly corner of Spring and Water streets, the end of the building facing Spring street, and the entrance by two doors on the western side. Fourteen persons associated themselves together for the purchase of the land and defraying the expenses of building, holding ownership of the pews in proportion to the sums invested by them. These pews, thirty in number, were large square pews, the prevailing, if not the only style of that day, and were assigned as follows: To Winthrop Sargent, thirteen; David Plumer, three; Isaac Elwell,

[15] See Appendix D.

two; David Pearce, two; Epes Sargent, William Pearce, William Hales, Samuel Sayward, Joseph Foster, Abraham Sawyer, John Somes, Bradbury Sanders, William Murphy, Philemon Haskell, one each. The cost of the building I have not been able to ascertain.

The records make mention of an organ loft in the building, which I suppose to have been erected for tho accommodation of the instrument that stands on the floor before you, and which was captured from an English merchant-ship, by Capt. John Somes, a successful Privateer during the Revolution, and was by him given or loaned to the Society. As a crank organ it was supplied with three barrels, each arranged for ten tunes, and as most of these were inappropriate for religious service, a fourth barrel, containing ten psalm tunes, was made for the new use to which the instrument was now put. This extra barrel shows much use, and has doubtless many times furnished the accompaniment for singing the hymns of James and John Relly, the collection then, and for many years after, in use by the congregation.[16] This limited number of tunes seems to have satisfied the people for about fifteen years, when a key-board was placed in the organ, and a greater variety became possible.

On taking possession of their House of Worship, the hopes of the congregation were doubtless ardent; and for a while they were free from molestation, but before long they were made to feel the most determined opposition and annoyance. The assessors of the First Parish claimed that they were still obligated to contribute, by taxation, to the support of

[16] See Appendix E.

that organization. The Universalists denied this liability, basing their denial on the Bill of Rights prefixed to the Constitution of the Commonwealth, which had recently been adopted, the guarantees of which were, that "All religious societies shall, at all times, have the exclusive right of electing their public teachers, and of contracting with them for their support and maintenance. And all moneys paid by the subject for the support of public worship, shall, if he require it, be uniformly applied to the support of the public teacher or teachers, of his own religious sect or denomination, provided there be any one whose instruction he attends." The assessors made answer that this provision could not apply in this case, because the congregation of Mr. Murray was not a Religious Society, or if it was, it had no Incorporation; nor was Mr. Murray a Teacher of Religion, or if so, he was not an Ordained Minister.[17] And so, on the assumption that they had the right to determine what was and what was not a religious sect, and who was or was not a religious teacher, they proceeded to assess and attempt to collect taxes from the Universalists, for the support of the First Parish.

There was a way out of this difficulty, which was suggested to our fathers, and to which many urged them without influencing their action. It was to apply to the Legislature for an Act of Incorporation. The answer to this was: "Providence has so ordered it, that we should in the first instance be called upon to contend for those religious liberties preserved by our excellent Constitution. The inconsiderableness of our party, and the prejudices raised by our enemies in the minds of our fellow-citizens, point us out

[17] "Answer to an Appeal." pp. 13, 16.

as the proper objects of the first essay for religious tyranny; and should we fly to the law-makers instead of that great law made by the people to govern the legislature itself, we should, in our apprehension, betray our country's freedom, and act a cowardly part. We should feel ourselves very unhappy if there was no other security in these matters than acts of legislation, which might be repealed at any time when a particular party should prevail." [18]

In 1782 the First Parish enforced their demand by seizing and selling at auction, the goods of three members of the Universalist Society. From Epes Sargent they took articles of silver plate; from another, perhaps Winthrop Sargent, they took English goods; and from another, probably David Pearce, the anchor of a vessel on the point of sailing. William Pearce, a brother of David, prominent in the mob which, as before referred to, attempted to ride Mr. Murray ingloriously out of town, had become a convert to Universalism, and on his resistance of the tax, was lodged by the Parish Committee in Salem jail. Failing to recover their goods by replevin, the society instituted a suit against the assessors, which was afterwards withdrawn as not being tenable in the form in which it was commenced.[19]

It was found that, in order for an action to be sustained in the Court, it must be brought in the name of the religious teacher from whom the money had been diverted. With the utmost difficulty could Mr. Murray be brought to consent to such a suit. For thirteen years he had preached in many places without accepting pecuniary compensation; and to be a

[18] "An Appeal to the Impartial Public." p. 31.
[19] "Answer to an Appeal." p. 13.

prosecutor for money said to be due him for preaching the gospel, which it had been a matter of principle with him to do without price, appeared like prostrating his integrity, and to be a claimant for what he had always affected to hold in contempt. His friends were on the point of giving up the case, so great was his agony of mind in regard to it;[20] but on a review of the matter it presented itself to him in this light: "that persistence in his resolution was a sacrifice of the personal interests of his friends, and would be a cowardly giving up of a right which the Constitution guaranteed to all." And so he consented to bring the suit.[21] Hon. Rufus King was retained as counsel, and the case came to trial in 1783, and was continued on appeal and review to 1786. Mr. King removing to New York before the final decision, Judges Sullivan and Tudor became Mr. Murray's counsel. Of the trial in 1785, Mr. Sullivan gave the following account, in a letter written to Mr. King:

"June 25th, 1785. On Wednesday last was tried the case of John Murray against the inhabitants of the first parish of Gloucester. The cause was opened by Mr. Tudor, and closed by me; Mr. Bradbury and Mr. Parsons for the parish. Many exceptions were taken to the form of the action; but the three Judges present, Sewall, Dana and Sumner, agreed the action to be well brought. On our part we proved that the Society under the teaching of Murray were a sect different from [Calvinists, or the Standing Order,] by denying the external rite of baptism. We rested it there. The Court thought we ought to prove him to

[20] Life of Murray. p. 330.
[21] See Appendix F.

REV. THOMAS JONES.
Second Pastor, 1804-1841.

be a teacher of piety, religion and morality, to entitle him to the action. To this we agreed, and therefore produced evidence that he professed to teach the Christian Religion, which we thought to be a moral system, and that the persons whose taxes were in consideration attended upon him as a teacher of morality, and were content to submit the cause. Upon the other side they moved to prove that his doctrines were opposed to morality because he denied punishment in another world. To this we objected, that although we were obliged to prove him a teacher of morality, yet they would not go so far as to bring before a civil tribunal the question whether the motives of rewards and punishments in another world were such as would induce piety; for, should we at once launch into that inquiry, there would be no end to it. For, suppose the Clergyman in suit was an Episcopalian, one of the thirty-nine articles might be produced against him, which perhaps he had sworn to, holding up the idea of election and reprobation, which would be deemed by those who dissented from the doctrine to be opposed to every incentive to virtue or determent from vice. All Calvinists were involved in the same observation; the Hopkintonians worse, still worse; and it might even be said of the Arminians that their distinction between foreknowledge and predestination was derogatory to the perfection of the Deity; and so no end could be had to the disquisition. The Court were, however, against us, and in summing up, or rather arguing the cause, gave it as their full opinion that no teacher but one who was elected by a corporate society could recover money paid by his hearers to the teacher of the parish. This excludes, you will observe, the Episcopalians, Baptists, Quakers, Presbyterians and Sandemanians, from all benefit arising from the third article. The jury thought otherwise, and gave us a verdict. John Tracy, foreman." [22]

This verdict being in direct opposition to the instructions of the Court, a review of the case was ordered, and the final trial was had the following June.

Before that time arrived, the Universalists published a pamphlet of thirty-nine pages, entitled "An Appeal to the Impartial Public by the Society of Christian Independents, congregating in Gloucester." [23] It was written by Epes Sargent, and contained a full statement of the facts and arguments in the case, as based on the Constituton of the Commonwealth. It was immediately followed by a pamphlet of twenty-three pages, entitled "An Answer to a Piece entitled 'An Appeal to the Impartial Pnblic, by an Association' calling themselves 'Christian Independents, in Gloucester.'" [24] In addition to the common arguments of that day against allowing churches to be founded in opposition to the regular parish organization, this pamphlet contains the letter of Dr. Stiles, before referred to, and a strong appeal to discountenance "this man Murray, and his pernicious doctrines, which have been more damage to this town than the late war." To this pamphlet Mr. Murray at once replied in a vigorous broadside.[25]

When the case was heard upon review, in June, 1786, Judge Dana had wholly changed his opinion as

[22] Amory's Life of James Sullivan, Vol. 1, p. 183.

[23] See Appendix G.

[24] See Appendix H.

[25] See Appendix I.

expressed in his rulings and instructions the year before. He was now of the opinion that "as the Constitution was meant for a liberal purpose, its construction should be of the most liberal kind;" it should not be interpreted to apply only to corporate societies, but to all religious bodies. That Mr. Murray was a teacher of piety, religion and morality, had, in his opinion, been fully proved. "It is my opinion," he said, "that Mr. Murray comes within the description of the Constitution, and has a right to require the money." The jury brought in their verdict that "The judgment obtained last year was in nothing erroneous." Thus our fathers triumphed at last, and in their victory every sect in the Commonwealth was assured of its rights. "I have been the happy instrument of which the God of peace and mercy has made use," wrote Mr. Murray, "to give a death wound to that hydra, parochial persecution." [26]

While this suit was pending, other societies of Universalists, which had been recently formed, desired instruction, counsel and encouragement as to legal duties and rights, and held an Association at Oxford, in this state, "for the purpose," as Mr. Murray states it, "of deliberating on some plan to defeat the designs of our enemies, who aim at robbing us of the liberty wherewith the constitution has made us free." [27]

In anticipation of this Association, which was held September 14th, 1785, the male portion of the congregation, at a meeting on the 6th of that month, adopted a "Charter of Compact," which provided for carrying on the affairs of the Society by voluntary

[26] Murray's Works, Vol 2, p. 351.
[27] Life of Murray, p. 337.

subscriptions, and sent it to Oxford as a model for the societies which might be represented there. On the return of Mr. Murray, most of the amendments which had been suggested by the Association were adopted, the Compact was engrossed on parchment, and signed by the male members of the Society, eighty-five in number.[28] This venerable document is before you, enclosed in a frame made from one of the timbers of the House of Worship in which it was drawn up and signed.

Great as was the relief obtained by our fathers from the decision of the highest tribunal in the state, their annoyances from their enemies were not at an end. Before this case was out of the court, a prosecution was commenced against their preacher for performing the marriage ceremony. He and his friends had assumed that, as the founders of a new sect, or at least as the organizers of an Independent Society, it was their right to Ordain him, by simply setting him apart as their religious teacher, without having recourse to forms and ceremonies in any way like those which distinguished other sects in conferring Ordination; and that their act was as public and notorious as it would have been if they had made use of such ceremonies.[29] But their enemies reasoned differently, and selecting a particular case of Marriage by Mr. Murray, brought suit against him in the Supreme Judicial Court, where a verdict was obtained, condemning him to the payment of a fine of fifty pounds. As he had frequently solemnized marriages, and had reason to expect that suits might be brought against him for each offence, and the sum

[28] See Appendix J.

[29] "An Appeal to the Impartial Public," p. 13.

of the fines imposed would involve him and his
friends in great difficulty, he drew up a petition to
the legislature, for relief, and pending action upon it,
left the country on a visit to his native land in January, 1788. Early in the session, the legislature, by
a handsome majority in the House, and almost unanimously in the Senate, passed an Act, "Indemnifying him from all the pains and penalties which he
may have incurred on account of having solemnized
any marriages;"[30] and he returned home the following July.

Nearly his first act on reaching this place was to
record, in the Town Clerk's book, his intentions of
marriage with Mrs. Judith Stevens, a daughter of his
friend Winthrop Sargent, concerning whom it might
be interesting to say many things, both as to her
intellectual abilities and reputation as an authoress;
her husband's pride in her on account of her position
in the world of letters; and her own devotion to him
and to the sentiments which he preached; but I cannot trespass on your time to say it here. The intentions of marriage were recorded in July, and the marriage took place in Salem, October, 1788.[31]

The next important event was his re-ordination, a
measure determined upon by the Society, that they
might not again be subjected to the annoyance and expense of litigations. This ceremony took place in the
House of Worship on Christmas day, 1788.[32] Winthrop Sargent, David Plumer and Barnett Harkin
were appointed a committee "on the behalf of the
church and congregation to transact the ceremonies,"

[30] Life of Murray, pp. 341-344.

[31] See Appendix K.

[32] See Appendix L.

which they did by first presenting him with a formal call to become their minister; then by announcing the vote of the Church that the ceremonies in which they were engaged were the act of Ordination; and finally by presenting him the "Sacred Scriptures as a solemn seal of his Ordination to the Ministry of the New Testament, and the sole directory of his faith and practice." Mr. Murray offered the prayers, and preached a discourse from Luke x : 2. "The harvest truly is great, but the laborers are few; pray ye therefore the Lord of the harvest, that he would send forth laborers into his harvest."

Up to this year, Mr. Murray had received no stated salary, his wants having been supplied by the voluntary contributions of his friends, as provided in the Charter of Compact. But in anticipation of his marriage, the society agreed, about a month before that event, to pay him the sum of "One hundred pounds per year," and to raise it by tax, "paying severally in such a proportion as we pay the town or state tax the year immediately preceding." This agreement was signed by seventy-six of the male members of the society.[33] As consent had been given, some two years previous to this, to a request from the society in Boston, that Mr. Murray should preach there once in three weeks,[34] I suppose a deduction to have been made of his time spent there, for I find that the first tax assessed on this vote was for Thirty-five pounds, thirteen shillings and seven pence, for six months beginning January 1st, 1789. This amount was assessed on one hundred and three persons, David Pearce paying Eight pounds, nineteen shillings and

[33] See Appendix M.
[34] See Appendix N.

ten pence; Winthrop Sargent, Two pounds, eleven shillings and ten pence; Joseph Foster, Two pounds, two shillings and eight pence; four persons paying upwards of One pound each, and the remainder varying from nineteen shillings down to one shilling, four pence. In 1790, one hundred and twenty-one persons were assessed, and Forty-one pounds, seventeen shillings and four pence raised in sums varying from Nine pounds, one shilling and six pence, to one shilling and six pence.

This year Mr. Murray was absent from May to November, first in attendance on a Convention in Philadelphia, and then engaged in preaching in various places in Pennsylvania, New Jersey, Connecticut and Rhode Island. On his return his enemies instituted another suit at law, serving a writ upon him within an hour of his arrival; [35] the occasion being a decision of the Courts that a resident of a corporate parish could not divert the tax imposed on him for the support of religious worship, to maintain an unincorporated society. This was a reversal of the decision of 1786, and of course threw open the whole question which it was supposed had then been decided. For some reason, the suit was not pressed to trial; but the Society, weary of such annoyances, and in dread of their repetition, petitioned the Legislature for an Act of Incorporation, which was granted June 28th, 1792, when David Pearce, Winthrop Sargent, and forty-nine others whose names are given,

[35] This information is based on an unpublished letter of Mr. Murray's, dated "Gloucester, November 1, 1790." In it he says: "My determined foes in this place have brought me into the law again. I had not been in this town one hour before I was served with a writ, and am obliged to defend myself once more."

together with all others who are or may be associated with them, were "set apart and Incorporated into a society by the name of 'The Independent Christian Church in Gloucester.'"[36]

While awaiting the result of their petition for Incorporation, the Society levied no tax, but resorted to subscriptions for defraying their expenses, made payable to Winthrop Sargent and nine others, who obligated themselves to Mr. Murray for the payment of his salary. On this subscription I find one hundred and three names pledged for sums ranging from Eight pounds, nineteen shillings and eight pence, to one shilling and six pence.

The Society may be said to have supposed itself at the time of obtaining its Incorporation, victorious over all hindrances to its peace and growth, and to have entered on a career of great increase in numbers, religious interestedness, and general prosperity; but in reality it was on the eve of its greatest trials and embarrassments. While at Philadelphia, Mr. Murray had with great difficulty resisted the importunities of the Church in that city to become its pastor. A yearly income of Four hundred pounds, exclusive of his house-rent, was promised him; and he was only permitted to depart by pledging to lay the matter before his Eastern friends, and to urge that they release him.[37] The Boston society would not consent to his leaving the state, but urged him to take up his residence there, promising to do as well by him, pecuniarily, as was done by any minister settled in the town. The society here preferred its claim, was anxious to employ him constantly, and

[36] See Appendix O.
[37] Life of Murray, p. 353.

promised to do better by him in worldly matters than could be done elsewhere. Mrs. Murray's family also brought forward their personal reasons why there should be no change, and the result was that Mr. Murray seemed to be more firmly located in Gloucester than ever before. But in the year 1793 Mrs. Murray's parents died, her family became scattered, and the special ties which bound her to Gloucester were severed. Mr. Murray had sought in vain for a pastor for the Boston society; the great importance of a well-established centre for Universalism there, was becoming more and more apparent, and he felt compelled to announce to this society that duty called him to Boston, whither he went, and was Installed Pastor, by the Deacons of the Church, October 23d, 1793.[38]

It was a most melancholy thing for this Society to have him leave the place that had been his home for nineteen years, and where they had shared so fully in his troubles and joys. They had increased in numbers and in worldly prosperity, and they would gladly have shared with him their material gains; but they could urge nothing against his convictions of duty, and parted with him, "stipulating that he should occasionally visit them, and that they should be allowed to command his presence upon every distressing or important exigence, until they should be favored with another pastor;" a pledge faithfully redeemed by him for the ensuing ten years, during which many shadows passed over this little flock. Although the times were oppressive, they had no pecuniary difficulties in the way of their prosperity, and were, at the time of his leaving them, possessed

[38] Life of Murray, p. 362.

of property representing one-third of the entire valuation of the town. But Universalist ministers were few, the demands for their services were numerous, and how to obtain a pastor was a matter beset with many difficulties. Nor was it always easy to obtain even temporary supplies. The attempt was made, however, and with quite an approach to success, to have preaching once in two weeks.

Rev. Messrs. Matthew Wright and Hosea Ballou officiated during the remainder of the year 1793.

In 1794, Rev. Thomas Barns supplied the pulpit about one-half the time, occasionally assisted by Rev. Messrs. Zephaniah Lathe and Isaac Mansfield. The Society raised Eighty pounds to defray its expenses, which it assessed on one hundred and eighteen persons, among whom seventy-seven estates were represented, aggregating a valuation of Fifty thousand seven hundred and eleven pounds, the largest estate being that of David Pearce, then probably the wealthiest man in town, valued at Nine thousand five hundred and seventy-five pounds. The total valuation of the town that year was One hundred and fifty-three thousand five hundred and forty-five pounds.

In 1795 the Society voted to raise the sum of Ninety pounds, and have preaching three-fourths of the time. The services of Mr. Barns were obtained for one-half the year, but the balance of the time could not be provided for.

In 1796 the sum of One hundred pounds was raised for preaching, but it was impossible to obtain a supply oftener than once in two weeks, when Mr. Barns officiated.

The same amount was raised in 1797. Mr. Barns

preached half the time, and Rev. Michael Coffin was here occasionally.

In 1798 the Society raised Three hundred dollars, and Mr. Barnes preached once in two weeks, till October, when he made a visit to Maine, where he located soon after. Rev. Hosea Ballou was here once in two weeks during the rest of the year.

In 1799, Rev. Messrs. Hosea Ballou, John Foster, George Richards, and Zephaniah Lathe supplied the pulpit for twenty-one Sundays. Not until this year did the Society establish their title to the land on which their House of Worship stood. It belonged to the estate of Winthrop Sargent; and "on the basis of the valuation of 1781," they assessed a tax on the proprietors of the pews, and raised the sum of One hundred pounds in payment for the land.

In 1800, preaching was had but fourteen Sundays, by Rev. Messrs. John Foster, Ebenezer Paine, and Thomas Barns.

In 1801 there was preaching once in two weeks, by Rev. Messrs. Hosea Ballou, John Foster, Thomas Barns, Edward Turner, George Richards and John Murray.

In 1802 there was preaching only seven Sundays, the pulpit being occupied by Rev. Messrs. George Richards, Joshua Flagg and Edward Turner. Mr. Turner was here at the request of Rev. George Richards, then settled at Portsmouth, N. H., who took a lively interest in the affairs of this Society, and aided it by all the means in his power during the long time it was without a pastor. This year the Society voted to take down the Organ loft in their House of Worship, at which time, I suppose, the ancient instrument before us passed into retirement.[39]

[39] The Organ reverted to the possession of Mr. Somes, and

At the Annual Meeting in 1803, "the Society Voted, To have Mr. Turner to preach with them the current year." But Mr. Turner declined the invitation, and it was found impossible to obtain supplies for more than fourteen Sundays in the year. These were furnished by Rev. Messrs. Isaac Root, Noah Murray, Mr. Gleason and Thomas Jones.[40] The latter came from Philadelphia, where he had been pastor since 1796. He was here at the urgent solicitation of Mr. Murray, who wrote to the Society that Mr. Jones was a superior preacher, and that they could do no better than to hear him and keep him.[41]

At the Annual Meeting in March, 1804, the Society "Voted, To have preaching the current year by settling a Minister. That a salary of Five hundred dollars be given by this Society to the Rev. Thomas Jones, together with the expense of removing his family to Gloucester, in case Mr. Jones shall conclude to settle as Pastor of this Society, after the trial of a term not exceeding six months to the satisfaction of all parties." The six months' trial hav-

remained in the keeping of his descendants till 1870, when it was loaned to the Society for exhibition during the Centennial. At the close of that celebration, it was thus donated to the Society:

"B. H. CORLISS, Esq., Treasurer of the Independent Christian Society:

SIR — Permit me to present, through you, to the Independent Christian Society, the 'MURRAY ORGAN,' and to assure them that it certainly affords me great pleasure thus to donate this most interesting relic of the olden times, knowing full well that in their keeping it will be preserved from ruin and decay, to the later generations. With my best wishes for the future prosperity of the Society, I subscribe myself,
HARRIET WEBBER."

---

[40] See Appendix D.
[41] See Appendix P.

ing proved satisfactory, the Society, at a meeting held September 3d, "Unanimously voted, That the Rev. Thomas Jones be Installed as Pastor over the Independent Society in Gloucester, during his natural life." His salary was at the same time fixed at Six hundred dollars per annum, to date from his Installation; which took place September 26th, the Sermon and Charge by Rev. John Murray, the Installing Prayer and Right Hand of Fellowship by Rev. George Richards. I believe this to have been the first Installation in the history of the Universalist Church, where the services were wholly conducted by preachers.

Then commenced a long and successful pastorate of an eminently devoted and faithful minister, one whose attention was early called to the sacred things to which he was wholly consecrated during a long and blameless life. Born at Narbath, Pembrokshire, South Wales, April 5th, 1763, he entered, at the age of nineteen, the Seminary established by the Countess of Huntingdon, at Trevacca, Wales, for the education of young men for the Calvinistic Methodist Ministry. Spending three years in this institution he graduated in 1785, and was immediately Ordained, and entered upon his work as a preacher, fully imbued with and heartily believing the doctrines of Whitefield. His settlement was at Berks, England, where for three years he was an earnest and sincere preacher of the doctrines in which he had been educated. But in 1788 he was brought by the study of the Scriptures to the belief of Universalism, which he at once openly professed, and began to preach. His church, instead of casting him off, severed its connection with the Calvinistic Methodists, and retained him till his removal to America, eight years later, whither he came at the earnest desire of John Murray, who was interested in obtaining a Pastor for the Church in Philadelphia. He had entered his forty-second year when he became Pastor of this Church, and forty-two years were added to his life before he changed his home among you for the home immortal.

During his long pastorate many things occurred which it would greatly interest the older of you to have again brought to your remembrance, and many which it might be of service to all to know; but I must not presume to mention, save in the briefest manner, a very few of those things which are most prominent in the history of the Society, as indicating its own growth and progress, and the influences which have gone forth from it in other parts of the territory then embraced in the limits of the town.

As early as the time of the adoption of the Charter of Compact, several of the signers resided at Sandy Bay, now Rockport. In 1804 they had so increased as to be one-fifth of the membership of this Society, and had contributed two-fifths of the amount raised that year for the building of a new Meeting House at Sandy Bay, then the Fifth Parish in Gloucester, for which they had received the promise of the use of the house twenty-one Sundays in each year. Shortly after Mr. Jones came here it was arranged that he should preach there every fifth Sunday; and as it was impossible to obtain supplies for the other portion of the time to which the Universalists were entitled to the use of the house, they temporarily relinquished their right to those Sundays to the Congregational Society. The arrangement with Mr. Jones continued two years, at the expiration of which, the parish voted to themselves the exclusive use of the Meeting House, and the Universalists were shut out. Meetings were then commenced in a school-house, a Universalist Society was subsequently organized, and a suit in equity for the use of the Meeting House, was commenced. After a protracted litigation of years, the Court, virtually acknowledging the justice of the Universalists' claim, dismissed the action for want of jurisdiction, and referred them for redress to the Legislature. Preferring rather to build a new house than to have further contention about the old, the corner stone was laid June 24th, 1829, and the frame, gotten out at Cambridge, and floated to Sandy Bay, was, by the volunteer services of the citizens, taken from the water, and raised on its foundation, the ensuing Fourth of July. On the 8th of October, the House was Dedicated, the Pastor of this Church preaching the sermon. The Pastors of the Society in Sandy Bay after the Dedication, and until 1840, when that portion of our old town was set off to make the town of Rockport, were Rev. Messrs. Fayette Mace, Lucius R. Paige, B. B. Murray, A. C. L. Arnold, Charles Spear, and Gibson Smith.

Mr. Jones' settlement at once drew the Society together, and so speedily increased the size of the congregation that on the 5th of February, 1805, a number of the members met together for the purpose of considering the pressing necessity for a new Meeting House, and there agreed to open a subscription for the erection of such a building, the number of shares to be subscribed for not to be less than one hundred nor more than one hundred and twenty. The whole matter was left to the supervision of a Committee consisting of John Somes, William Pearce, Israel

Trask, Joseph Foster, and Isaac Elwell. Mr. Pearce having bargained for a large lot of land, the "Subscribers to the New Meeting House," at a meeting held in April, "Voted, To take the whole land as purchased by Col. William Pearce for the Meeting House upon the same terms on which he bid it off, and that a part of the same be reserved for a Burial Ground. That the Meeting House be erected near the eminence back or north of the brook, and that a handsome gravelled way be laid from Middle street to the front of said house, and that there be gravelled sidewalks for foot passengers, with rows of trees on each side, and terminating with turnpike gates." The price of the land was Twelve hundred dollars, and the lot extended from Middle to High street, the front on Middle street being sixty-three feet on the line of the Northern side of the street, and thence extending in a North-eastern direction, back of the present Northern line of Middle street, about Two hundred feet, and thence in an irregular course to High street, thence West on High street about One hundred and seventy feet, thence South to Middle street.[42] A large lot near the Northern end was reserved for a Burial Ground, so much of the Southern end as extends from Pine street to Middle street, together with the Meeting House, when completed, except the pews, was given by the Subscribers, to the Society. Three-fourths of the Burial Ground was laid

---

[42] The bounds are thus given in the deed from "Patrick Jeffrey, of Milton, in the County of Norfolk, and Mary his wife. A certain piece of land lying in Gloucester, upon the Northerly side of Middle street, and bound at the Eastern corner by land of Philemon Haskell, dec'd, and running by said street South 67 degrees west four rods and one tenth to Sam'l Whittemore's

out in lots corresponding to the number of the pews in the Meeting House, and one lot assigned to the owner of each pew; the remaining fourth was given to the Society. The gravelled walks were laid out, and Poplar trees were planted, which, some twenty years after, were taken up, and the present Elms took their place. There were Fifty-two Subscribers, and the Shares were One hundred, at One hundred dollars each. William Pearce was the largest subscriber, having fifteen shares, John Somes had thirteen shares, two of the subscribers had four shares, four had three shares, eight had two shares, and thirty-six had one share each.[43]

The Corner Stone of the new building, the one in which we are now assembled, was laid September

land, thence running north 4 degrees west by said Whittemore's land, and land of Jonathan Brown, jr., and land of Aaron Burnham to a stake twenty-six rods and four tenths, thence running North 53°. West by said Burnham and land formerly owned by Nath'l Ellery and land of Benjamin Stacey and land of Zebulon Parsons and land of Robert Cleaves, former owners, twenty-one rods and three-tenths, thence running North 41½°. East by land formerly owned by Benjamin Appleton five and one-half rods, thence running by land of Thomas Millet six rods to the highway, thence by said highway or back street about South 80°. East ten rods and four-tenths to Jacob Smith's land, then by said Smith South 42°. East fourteen rods and four-tenths to land formerly owned by said Philemon Haskell, thence by said Haskell's land South 13°. East nine rods and six-tenths to a stake, thence by said Haskell North 84°. East, two rods and one-tenth to the corner of the wall, thence by said wall 16°. East about sixteen rods and four-tenths to the brook, thence by said wall and brook South 84½°. West twenty feet, thence Southerly by said Haskell's land about fifteen rods and three-tenths to Middle street, to the bounds first mentioned, the whole containing more or less."

[43] See Appendix Q.

5th, 1805, by John Tucker, Master of Tyrian Lodge, F. A. M.[44] Col. Jacob Smith was the Architect and Builder. The timber of which the frame of this house is constructed, was felled in the British Provinces, and shipped for England in the Barque "Theodosia," which, becoming disabled near our harbor, was brought in here and condemned as unseaworthy. Her cargo was bought by Col. Pearce, sometime in 1804. The building was completed and ready for use in October, 1806. The first Sunday in that month a Farewell Service was held in the old House of Worship. The conclusion of the Discourse on that occasion I now read you from the Manuscript used by Father Jones:

"I have now closed my subject. I beg your patience a few minutes longer, My Friends, till I make a few remarks on this our eventful Day, and our present circumstances. This Day we close our assembling in this consecrated spot. Many of the Fathers who dedicated the House to the God and Father of all, and to His Christ, are gathered unto their Fathers, within the Vail! We shall see them no more until the General Muster of our race, when we hope to join them in triumph and perfect worship before the throne of the Son of God.

"We rejoice that *some* of the Elders are still amongst us,—who will not weep for sorrow at our approaching Dedication, as the Elders of Israel wept at the laying the Foundation of the Second Temple, because it was far inferior to the first,—but will rejoice with our young men and maidens, in our latter house. Many can, and could have said of this place, This is the House of God! this is the Gate of

[44] See Appendix R.

Heaven! I trust they will continue to find Every place consecrated by the sound of the Saviour's name, Hallowed Ground!

"Here they first heard that Christ died for all! that His Grace and Mercy was as extensive as the Light of the sun, and as free as the Air.

"Here you have heard various Gifts, and divers Talents, uniting, however, in one point — to ascribe to God Goodness and Mercy consistent with Justice and Holiness. Here you obtained freedom as an Independent Church or Society of Christians, the Charter of which you will transmit inviolate to your children, and they to theirs.

"It is twenty-six years next Christmas since you first assembled in this place. When your Candlestick was removed to another place, you were not left in darkness. A Degree of the true light had been emitted unto you. God in His Providence commanded the emitted Blaze to stand still in your Gibeon; and here we are this Day. A new Day hath visited us. We say with surprise, thankfulness and gratitude, What hath God wrought! He hath done for us Great things, whereof we are Glad!

"This Day and the approaching one I esteem as the most eventful of all my eventful life. Born in the Northwest extremity of Britain — where the Atlantic Ocean dashes her shores — strictly educated in the religious tenets of John Calvin, who sincerely thought Christ Sovereignly excluded a part of Mankind from Redemption. But I was enabled to break these Bands as Sampson did the Green Withs, and think freely for Myself; for which I suffered persecution several years. God hath given me an Asylum of peace among you, where I am willing to close my

Eyes, and Open them no more till upon the Son of Man in His Glory and Kingdom.

"My Friends, I count it one of the most Honorable of all my Deeds to lead you out of this House, where you have enjoyed so much religious pleasure, into your new House about to be Dedicated to the Head of the Church.

"May the Holy Fire continue burning clear upon our new Altar.

"May the Divine Presence and Blessing go with us.

"May your religious pleasures increase and multiply.

"May our lives be prolonged so long as useful, and we finish our course with joy.

"I congratulate you all on this Occasion, Especially the Elders of the Congregation, in the prospect of your children's worshipping the God of their Fathers; and pray that our Sons may be as plants grown up in their Youth; that our Daughters may be as Corner stones, polished after the Similitude of a palace.

"I conclude wishing God may prosper your handywork, and that His Glory and Blessing may rest upon us; that we may continue to add to our Faith Virtue, and Go on toward perfection, adorning the Doctrine of God our Saviour by Christ, in all Things. Amen."

The following Thursday, October 9th, this House was Dedicated to the Worship of God. Rev. John Murray offered the Introductory and Dedicatory Prayers, and Rev. Thomas Jones preached the Sermon, from Ephesians ii: 19, 20, 21. I regret that this sermon has not been preserved, and that the above meagre statement, taken from the *Columbian Centinel*, Boston, is all that can be known by us concerning services which must have been so deeply interesting.[45]

This House, as dedicated, contained Seventy-eight pews on the lower floor, and Twenty-two in the gallery; but these latter were not, I suppose, equally distributed on each side, as in 1828 it was "Voted, That the Committee build Six new pews in the Eastern gallery, if they find it necessary." The Pulpit was high and circular in form, and over it was suspended a Sounding Board. The old style square pews prevailed entirely on the lower floor, and were elaborately wrought in panel work.[46] The seats, for

[45] The full account given in the "*Columbia Centinel*, Boston, October 11, 1806," is as follows: "DEDICATION. On Thursday last, the new and elegant Meeting-House erected in *Gloucester* (Cape Ann) by the Society of Christians believing in the *Universal Salvation* of men, was solemnly Dedicated to the Author of that Salvation. The Rev. Mr. Murray, of *Boston*, read the introductory service, and made the Dedication and concluding Prayers; and the Rev. Mr. Jones, (the Pastor of the Society), delivered an excellent sermon, from Ephesians ii: 19, 20, 21, '*Now, therefore, ye are no more strangers and foreigners, but fellow-citizens with the saints and of the household of God; and are built upon the foundation of the apostles and prophets, Jesus Christ himself being the chief cornerstone; in whom all the building fitly framed together, groweth unto an holy temple in the Lord.*' The services were interspersed with music from an excellent choir. The House is capacious, and completely finished, and has a beautiful spire: and the whole work has been executed in a style which confers honor on the architect, and shows the liberality of the Society. The bell is from the *Revere* foundery of Canton."

[46] In this discourse, as read at the celebration, I said of these pews, "The top style and cap rested on a series of upright rounds, which were occasionally turned about by some indifferent hearer, or mischievous boy, and emitted disagreeable squeaks." In this I was mistaken. It was true of the old Meeting House, and not of the one erected in 1806.

the convenience of turning them back, and so making more room as the congregation rose in prayer, were hung on hinges, and the clatter made by letting them down, especially when the children, who delighted in that part of the exercise, took the matter in hand, is said to have borne no small resemblance to an irregular discharge of musketry; which at length became so annoying that the Society "Voted, To request the pew owners to fasten down, or otherwise prevent their seats falling so hard as to disturb the meeting."

The same style of pews were built in the front of the galleries, while at the rear were long benches. These gallery pews were favorite resorts for the children, and their presence in them, only manifest by the noise made — since the pews were so high that the small people could not be seen — was the occasion for frequent legislation in the Society meetings. In 1809 it was "Voted, that Mr. Benjamin Stacy have the use of the pew in the gallery which remains unsold, provided he will take care of those boys in the gallery, and keep them in order." It seems to have been more than Mr. Stacy could do; and so the next year "a committee of four was appointed to preserve order." The following year a committee of seven was chosen, "for the special purpose of noticing any rude or unbecoming behaviour, either of the boys or girls, during services, by writing their names in their pencil books and informing their Parents, Masters or Mistresses, as the case may be, of such conduct, in writing, and requesting them to punish them for the same." This seems to have reached the case, for thereafter, one man, who was paid Fifteen dollars a year for his services, was able to maintain order in the gallery. Armed with a long wand, on one end of which was a large feather, and on the other end a gilded knob, this guardian of the peace moved quietly through the galleries, brushing the faces of the rude girls with the feather, and bringing the gilded knob vigorously down on the heads of the refractory boys.

The Bell which still hangs in the tower was placed there before the day of Dedication. For many years it was the only large bell in town, and was long spoken of as "The heavy bell of the New Meeting House." Its constant service these sixty-eight years indicates the good quality of its material.

The Clock which projects from the gallery was also an original part of the furnishing of the house by the Subscribers. At least it is remembered, by a gentleman now present, to have been there the year that the House was dedicated.

At the rear of the house was a small one story building known as "The Vestry." It was provided with a fire-place, was used for ordinary Society meetings, for the Sunday School when that was first organized, and for some time was rented for a day school. Its full size may be seen by a glance at the Organ loft, which is but another story added to the original frame.

No provision was made for heating the Meeting House till Christmas, 1820, when stoves were used for the first time.[47] Prior to this, and some extended the custom a few years longer, the elderly people

---

[47] This innovation was stoutly resisted by a few, on the plea that the air would be rendered unhealthy, and sickness would be caused. One who was present at the first service after the stoves were put in, but when, owing to a lack of stove-pipe, no

and the ladies brought foot-stoves, or hot bricks or stones, to keep their feet from freezing, and bravely bore the cold in other parts of their body.

Candles at first furnished the lights for evening services. These were placed chiefly on the pulpit and the gallery in front of the singers' seats, and in two or more chandeliers which were suspended from the ceiling. These chandeliers were superseded by a large one, fitted with lamps, in 1823, at an expense of One hundred and seventy-five dollars. It was a grand affair, as the remnants of it, still preserved in the attic, will show, and suspended by its gilded rope, was a wonder and delight, especially to the young people. At the same time ornamental branches were placed on each side of the pulpit, each containing three large lamps.

No instrumental music was used in this house till 1814, when a Bass viol was purchased, not without considerable opposition, however, at such an innovation; and was in a few years followed by Clarionets and Violins, which were continued in use till 1826, when an Organ was procured, which, after Thirty years' service, gave place to the present Organ, first used July 31, 1856, a Concert being then given by the "School street Choir," of Boston. Vocal music received early attention, and liberal provision was made for it from the treasury. The singers' seats were always well filled, and under the leadership of Thomas Ireland, Samuel Friend, John and Denmark Procter, the singing was powerful and spirited. Relly's Hymns continued to be used till 1808, when

fires were made, relates that during the service several of the ladies, and among them the wife of the minister, fainted, and had to be taken into the open air before they could recover.

the Society, through a Committee, of which William Saville was Chairman, published a collection. The last hymn in the book was written by Mr. Saville, and the others were selections from Relly, Watts and others.[48] This book was in use till 1838, when it gave place to the Collection compiled by Rev. Hosea Ballou, 2nd, which in turn was superseded, in 1855, by the book now used, Adams and Chapin's.

At the first Sabbath service in this house, October 12th, 1806, Clara Sargent, an infant daughter of William Pearce, jr., was Dedicated to the Love and Service of God; a Ceremonial instituted by Rev. John Murray, and probably first observed by him, at least frequently observed by him, in this town. Baptism, he said, was wholly connected with Profession of Faith, and as such profession could not be made for another, least of all for infants, he would not baptize infants. But he thought it seemly and wise to acknowledge children as God's gift, and to Dedicate them, as such, to God's love.[49] Mr. Jones saw no impropriety in the use of water in this ceremony; and in this I suppose that the pastors who have succeeded him have agreed. At all events, either with or without the use of water, the Dedication of children has been observed by the Universalists of Gloucester for nearly, if not quite a century.

On the same first Sabbath, measures were taken for the organization of the body of Communicants into a Church distinct from the mere business Society created by the Act of Incorporation. On the 23d of the following November, a Covenant and Articles of Faith were adopted by the male members of the

[48] See Appendix S.
[49] See Appendix T.

Society, and Thirty-three persons, Nine Men and Twenty-four Women, organized under them as a Church.[50] The first Wardens, or Deacons, were Isaac and Payne Elwell. The business of the Church was wholly in the hands of the male members, which the worthy pastor never ceased to regret, and to fight against; some of his recorded resolves and protests being very vigorous and decided; but the chief opposition to a change coming from the proscribed sex themselves, no change was made until the reorganization of the Church, thirty-two years later. Mr. Jones has also left on record his firm convictions in favor of an Open Celebration of the Lord's Supper, a belief that this Ordinance of the Gospel is no more sacred than are the Doctrines of the Gospel, and that all members of a Christian congregation should have a right to the Communion without the intervention of Ceremony. These views he urged upon the Church, but failed to obtain their endorsement. Succeeding pastors have held various opinions on this subject. The Church, though passing through several modifications, has continued to the present, never a large body, but always a recognized power and influence in the religious life of the congregation.

In 1811 an event occurred connected with the history of Universalism in Gloucester, which gave sudden strength to the cause here, and great rejoicing to its professors everywhere. The Third (Annisquam) Parish had settled as its Pastor, in 1804, Rev. Ezra Leonard, a graduate of Brown University, and a student in orthodox theology with Rev. Perez Fobes, LL.D., of Taunton. Finding in his congregation at Annisquam a number of persons who had

[50] See Appendix U.

embraced the doctrine of Universalism, and being often brought in contact with Mr. Jones on funeral occasions, he was of necessity frequently engaged in arguments and conversations on the subject of Universal Salvation. Among the MSS. of Mr. Leonard, which have come into my possession, I find a fragment of what I suppose to have been the first Sermon which he preached after being convinced of the truth of Universalism. In this he enumerates the Works and Arguments for and against the Doctrine, which he had read, and with which he had made himself familiar. He then adds: "About six months ago I put them all aside, and began to search the Scriptures anew, prayerfully and very attentively. And at present I am convinced by the Spirit of Truth which I find there, that Grace will reign as universally as sin has reigned." The result of this avowal was, that a very few of the parish withdrew from his ministry, while the great majority, having confidence in their pastor as an honest and learned man, remained. The only action taken in Parish Meeting was a vote, passed in December, 1811, "that he should continue to preach to them till the next March meeting." At the March meeting the opposition was feeble, and he continued to be the Parish Minister till his death in 1832. Dying, he left no enemies, but is remembered as a faithful Christian Minister, richly imbued with the Spirit of his Master. His successors in the pastorate have all been Universalists, and the society, though weakened by deaths and removals, still preserves its integrity and zeal.[51]

[51] The Ministers of the Society since Mr. Leonard's death, with the dates of their settlement, have been, Abraham Nor-

The War of 1812 was a time of severe trial to this Society, as the business of the town was at once destroyed, and the inhabitants were nearly equally divided in sentiment, the anti-war party being slightly in the ascendant when the difficulties commenced. All the Churches suffered, and it became a burden and sacrifice to maintain the preached word. It was found necessary to reduce Mr. Jones' salary, and at one time it seemed inevitable that the meetings must cease, so small was the attendance, so absorbing were the political troubles. But there were brave and true men who stood by, and who were more than sufficient for the demands of the occasion. The Patriotism of the pastor was of the highest order. He knew by the contrast gained in personal experience, how great were the political blessings in the land of his adoption; and "the claim of Great Britain to the Right of Impressing Seamen, is," he declared, "as absurd and wicked as is the claim of the Southern Planter to Ownership in man;" a comparison which shows his hatred of that which he so often denounced in no measured terms within these walls — American Slavery. His Sermon preached on the occasion of a Special Fast appointed by the President, in 1813, has the ring of an old anti-slavery Oration.

Just after the Treaty of Peace, the society was called to mourn the death of their first pastor. Many of the early friends of Mr. Murray had died, wood, 1832; Elbridge Trull, 1833; John Harriman, 1834; George C. Leach, 1837; Maxcy B. Newell, 1842; Joseph A. Bartlett, 1845; Benjamin H. Clark, 1847; E. W. Coffin, 1848; N. Gunnison, 1854; Emmons Partridge, 1857; Lewis L. Record, 1859; J. H. Tuller, 1863; J. H. Willis, 1865; F. A. Benton, 1868; William Hooper, 1871.

but quite a number remained, to whom his death, September 3d, 1815, although the event had long been looked for, brought deep grief. Mr. Jones officiated at the Funeral, and, by special request, preached in Boston the following Sunday; and then by desire of the Society here, preached a Commemorative Discourse in this house, the Sunday after. So much of the Funeral Oration, and of these two Discourses as contain special allusions to Mr. Murray, are preserved, but have never been put in print.[52]

In the Spring of 1819 Mr. Jones commenced a series of Twelve Short Sermons to the Children. From 1807 it had been his custom to give at least two such sermons each year; but a result followed this last and special course, which probably had not been sought before. It was the Establishment of the Sunday School, June 25th, 1820, which has continued to the present time. Dr. William Ferson was the first Superintendent. As it is not long since I gave a Historical sketch of the School, I need make no further mention of it here, save to say that I believe it to have been the Third Sunday School organized by Universalists, and since 1826 the oldest school in the denomination.[53]

October 3d, 1824, a meeting of the congregation was held, at the suggestion of Benjamin K. Hough, to consider the propriety of observing the approaching Semi-Centennial Anniversary of the First Preaching of Rev. John Murray in Gloucester. The Pastor proposed that the whole day be used in Religious Services, which was unanimously agreed to, and Rev. Thomas Jones and Col. William Pearce were asso-

[52] See Appendix V.
[53] See Appendix W.

ciated with William Babson, jr., William Collins and Samuel Pearce, the Parish Committee that year, to make the necessary arrangements.

Fifty years ago to-day the Celebration took place. All the Ministers specially invited were in attendance except Rev. Messrs. Hosea Ballou and Edward Turner. The Morning Services were conducted by Rev. Thomas Whittemore, of Cambridgeport, who offered Prayer and made a brief Introductory Address; Rev. Paul Dean, of Boston, who read the Scriptures and preached a Sermon from 1 Samuel vii : 12, "Hitherto hath the Lord helped us"; and Rev. Zelotes Fuller, of Charlton, who made the Concluding Prayer. In the Afternoon, the first Prayer was made by Rev. Barzillia Streeter, of Troy, N. Y.; the Sermon by Rev. Sebastian Streeter, of Boston, from 1 Cor. ii : 10 ; and the Closing Prayer by Rev. Ezra Leonard, of Annisquam. The Evening Services commenced with Prayer by Rev. Hubbard H. Winchester, of Wilmington, Vt.; the Sermon was by Rev. Hosea Ballou, 2nd, of Roxbury, from Isaiah lx : 2, 3, 4 ; and the Concluding Prayer by Rev. Thomas G. Farnsworth, of Newton.

Including the Pastor of the Society, there were Ten Preachers in attendance, all of whom, except Rev. Thomas G. Farnsworth, who is with us to-day, Rev. Zelotes Fuller, now residing in Philadelphia, and Rev. Hubbard H. Winchester, living in Iowa, have passed on to their Heavenly rest. It was a day of great rejoicing to the society. The congregations were large at each service, and the singing on the occasion was spoken of in the highest terms. Fifty singers occupied the gallery, and extra instruments were brought into use; the whole being under the lead of John and Denmark Procter. Mr. Jones has recorded that the first hymn sung after the opening Anthem, in the Morning, was the one commencing:

> " Blow ye the trumpet, blow
>   The gladly solemn sound!
> Let all the nations know,
>   To earth's remotest bound,
> The year of jubilee is come;
> Return, ye ransom'd sinners, home."

Rev. Paul Dean was instructed to prepare an account of the Exercises for the Universalist periodical publications, and to express therein "the hope and belief that the semi-century returns of this day will be celebrated with religious gratitude and joy until Christ shall have an altar in every place, and at every altar an herald of salvation ministering to his redeemed." [54]

In 1830 another Universalist Congregation was gathered in the town, in the Second, or West, Parish. Rev. Daniel Fuller, who had settled there in 1770, and whose active ministry continued for Fifty-three years, died in 1829. In the Warrant for the Annual Parish Meeting following his death, this Article was inserted: "To know of what Denomination the Parish will be most united." The vote was just three to one in favor of the Universalist Denomination. Rev. Calvin Gardner was, I believe, the first Minister under this vote, and his support was provided for by subscriptions. The following year the Parish voted to assess a tax, and to grant to each person assessed "the privilege of having his own money appropriated to support Ministers of his own Denomination." Under this just arrangement there was, of course, a

[54] See Appendix X.

variety of preaching, but by far the greater part of it was by Universalists. The so-called Orthodox portion of the parish withdrawing about this time and organizing a new Society, the meetings in the Old House of Worship were thereafter conducted by the Universalists, who continued meetings a portion of each year till 1846, when the house, erected in 1716, having become greatly out of repair, was sold and removed. The purchaser worked most of the timber into a new building, afterwards called "Liberty Hall," where a Society of Universalists has been organized, a Sunday School is held every Sunday, and preaching is had a portion of each year.[55]

[55] The Universalist preachers at West Parish since 1830, until the arrangement under the old Parish organization ceased, in 1843, were Rev. Messrs. William A. Stickney, Ezra Leonard, Robert L. Killam, Joseph P. Atkinson, Henry Belding, Charles Galaca, George G. Strickland, James M. Usher, Thomas Jones, William Hooper, Henry C. Leonard, John M. Spear.

A Farewell Service was held in the Old Meeting House, Sunday afternoon, September 7, 1846, Rev. A. D. Mayo preaching the sermon, on Continuance in well doing; text, Gal. vi : 9. The following hymn, written by Mrs. S. C. E. Mayo for the occasion, was sung:

>   Thy temple, God, not built with hands,
>   Unharmed through endless ages stands;
>   Its great dome still in glory spreads
>   Its myriad star-lights o'er our heads.
>
>   Its columned aisles with music ring,
>   Poured forth by every living thing;
>   Ocean its awful anthem roars,
>   And winds sigh soft along its shores.
>
>   But Thou, though worshipped day and night
>   In fanes of boundless breadth and height,
>   Wilt hear a simple song and prayer,
>   Breathed from a true heart anywhere.

REV. DANIEL D. SMITH.
THIRD PASTOR (ASSOCIATE WITH DR. JONES), 1838-1841.

Whether it was on account of the evident spread of Universalism on the Cape, or from some other reason, I have no means of knowing, but at this period of its ascendancy in the Second Parish, great zeal was manifest by several sects in sending Missionaries to Gloucester, some of whom caused most abusive articles to be written and circulated in the religious papers of the state. A paper called the "Anti-Universalist" was printed in Providence, R. I., in an early number of which appeared one of these articles, charging that the Universalists of this town were drunkards and immoral, and declaring that it was notorious that Murray was grossly immoral while residing here. So sweeping a charge killed itself, and so roused the indignation of those who honestly opposed Universalism, that, through their instrumentality, the paper fell into such disrepute as to speedily lose its supporters and its life. A Missionary sent from Salem made a lamentable report that "at the Squam Sabbath School no book but the Bible is in use," and he was "sorry to say that the School is under very bad influence." This was an unfortunate statement, in view of what the Missionary was

> E'en here, beneath this mouldering roof,
> Far from the crowded world aloof,
> Mid these old aisles, so worn and grey,
> E'en here our souls may sing and pray.
>
> May those old sires who built this fane,
> In spirit meet with us again;
> And blending their high souls with ours,
> Make this the holiest of life's hours.
>
> And may the soft winds, breathing through
> This old church, from the waters blue,
> Bear up to Heaven as pure a strain
> As ever rose from royal fane.

seeking, and all his work came to nought. An Agent of the Massachusetts Missionary Society came here, and in his published report said of Universalism, that "at Cape Ann, it issues from every dark cavern there, and is echoed by every rock and shrub that deforms the fair face of nature." Mr. Jones, who was an ardent lover of the scenery of the Cape, published a spirited reply, in which he so rebuked the Agent's want of appreciation of the beauty of the coast, as also so clearly exposed his ignorance of what he was attacking, that there was no further opposition of that kind.

In 1837, the health of the venerable Pastor being feeble, a special meeting was called in December to consider the propriety of soliciting his views with regard to the settlement of a Colleague; and three of his long-tried friends, Benjamin K. Hough, Richard Friend, and William Pearce, jr., having reported for him that such a step would be perfectly satisfactory, it was determined that measures should be taken at once, to either obtain a supply till such time as Mr. Jones should be able to resume his duties, or to settle an Associate Pastor.

The following January, a Committee who had been authorized to do so, extended an invitation to Rev. Matthew Hale Smith to settle as Colleague with Mr. Jones. Mr. Smith declining the invitation, "the Committee were instructed to supply the pulpit with such suitable preachers as may be obtained with a view of securing some one on whom the society can unite." In August a unanimous invitation was extended to Rev. Daniel D. Smith, of Portland, Me., who accepted, his labors to commence as soon as he could make satisfactory arrangements at Portland.

The Society having already voted to make an alteration in their House of Worship, at once perfected their plans, and the work was finished before the installation of the new pastor. The square pews were all removed from the lower floor, and Ninety-eight pews, of about nine feet each in length, took their place, giving a gain of Twenty pews. Nineteen of these pews were sold, to defray the expenses of the alteration, the remaining one being kept by the Society. The old Pulpit was also taken down, and a more modern one was built.

Mr. Smith was Installed as Junior Pastor, December 20th, 1838. The Installing Prayer was by Rev. Thomas Jones, and the Sermon by Rev. Otis A. Skinner, of Boston.[56]

The popular talents of Mr. Smith at once drew in a larger congregation than could be accommodated with sittings. To remedy this, the Society voted on the 29th of January, 1839, "to make an alteration in the gallery by which they could obtain Fifty-four pews," being an addition of Twenty-six to the number then located there. This was no sooner done than the new pews were sold and occupied; and for several months the attendance on Public Worship was larger than ever before. A movement was also set on foot to build a large Vestry and School House, stock in which was readily taken; and a commodious two-story edifice, called the "Murray Institute," was made ready for Dedication, October 31st, 1839. This

[56] The other services were: Scripture Readings, Rev. Charles Spear; Introductory Prayer, Rev. J. M. Austin; Delivery of the Scriptures and Charge, Rev. Hosea Ballou, 2nd; Right Hand of Fellowship, Rev. Thomas F. King; Address to the Society, Rev. Hosea Ballou; Concluding Prayer, Rev. Samuel Brimblecome.

was located on the lot now occupied by the Episcopal Church, the expense of land and building being about Forty-two hundred dollars. The "Liberal Institute," a school formerly located at Methuen, was moved here and opened in the new building in November. Philosophical and scientific lectures were given, a large amount of apparatus was bought, an extensive library gathered, and the social as well as the religious affairs of the Society seemed to be in as prosperous a condition as the most sanguine could desire. But in the midst of this great prosperity came the severest trouble and disaster. Difficulties were gathering which soon burst with volcanic fury, and threatened utter ruin. This hitherto steadfast and united Society was shaken and disunited. Friends who had always been one in all good aims and efforts, became alienated and embittered; families, even, were rent asunder; and, to set forth in few words this melancholy part of our history, so many of the Society had withdrawn, and so large a number of the congregation had ceased to attend his ministry, that Mr. Smith deemed it expedient to send in his resignation in October, 1840. It was accepted; but subsequently, at his earnest desire, his services were continued from January, 1841, till the Annual Meeting in April.

The friends of Mr. Smith, who were numerous — and among them were some of the most useful and influential members of the Society — withdrew when he ceased to preach; and not long after formed a new organization, called the "Independent Universalist Society," and commenced meetings in the Murray Institute Hall. In 1843 they invited Mr. Smith to become their pastor, and in September,

1845, they Dedicated a small House of Worship, on Elm street, which they had built at an expense of about Three thousand dollars. A Church of about forty members was organized, Richard Friend, jr., and Joseph Friend being the Deacons. Mr. Smith continued with them till the Summer of 1848; and the following year was succeeded by Rev. David H. Plumb, who remained three years. In April, 1853, Rev. George J. Sanger became their pastor, and preached his farewell discourse, March, 1856. The dissolution of the Society soon followed the close of his services, and in 1858 the property was sold to the Methodists.

From April, 1841, till December, 1842, this Society had preaching, a large portion of the time, from ministers living near. An arrangement was made with Mr. Jones, in May, 1841, by which his connection as Pastor was dissolved; the Society making provision for his maintenance during the remainder of his life, and for the support of his wife if she should survive him.[57] His health was gradually failing, the troubles of the Society were a source of great annoyance to him, and he was no longer equal to the work which the circumstances demanded. Mutual love and confidence and interestedness dictated the separation, and the same feelings characterized the remainder of his stay upon the earth. For some little time after his release from duty as pastor, he was able to preach occasionally, in places

---

[57] The sum of $400 per annum was settled on Mr. Jones, and $200 on his wife, if she should survive him. Mr. Jones kept very accurate records of his ministerial labors; from which I ascertain that while pastor here he solemnized 658 Marriages, Baptized 711 Persons, and attended 1162 Funerals.

not far distant from home. When here on Sunday a seat was reserved for him in the pulpit, on account of his great deafness, and he frequently took part in the services, especially in the Administration of the Lord's Supper. His last service of this kind, and, I suppose, his last religious service of any kind, in public, was on Sunday, November 3d, 1844.

In March, 1843, the Society invited Rev. Frederic F. Thayer, of Cambridge, who had supplied the pulpit the preceding three months, to become its pastor. The Invitation was accepted, and Mr. Thayer was Installed on the 28th of that month, Rev. Otis A. Skinner preaching the Sermon.[58] It was Mr. Thayer's first settlement, and to his office he brought a well-cultivated mind and a warm and zealous heart. His pulpit services were acceptable and the Church records show a quickened religious interest and an increase in the number of Communicants. But the circumstances peculiar to that time of division and estrangement were not favorable to such results as fire the ambition of an earnest pastor. Measures which were taken for the reconciliation and return of those who had separated from the Society failed of accomplishing their object. Annoying debts had accumulated, and discouragements were numerous.

[58] The other services were: Reading of the Scriptures, Rev. Maxey B. Newell; Introductory Prayer, Rev. Thomas B. Thayer; Installing Prayer, Rev. T. P. Abell; Charge and Delivery of the Scriptures, and Right Hand of Fellowship, Rev. E. G. Brooks; Address to the Society, Rev. L. S. Everett; Concluding Prayer, Rev. Hosea Ballou. The hymns, three in number, were written for the occasion; one by Rev. J. G. Adams, the 715th hymn in Adams and Chapin's Collection; one by Rev. E. H. Chapin, the 710th hymn in the same collection, and one by Rev. Hosea Ballou.

Under these circumstances, and impelled by them, Mr. Thayer tendered his resignation in September, 1844, and his connection with the Society ceased in December.[59]

From this time until the next Annual Meeting, the Society devoted its energies to the payment of its debts, amounting to about Twenty-three hundred dollars. Being successful in this, it extended an invitation, in June, 1845, to Rev. Henry B. Soule, of Boston, to become its pastor. Accepting the invitation, Mr. Soule at once commenced his work, which, however, was of brief duration; for in October he informed the Committee that he was discontented in Gloucester, and had been from the first, and being thus in no condition to do justice either to the Society or to himself, he desired them to accept his resignation, to take effect at the close of the quarter, in December. Action on this resignation seems to have been deferred until the Annual Meeting the following April, when it was accepted.[60]

Rev. Amory D. Mayo, of Warwick, was invited to the pastorate in June, 1846, and commenced his ministry here, which was also his first pastoral settlement, in July. He had not been here a month when this house was heavily draped in mourning, and all its spaces were occupied by an immense throng, who gathered in great respect and affection to perform

[59] The other pastoral settlements of Mr. Thayer were at Brooklyn, N. Y., 1844; Chelmsford, Mass., 1845. In 1847, Mr. Thayer, in consequence of a severe affection of the throat, left the ministry and went into secular business.

[60] Mr. Soule was subsequently settled at Hartford, Conn., 1846; Granby, Conn., 1851; Lyons, N. Y., January, 1852, where he died, after a very brief illness, with the small-pox, on the 30th of that month.

the funeral rites of the venerable Man of God who for Forty-two years had been so intimately identified with the Church and with the history of the town. Father Jones, after long confinement to his house and gradually yielding to the slow decay which waits upon advanced age, "put off this tabernacle of flesh" and entered "into the house not made with hands," on the 20th of August. Two days after, his mortal remains, borne on the hands of long tried and faithful friends, were brought hither and the new pastor, in well-chosen words, preached a discourse from the passage of Holy Writ which was of all others most eminently suitable for the occasion: "Mark the perfect man, and behold the upright; for the end of that man is peace."—Psalm xxxvii : 37.[61]

[61] The following Hymn, written for the occasion by Mrs. S. C. E. Mayo, was sung at this Service:

"Softly breathe the low lament
O'er the aged warrior, spent;
Weary, worn, he hath lain down,
Sleeping in his victor crown.

Bear him down these aisles once more,
Gently through the old church door;
Let the green trees o'er him wave,
In his slow march to the grave.

Give to earth its solemn trust;
Give to dust its kindred dust;
Lay within its narrow bed
All the perishing and dead.

But the life that made its shrine
In yon pale form, was divine!
An undying, quenchless flame,
From the Lord of life it came!

Mr. Mayo's ministry was attended with many gratifying results. His preaching was attractive, instructive and profitable; the attendance at Public Worship greatly increased; there were no discordant elements in the Society, but a large measure of its former united and prosperous state was restored. The only hindrance to its most complete success was the uncertain and frequently feeble condition of the pastor's health. This sometimes compelled him to ask for a respite from his labors; but in spite of such disadvantages and interruptions, his work was blessed to him here, and he has, we trust, been able to feel what so many others see, that what he prepared for the enlightenment and faith and Christian growth of this people, has, through the instrumentality of the printed page, been light, and cheer, and strength to great multitudes. His book on "The Moral Arguments for Universalism," made up, I suppose, of sermons preached here, has not yet finished its work. It is a strong and unanswerable statement, in its peculiar line of reasoning, of the utility, philosophy and reforming power of our Faith in God's Infinite Love. Another volume of his sermons prepared for this people, the "Graces and Powers of the Christian Life," is also an honor to our denominational literature, and its perusal cannot fail to in-

> It hath sought its source above,
> In the Infinite of love!
> Where, throughout a round of time,
> It will rise through heights sublime!
>
> Through the ambient fields of Heaven,
> Far, even now, that life hath striven;
> Upward, onward, evermore,
> Will the Immortal rise and soar!"

struct and help Christian people of every name. I find also, in some of your homes, several of his sermons preached on special occasions, which, and particularly those containing lessons drawn from the lives of the older members of the Church, several of whom passed away during his ministry, are highly prized, and will be faithfully handed down to others, and through them the fathers shall still speak to others who will come after us.

The pastorate of Mr. Mayo was brought to a close on the 1st of October, 1854, by his own request; from a conviction that an opening in the city of Cleveland, Ohio, offered him an opportunity for building up a Church whose influence would be widely felt in the great West.[62]

In April, 1855, the Society invited Rev. W. R. G. Mellen, of Auburn, N. Y. The invitation was at once accepted, and Mr. Mellen commenced his services in May. During his ministry there was a manifest growth in the town, and his abilities drew large numbers of the new comers to this Church, and retained them as permanent members of the congregation. The old disagreements in a large measure subsided on the dissolution of the other Society, and many who had been estranged returned to their first love. The Sunday School felt the impulse of these changed conditions and improved surroundings, and grew and prospered under his fostering care, the Bible class proving especially interesting and profitable. Without noise or excitement the congregation became large, and the Society set on foot several

---

[62] Mr. Mayo's settlements since leaving Gloucester have been, Cleveland, Ohio, 1854; Albany, N. Y., 1856; Cincinnati, Ohio, 1863; Springfield, Mass, 1873.

improvements looking to greater convenience and comfort in this House of Worship. The galleries which had been made so much more available than formerly, by the alterations in 1839, were still inconvenient and undesirable to those who sought sittings there. They were therefore remodeled in the winter of 1861, and changes were also made in the vestibule, the present circular stairs being substituted for the old-fashioned staircases. The lamps were at the same time abolished, and gas fixtures took their place.

Both Mr. Mellen and Mr. Mayo favoring the method of open communion, no Church records were kept during the pastorate of either, and it is therefore impossible to tell what additions, if any, were made to the Church for about fifteen years; but it is known that a good degree of religious interest, earnestness and devotion was cultivated by both of these faithful ministers; and not a few who were old enough to have their attention understandingly drawn to spiritual affairs when Mr. Mellen was pastor, attribute their deepest and most lasting religious convictions to his instructions and counsels. In October, 1861, Mr. Mellen resigned, having accepted the Chaplaincy of the 24th Regiment of Massachusetts Volunteers.[63]

The next pastor was Rev. George W. Skinner, who was called in June, 1862, and immediately accepted. Previous to his coming here, Mr. Skinner

[63] Mr. Mellen remained in the Army till January, 1863. In February, 1863, he was commissioned Consul to Mauritius, where he remained till 1867. In 1869 he settled as Pastor, at Detroit, and subsequently at New Brighton, Staten Island, 1871; Albany, N. Y., 1874.

had been for a few months connected with the Army, as Lieutenant in the 97th Regiment New York State Volunteers. His ministry was during days of trial for the Country, days of anxiety and trial to all faithful ministers. His patriotic utterances in the pulpit were frequent, and he also embraced the oft-recurring opportunities of addressing the citizens at the many War Meetings which were then held, and of further helping them for the discharge of loyal duties; while at the same time he was prompt and responsive to the ordinary demands of the pulpit, and of his people. But his stay here was too brief, and the circumstances of the times too exacting in other directions, to mark his pastorate in any special manner. Mr. Skinner resigned, and his connection with the Society ceased, February, 1865.[64]

Rev. Elmer H. Capen, of Stoughton, was invited to minister here in March, 1865. His Ordination took place in this house in October of that year, the Sermon being preached by Rev. A. A. Miner, D. D., of Boston.[65] Mr. Capen's pastorate, which terminated by his resignation in October, 1869, is too

[64] Mr. Skinner settled in New Bedford, Mass., in 1865; in Stoneham, Mass., 1866; Leavenworth, Kansas, 1867; Quincy, Mass., 1869; and Lawrence, Kansas, 1872.

[65] Other portions of the Service were: Invocation, Rev. B. K. Russ, of Somerville; Prayer, Rev. J. H. Willis, of Annisquam; Ordaining Prayer, by Rev. Geo. W. Skinner, of New Bedford; Charge and Delivery of the Scriptures, Rev. A. St. John Chambré, of Stoughton; Right Hand of Fellowship, Rev. J. F. Powers, of East Cambridge; Charge to the Society, Rev. H. C. Leonard, of Pigeon Cove, who also wrote a Hymn for the occasion.

Mr. Capen's pastorates, since leaving Gloucester, have been: St. Paul, Minn., 1869; Providence, R. I., 1871; President of Tufts College since 1875.

recent to need any special notice at this time. You all remember it, and can testify to his doing the work of an earnest, faithful Christian minister. One thing, however, connected with it, and to secure which he was untiring in effort, must be mentioned —the great change which took place in the ownership of the pews, and the convenience, comfort and enlarged accommodations of this House of Worship. By gift in some cases, and by purchase in others, the pews became the property of the Society. Alterations and improvements costing about Fifteen thousand dollars gave the following results: the removal of the pews placed here in 1838, and the introduction of the present greatly increased and comfortable sittings; the removal of the Organ from the gallery to its present position, thereby gaining more pews in the gallery; the present platform arrangement of the Pulpit; and the elevation of the floor of the house thirty inches, relieving the galleries of their appearance of great height, and producing symmetry in the whole interior arrangement of the building. The house was raised seven feet from its old foundation, and a commodious vestry for the use of the Sunday School, with suitable ante-rooms and other conveniences, was obtained. The whole was completed in the Fall of 1868, and Re-opening Services were held on the 30th of December, the Pastor preaching a a Discourse on Temple Worship, from Genesis xxviii : 17.[66]

[66] The other services were: Prayer of Consecration, by Rev. C. H. Leonard; Address, by Rev. A. St. John Chambré; Prayer, by Rev. J. H. Chapin. The following Hymn was written for the occasion by Rev. Henry C. Leonard:

My own ministry here commenced in May, 1870, — a year memorable in the history of this Society, as also in the history of the Universalist Church, as completing a century since the arrival of Rev. John Murray in America. The Session of the General Convention, appropriately held here — with the oldest Denominational Organization — in September of that year, was the occasion of the largest gathering of Universalists ever known. In every respect a success, that event was a joy to all who participated in it, an honor to this Society which so liberally provided for it, and an inspiration and impulse to the Universalist Church everywhere.

As we have now, at great length, it may at first seem — but really only by glimpses and hints of the facts to which allusion has been made — reviewed the Century which closes this day, some of the things that belong to our history are worthy of being mentioned with greater emphasis than has been laid

> "O Thou! whose thought pervades all space,
>   Whose light illumes the earth and skies,
> Within these walls reveal thy face,
>   And smile upon our sacrifice.
>
> We give to Thee this house once more,
>   Improved by human art and skill;
> Oh, may the power of sacred love,
>   And Thine own love, this temple fill.
>
> Through all our Sabbaths here below,
>   May we within this temple wait;
> And unto Thee, as moments go,
>   Our souls divinely consecrate.
>
> And when have run our life's quick sands,
>   And we shall reach the fane on high,
> Within this temple made with hands,
>   Our children's spirits sanctify."

on them as spoken of in connection with the general facts. And yet I can only call your attention to them, at the best, and leave to yourselves that more extended thought which meditation upon them as causes of gratitude to God, and as reflecting honor on our fathers, will suggest and urge.

I. From the first, this has been an eminently Christian Society. Its pulpit has illustrated and defended the doctrines of Revealed Religion, and the congregation have reverenced and trusted the truths of the Bible. Never has it been taught to, or assumed by this people, that Revelation is a fiction, or the Gospel of Jesus Christ a myth. Amid all the diversities of gifts, and differences of administration, no man has ever ministered to this people who sought to weaken their faith in the Authority of Divine Revelation. No substitute for the Gospel has been proposed, none accepted. What has been taught to, or accepted by this Society, as doctrine and duty, may have been illustrated by many facts outside of Revelation, may have been commended by its agreement with science, with philosophy, with the utterances of ancient and of modern wisdom, but its foundation has always been on a "Thus saith the Lord." Our fathers built upon this rock, an unshaken confidence in God's Revealed Word, and to the present day their descendants countenance no departure from this. The Sermons of Murray reveal a depth of faith in the Bible, and in Jesus Christ as the Son and Sent of God, which the leaders of other sects may have equalled, but none of them have surpassed. His immediate successor was emphatically "A man of one book," and that the Bible. To no other authority would he bow, but this was his complete

Counsellor and Guide; he defended it against all attacks, and sought in his teachings, as he also devoutly supplicated in his prayers, "the spread of the Everlasting Gospel," as the only cure of the world's ills and miseries. Those who came after him have had no different conviction. Forty years ago, when the now prevalent phases of skepticism and unbelief first came across the waters and were being disseminated in every community by a portion of the secular press, as also by numerous tracts and pamphlets, the Young Men of this Society set on foot an Organization having as its aim the Defence of Divine Revelation, and under their auspices a Course of Lectures was given in this and the other churches in town, on the Evidences of Christianity. Among the eminent men who took part in that Course, I find the honored name of Bp. Griswold, of the Episcopal Church. Our record, in this respect, is one for which we may justly indulge in great satisfaction.

II. This Society has also been characterized by a free and progressive spirit. Its pulpit has never been hampered, nor has the congregation been bigoted against the light and truth of new investigations. Murray's belief is now wholly a thing of history with the Universalist Church. He accepted most of the peculiarities of the Calvinism of his day, except the dogma of reprobation. He advocated the doctrine of special election to the light and knowledge of the gospel in this life, and a general election to be manifest in the life to come. His peculiar doctrine, the Union of all souls with Christ, who bore all the penal sufferings due to the entire race, he grafted to the phases of Calvinism which he accepted,

REV. FREDERIC F. THAYER.
Fourth Pastor, 1843-1844.

including the Sabellian modification of the trinity, personal devil, universal forfeiture of the divine favor, and arbitrary sovereignty. His methods of interpretation seem fanciful to us, and his treatment of Bible history, narrative, ritual and psalms, as having allegorical reference to Christ, strikes us as extremely grotesque; but certainly it was not more so than was the common exegesis of a hundred years ago; while it had this decided advantage over the popular theology, that, in pushing the Universal Promises and Invitations of the Gospel, against the dogma of eternal reprobation, it let in a flood of light and cheer to the human soul, such as the common preaching could not impart. Joy, deep and intense, was the result of receiving and believing the views which he gave of the plan of Salvation; a joy whose fulness we of the present day, who know nothing of the bondage of soul into which men were brought by a sincere acceptance of what Coleridge justly calls "that superfetation of blasphemy," the Calvinism of a century ago, can form no adequate idea.

The early Universalists of Gloucester were believers in the theory advocated by Murray; but they were also tolerant of other theories, as is evident from their receiving and hearing such men as Wright and Winchester; the former an advocate of the Universal Restitution, from the modified Calvinistic theory of the Moravians; and the latter, a still more modified Calvinist, if not wholly an Arminian, who denied that any such mystical union of human souls with Christ, by which his acts released men from self-incurred penalties, had any foundation; and who advocated such a personal bearing of punishment for sin as would necessitate, in the case of the most incorrigible, the endurance of sufferings hereafter, for the space of fifty thousand years. Their tolerance is still further manifest in their giving such frequent hearing to Hosea Ballou, whose independent views were so unlike those of any one who could then have preached to them.

Mr. Jones, at the time of his settlement, seems to have been quite in accord with the views of Murray, but his theology underwent several modifications in process of time, and in his later days he came to advocate a system not materially differing from the Unitarian basis on which Universalism has been generally placed since the early part of the present century. In some few particulars he retained his trinitarian views, although they were evidently very much modified by his rejection of the doctrine of vicarious sacrifice. He also retained to the last his old belief in the resurrection of this body of flesh.

None of those who succeeded him have had uniform views on all points of theology; and since their peculiarities of belief have been honestly entertained, the differences were no doubt freely presented and discussed. On such discussion the Society never imposed restraint, and the result has been that a free and instructive pulpit has been encouraged.

The early experiences of intolerance made the Society cautious how it gave aid or encouragement to any combinations based on statements of doctrine. It was eager to enter into alliance with those who are struggling for liberty of conscience, and the enjoyment of legal rights, and so took an active interest in the Association of 1785; but for many years it stood wholly aloof from the Convention organized in 1793, one avowed aim of which was the establishment of uniformity of belief.[67] So Independent was its spirit, as well as its name, that for twenty years it sent no representative to that body. Subsequently it became connected with the Convention, and when, years after, one of its Pastors argued strongly for ultra Congregationalism, and declaring himself "no longer a sectarian Universalist," urged the Society to the same position, he was quietly heard, but no measures were taken to change the course of action. Later, under a Pastor who was indifferent on this subject, the Society became indifferent; but never any other than a Universalist Church and Society, it afterwards responded to the appeal of another Pastor and identified itself with all the interests and organizations of our faith.

III. The attitude of this Society towards the Country, and the moral and social Reforms of the land, is one that has always been creditable to it, and to the truths which it has professed. I need not further enlarge on Murray's patriotic position during the Revolution; but it is due to the memory of his early associates in Gloucester, to say that, with few exceptions, they were patriotic men at a time when patriotism meant opposition to the mightiest and proudest government in the world. Several whose names are attached to the first form of organization, were eminent in their part in the struggle which gave us our Independence. And for several years after Mr. Jones came here he records his attendance of the funerals of no small number who were soldiers at Bunker Hill, at Monmouth and on other illustrious battle-fields. During the second war with Great

[67] See "History of Universalism in America," Vol. I.

Britain, this Society also furnished many for the maintenance of the rights of the nation. And on the breaking out of the late rebellion, a large number of the descendants of the old heroes went out to defend and perpetuate the Government which their fathers had called into being. Many of them were spared to return to their homes and are to-day with us, bearing honorable scars, and rejoicing that they have not been unworthy of the men in whose places they now stand. Others fell on the field and still others wasted away their lives in loathsome prison-pens. From first to last, it is a record of which we may well be proud, that this Society has neither withheld its money nor its blood when the Nation called for aid and for sacrifice.

I have already alluded to the attitude of Father Jones on our great National Evil, Slavery. He stands not alone as the representative of this pulpit on that great sin. Not one of his successors ever so far disgraced himself and his profession of Faith in Universal Brotherhood, as to be an apologist for human bondage. But often and at times when it has required no small degree of courage, has this pulpit faithfully instructed men in their duties towards those who were in bonds.

As the Universalist Church has it among the grandest things borne on its record, that it took an early stand against Intemperance, so this Society has been a consistent member of that Church in its position and efforts in this direction. In 1827 the Universalists of Gloucester were prominent in advocating the Suppression of Intemperance, by the action of the town authorities against it. Four years later, when the first Temperance Society of which I can find any account, was organized in this town, this Society furnished its full proportion of the membership; and its Ministers have done at least as much as any others in calling attention to the subject and enlightening and directing public thought with reference to it.

IV. Finally, it is not unbecoming in us, at this time, to bear testimony to the high Religious Character of this Society. We have already seen that the Founders of this Church were members of another Communion when conscience called them to rally around him whom God had chosen as the means of their enlightenment and joy. They were men and women of devout spirit and of truly Christian Character and Life. Their mantle descended on those who came after them; and rich are the lessons of devotion and of true Christian Manhood, furnished by those who have here been taught of God and have manifested in the world their Discipleship with the Lord Jesus Christ. I need but mention the names of Sargent, Pearce, Elwell, Friend, Hough, Babson, Sawyer, Moore, Ferson, Dale, Trask, Saville, to bring before many of you forms and faces with which you always associate honesty, benevolence, piety, and all the graces of the Christian Character; and the remembrance of whom also suggests to you the goodly company of men and women with whom they were associated in the House of God and whose Name they glorified among men.[68]

[68] See Appendix Y.

Behold, my brethren, how grand an Inheritance has come down to us, from our fathers, who trusted in God! What rich memories of teachers, alive and dead, are ours! How all these encourage, and also admonish us; teaching us how sure is God's blessing on faithful effort, and how necessary our present and continued fidelity is, if we would be worthy of what the past has put into our hands. While, then, we rejoice in the assurance of God's presence and blessing in the past, let us not cease to labor and to pray, that the Lord our God may be with us, as He was with our fathers.

Evening Services.

After partaking of a bountiful collation, provided by the ladies of the Society, in the Vestry, the Congregation reassembled in the Church at half-past seven o'clock. After singing by the choir: "Again within these hallowed walls," Prayer was offered by Rev. C. C. Clark, of Pigeon Cove.

The Congregation then joined in singing Hymn 657, Adams & Chapin's collection: "I love Thy Church, O God."

The Pastor then remarked that this House of Worship was dear and sacred to other denominations; for here, in 1832, the Orthodox Society had Ordained their first Pastor, Rev. Charles S. Porter, Rev. Lyman Beecher, D. D., preaching the sermon. Here, in 1846, while these walls were draped in mourning for the decease of Rev. Thomas Jones, the Methodists brought the mortal remains of one of their venerable ministers, the Rev. Joel Steele, and his ministering brethren here performed his funeral rites. But to none can this place be so especially sacred as to those who have made it their Religious Home, and have here learned how to discharge life's duties, and to find comfort amid life's trials and sorrows. We wish to give this service to tender memory, to the revival and the recital of reminiscences, that the story of the past may be pleasant to those who participated in its realities and profitable to those who are succeeding them in the delights and duties of this place. We have with us one who participated in the Semi-Centennial Services, in 1824, and from him let us hear first.

Rev. Thomas G. Farnsworth then responded substantially as follows:

MY DEAR FRIENDS:— I have not language adequate to express the pleasure I feel at this hour. I feel as if I were living beyond my time. When I look back fifty years, I think of a multitude of those who were with us then, whose sympathy was with us, who rejoiced in our faith, that are no longer here; they are gone, yet still I linger, not very old, not yet have I reached fourscore years. It rejoices my heart to believe unwaveringly and with faith, that all these souls still live. It may be that their ear is open to our prayers and songs to-night.

In the summer of 1821 I was in the study of Father Ballou in Boston, with Benj. Whittemore, Zelotes Fuller and M. B. Ballou. A member of the parish at Stafford called on Father Ballou and he told him that he had a young man for them. I received a call from them and settled there. I was there two and a half years. I went to Newton Corner in the Spring of 1824. In November of that year I visited Gloucester and attended the Semi-Centennial. During my ministry in Haverhill, some years later, I became acquainted with Father Jones and sometimes exchanged with him. There was no man living, save father Ballou, whom I respected so thoroughly and loved so tenderly as Father Jones. The last time I saw Father Jones was in 1839. He exchanged with me. I was then preaching in Georgetown. I believe you cannot hold in too high estimation the fathers of this Society. You can never estimate fully how much you are indebted to their fidelity, their Christian worth and the power of their example; how much they loved our cause; how much they were willing to sacrifice for its advancement and defence. They and the upholders of our faith in other places showed a spirit of consecration and self sacrifice that Heaven smiled upon. May the mantle of these worthy souls fall upon those who follow in their footsteps.

When this faith of ours was established here, there was a feeling of discord between the different churches. The Orthodox, Baptists and Methodists were at war with each other. Now they clasp hands. This faith our fathers cherished has transformed them. It has been the leaven that has worked through the whole Christian Church; it is still working and by and by we shall all be Universalists. Men are beginning to see and believe that God is the Father of the whole race; all men are brothers, all heirs of the same inheritance, with a common destiny. Let me beseech you to cherish with the utmost reverence the memory of those who built up such a faith and to whose devotedness and unswerving fidelity you are so strongly indebted.

I pray God that he may keep you, may make his face to shine upon you and finally and eternally give you peace.

This Church, said Mr. Eddy, has had ten pastors. It is matter of regret that of the seven yet living, more are not with us on this occasion, but unavoidably, several are absent. The immediate successor of Father Jones, Rev. Frederic F. Thayer, is with us and will now address you. Mr. Thayer responded:

RESPECTED FRIENDS:— Thirty-two years ago this autumn, I made my first visit to Cape Ann — a stranger alike to the people and the work of the Christian ministry. I was invited to take up my residence here, and learn of both; and whatever may have been the results of that connection to this people — and I have never been led to regard them as unfortunate — to myself I have ever counted it among the fortunate events of my life. The young pastor found here obstacles, for which he was in no sense responsible, which might well dishearten the bravest. Out of the same soil, however, came encouragement and strength. The counsellors of those days were of the older men, while those younger and more active were ready to follow their leading. Among such competent and considerate advisers, who loved the cause of their Master and were willing to spend and be spent for it, the young pastor found co-workers and companions. A large congregation attended upon the Sabbath services, and the Sabbath School became as prosperous as in its previous history. But the embarrassments of past years, the support of the senior pastor, who was settled for life, the burden of a heavy debt, added to the current expenses of the Society, all of which were to be borne by a fragment of what had been one of the largest societies in the denomination, made it advisable that something should be done to remove some of the hindrances to success. The generation of veterans, who until then had controlled the affairs of the Society, were reminded by their approaching infirmities that what remained for them to do must be done quickly; and they were especially desirous to extinguish the debt which they had been instrumental in contracting. By the persistent labors of a few, to whom the Society should ever be grateful, this portion of the work was handsomely performed.

From that time, the generation of men who had so long been prominent as officers of the Independent Christian Society surrendered the prudential affairs to the control of younger men. And here I take occasion to say in regard to these men, who at this time laid aside the harness, that they were in some respects remarkable men. Their names may not illuminate any page of their country's history, but their virtues, as illustrated in the circle where they were best known, have given them an enduring place in the Book of Life, and the generation of to-day, who worship here, may look back to a noble ancestry. In a life not altogether secluded from the world, I have never found such men elsewhere; and it is but a grateful tribute to their worth that I speak of them on this occasion. My youthful efforts were encouraged by their acquaintance and their confidence, and my subsequent career cheered by their continued blessing, until we were separated by the impenetrable veil. My faith in the possibilities of human nature was strengthened by what I had seen of them, and the confident belief of a hopeful pastor confirmed, that a plant, nurtured by their efforts and their prayers, must deserve and secure the blessing of the Most High.

Did this occasion belong exclusively to me, I should delight to speak of many of these men individually; for they stand as distinctly before me in their personal worth, as they do by name, or in their places at the head of their families; but I must not so far trespass on time which belongs to others. Of two of these men, however, with whom I was intimately associated, you will allow me to speak. One of them, prominent among the founders of this Society — one of the most influential of the merchants of his time, who, when the infant Society had outgrown the meeting house on Front street, purchased the timber of which this edifice is constructed, from a vessel which the Fates had compelled to make harbor here — was especially prominent as a devoted disciple of John Murray and his worthy successor. So fully was he indoctrinated with the early instructions of the founder, that, regardless of any modification of the views of such as called themselves Universalists, which had taken place long before his death, I have reason to believe that he passed from earth trusting for his salvation to the merits of the crucified Son of God, "who was the propitiation for our sins, and not for ours only, but for the sins of the whole world." He believed in the brotherhood of the race, and exemplified the doctrine in his days of prosperity, by striving to make those around him happy. In adversity he bowed to the discipline of his Father in Heaven, not permitting himself to doubt the love of Him "who so loved the world, that he gave for it and to it his only begotten Son." Having completed nearly a century in years as a citizen and a merchant, an ornament to his native town, as a worshipper in this church, one of its most reliable and worthy, nearly thirty years ago he was borne to an honored grave.

Of the other one to whom I have alluded, I knew more, because I knew him longer. Younger by many years than the former, he lived many years after, during which I never failed in my visits to him until a cloud received him from sight. I can best express my estimate of him by saying that he was the best man I ever knew. He possessed the most virtues, offset by the fewest faults, I have ever seen combined. His smile was a benediction, and wherever he went he carried joy. His discriminating liberality commanded the blessing of the poor. His considerate regard for his associates made them love him. His integrity insured confidence in every relation. His wisdom in council enforced respect. His devotion to all outward religious observances and his compliance with the Master's commands, entitled him to be called a Christian. His house was a sanctuary where the Bible was honored, the blessing of God invoked for the labors of the day, and the prayer of gratitude offered at its close. Herein is found the germ of all that gives occasion for any eulogy. He of whom I speak was a disciple of Christ and as such we believe was approved of God and honored by men. His virtues were the offspring of his religion and it need not be counted strange that many a parent has pointed his child to such an one as a model for imitation. Modest and amiable, he yet was firm in resisting evil; and what appeared to him right was sure of his support. When the adversities of life, of which he had fully his proportion, came upon him, he leaned upon the same arm that had brought prosperity, and he found support in his confidence in his Father in Heaven. With the same meekness and trust he met the infirmities of age, until, ripe in years and in honors, he was taken home; and if our faith does not mislead us, he has found a world to whose scenes and occupations he was not entirely a stranger and to a presence where his fidelity here has won for him the welcome congratulation — the approbation alike of what has been and the prophecy of what is to be — "Come up higher." This community lost an exemplary citizen, whose name for many years to come shall be mentioned only with respect and this Society lost one of its shining jewels. He could always be referred to as illustrating in his life the teachings of this pulpit and when the clouds gathered around this church he led the noble efforts which were made for their dispersion. Here, of all spots, should his name ever be cherished, and when the Universalist denomination shall make up its calendar of sainted ones for exaltation, his name will be early found.

I have not mentioned any names, but there is not a parent present who will not delight in the opportunity to tell his asking children to whom I have referred and to confirm, so far as his opportunities permit, all I have said. If it shall be said that my eulogy has become flattery, I reply that I know whereof I affirm, for I have lived under the same roof with both these men; and although it was at a period of their lives when their active participation in worldly affairs was mostly over, yet in the matured fruit I could see indications of what must have preceded. I have seen a character almost spotless, I infer the rest.

These reminiscences will suffice to show on what my pleasant associations with this place are founded. With fathers such as I have described, I found worthy successors among the children, and from that day to the present I have reason to believe that I have found only friends. The time of my residence in Gloucester abounds in precious memories and my heart is filled with gratitude to God that I am permitted to be with you on this memorial occasion. I miss many faces that would look familiar here, but I can find some esteemed representatives of the dead or the absent living. Although not often with you in person, I know of your prosperity as a religious society, and I rejoice in it. The tidings of your domestic sorrows have often reached my ears and commanded my fullest sympathy. Therefore I cannot feel that I am a stranger, although many of those who are now active co-workers with your faithful pastor have grown to maturity since I left Gloucester. While the cheerful recollections of the worthies who have passed on, the pleasant welcome of those who have grown from youth to middle age and now bear the burden and heat of the day; while these remain, I can draw a little upon the good-will which must come by inheritance. Under these circumstances I have ventured to make the preceding remarks. It would give me pleasure to mention some reminiscences of Father Jones, as I was thrown in his way; but if I say only, that I saw in him the beauty of a character chastened in the work of life, and a devoted servant of Christ confidently awaiting his well-earned crown, it is enough to show his connection with the venerable men of whom I have already spoken. I would gladly recite what I have learned of the faithful ministers of this church for the last quarter of a century, but one is here who can do this more fittingly, and who by his eloquent words will manifest to you how the young pastor of another generation, feeble in body but strong in faith, who went forth bearing precious seed, has thrilled the hearts of thousands by his manly words for Christ and his cause, and now comes back rejoicing, bringing his sheaves with him. I would like to speak of some dear to my memory, who, having completed their tasks, in infirmity wait only the summons to depart; but must content myself by commending to such the blessed thought, that a kind Father has for all a higher field of service, to which, at His own time and in His own way, He gently leads us for nobler triumphs.

Having occupied the time allotted to me, I close with an earnest prayer for your continued prosperity, individually, and as a church of Christ; with the hope that the life of your devoted pastor may long be spared and his days of usefulness in this field be long protracted; and in the faith, strengthened with my years, that the fundamental doctrine of this church, as proclaimed here by John Murray, of the Divine Paternity, however interpreted by men, will finally be illustrated in the complete success of the Saviour's mission — the ultimate triumph of good over evil, and the consequent redemption and exaltation of the whole brotherhood of man.

The Congregation then sung Hymn 970, "Long be our fathers' temple ours."

The Pastor then remarked that the immediate successor of Mr. Thayer, Rev. H. B. Soule, had departed this life; and that the next in the order of service was Rev. A. D. Mayo, who would make such remarks as to him seemed most pertinent. Mr. Mayo thus responded:

It seems to me, to-night, as if I were looking across

REV. HENRY B. SOULE.
FIFTH PASTOR, 1845-1846.

the sea to some dim, fading land, as I recall the events of the years when I was here with you. It is now twenty years since I left you, to undertake the ministry of Liberal Christianity in the West. I did not go because I was tired of you, and I do not think you were tired of me. But when I entered the ministry I resolved that I would try to stay with one people until my health became firm, and I knew what I wanted to teach; and then go to some Western community to establish a church of Liberal Christianity. After a service of twenty years at Cleveland, Ohio, Albany, N. Y., and Cincinnati, Ohio, I was providentially called back to my native State. But the old "Commonwealth of Massachusetts," that God has been implored to "save" in the Thanksgiving Proclamations for the last hundred years, no longer exists. What changes have come over our dear old State within the last twenty years! I left Gloucester an old village; now you are a thriving young city. The crooked old Boston of that time has partly gone up in flames, and old Boston glorified into perhaps the most beautiful of our metropolitan cities. The valley of the Connecticut, that I left, thirty years ago, dozing in its sleepy meadows and elm-shaded village streets, has been touched by the great magician of Progress, and a hundred thousand people are now gathered in the dozen busy manufacturing towns within half an hour's ride of Springfield, my present home. Even the interior of this old church is all changed, and the rocky hills over which I tramped in the past days are now graded for city streets. Emerson used to tell us that England extended to the Alleghanies, and America began the other side. But the great war of reconstruction has changed all that. The mighty West is now overflowing the East, and all provincial distinctions disappear. As I stand at the street corners of New England cities, I see the children of every nation and clime flocking to the public schools. So are we trying to work out the problem of organizing the world's Republic on the basis of the Golden Rule. But through all these changes of past and present, one thing remains stable and equable. I have brought back to New England the same old Gospel of Christ that I began to preach to you twenty-eight years ago. That blessed Gospel of the paternity of God, the brotherhood of Man, the life of love, and the final restitution of all things, remains;—the same "yesterday, to-day and forever."

It would not be best for you or me that I should attempt to recall the personal events of that eight years' ministry among you. Those of you who knew me then will remember all those things, and they could not be understood by others. But three points in my recollection of that eventful past come up to me to-night, and of them I will briefly speak.

First, as I look into these faces before me, I see many that are familiar, though somewhat changed by the passing years; while in many a young countenance I behold glances and gleams that strongly remind me of those who have passed away. And those familiar looks, which become more familiar as I gaze, revive the recollection of the amazing kindness and forbearance of these Gloucester people towards me during my entire ministry in this church. I came to you little more than a boy, yet bearing about in my body the infirmities of an old man. And my bodily feebleness was not the worst of it. For my whole term of collegiate and theological education had been comprised in one year's study and two years of such reading as a desperate invalidism would permit. I had been reared in the old, obstinate school of New England Unitarian Independency, which practically puts every young man on his spiritual muscle, and sends him out into the wide world to conquer a faith. I came as full of theories and personal crotchets, as an earnest-minded boy who fancied himself a man, could be. As I look back upon some of these juvenile performances, I am filled with amazement at the way you bore with them. I remember being called to officiate at the marriage of three fair sisters, and thinking I had done a great stroke of business when I made them stand in a row and be married "at one fell swoop," by the same ceremony. When I came to my first communion service my heart failed me, and I did not think I could go through the ceremony. But good old Father Ferson talked it over with me, in his library, and gave me courage to come to the Lord's table, where I always have found a blessing awaiting me. For a long time I could not bring myself to lay my hand in baptism upon the forehead of a child, till one who has long since passed on to the better land persuaded me. I recollect in those old, explosive days before the war, when they sent back slaves from Boston to South Carolina, I used to stand up periodically, having packed my trunk the night before, and blaze away, like a whole battery, right in the face and eyes of you all, and then go home wondering at the little sensation my tremendous demonstration seemed to make. I didn't understand then, that under the quiet surface of your Yankee reticence you all agreed with me, and listened to the discharge of my artillery as soldiers hear the stray shots of the skirmishers in the early morning of a day of battle. But through all this, and a great many things I cannot now speak of, your patience and forbearance was simply astonishing. I do not remember an instance when any man of you reproached me, or in any unfriendly spirit said, "Why do you so?" I now realize what an advantage it was for me to spend those early years of my ministry with a broad-minded, generous, uncritical set of men, many of whom had seen and known a thousand fold more than myself; who were accustomed to the "tricks and manners" of boys, on sea and land, at home and in foreign parts. You evidently had made up your mind there was something in your young minister, and were willing he should work it out, even, sometimes, at your expense. How kind you were to me during those years of early toil and affliction. And perhaps the kindest thing of all was to let me go.

The second thought that occurs to me is that Gloucester and this church were the university where I was trained for the Christian ministry. Here I was brought by a Divine hand, that through quiet study and some experience of life, I might establish myself on a foundation of Christian faith, from which, thank God, I have never found occasion to swerve since the day I left you. Every day since I went I have felt the great advantage to a young minister to go first to a quiet place and abide with an indulgent people, until he knows in whom he believes, has somewhat measured himself and made some fit trial of his own powers. Especially, let not our young men go forth into the West, that great, chaotic realm of dissolving faiths and social experimenting, "not knowing whether there be a Holy Ghost;" whether Christ is an Oriental myth, or the Lord of Glory; whether man is a snarl of bewitched nerves, or a living, immortal soul; whether God is an infinite, impersonal uncertainty, or the "one God and Father of all, above all, through all and in you all." My years of sickness, that shut me in my study, gave me time for a great deal of careful reading. And no emergency has since come to me in which those studies have not borne invaluable fruit. But more than my books taught me did I learn of Christianity from teachers like Fathers Hough, and Babson, Friend and Ferson; from daily contact with men and women whose lives glowed with the fervor of their own beautiful faith. To me they were incarnate Christianity.

Then I was all the time enfolded in this wonderful gospel of nature on this New England coast. The restless ocean; this tumble of hills, sown with rocks, the deep, quiet pine woods; the summits from which I looked off on the silver circle of the all-surrounding sea; the fleets of fishing boats, like troops of white-winged spirits of the deep, dimly seen through the morning mists along the horizon line; all were familiar as the floor of my own study. Almost every foot of this Cape, its highways and by-ways, I remember, with the beloved friends who walked with me there. And never can I forget the old church with its avenue of elms, the songs of birds and the rustling of leaves mingling with our summer service, as I looked from my pulpit through the open door. All these things were the university in which I was trained for the ministry of my later years.

And the final thing I would say, is, that I believe I owe the best success I have had to the right beginning here. I always have looked upon the different Christian denominations as doors through which people of different types of nature could enter and make their way upward to the high table-land of our common Christian faith. As for myself, I fear if I had tried to enter through one of the old ecclesiastical gates, as I knew them in my youth, I could not have borne the burden of their theologies, and would have been swept off into the great throng of those who have no resting-place for their faith. I think it was well I was not launched into the strife of criticism that raged about the Unitarian Schools of that period. Perhaps if I had been, I could now better appreciate many of the theological and philosophical feats of the performers in the "radical" gymnasium of to-day. I make no boast of superior intelligence or sounder faith than others; only I bless God that I was led, providentially, into the Kingdon of Christ through the heart-door of faith in the Infinite love of God; and that all my early experience in this church, and the branch of the Church Universal to which it belongs, fixed me for life in a confidence and trust in the love of God and the salvation of men that has never been disturbed.

So, I come back to you and to my native State, after an absence of twenty eventful years, with this thing especially to say to you;—that I have seen human nature in many of its forms, have studied society in its varied phases, have tried to learn the secret of every church and every theory that has done any good thing for mankind; and it seems to me more clear than ever before that the living side of every church, and the vital truth in all our new science, philosophy, literature, society and statesmanship converge upon that high table-land of Christian faith which was seen in vision by the fathers of our Liberal Christianity. A great deal that is now called the Christian Religion is doomed to go down stream and be forgotten; the rubbish of Catholic superstition; the dry lumber of evangelical theologizing; the drift of liberal skepticism; and with them a whole world of social and political speculation for which humanity has no farther use. But as the great mountain ranges look down unmoved upon the lowland floods, sweeping the wrecks of the generations onward to the sea; so will abide forever the religion of the Lord Jesus Christ, as the central highland amid the changing history of the human race. Believe in God Almighty, the Infinite Spirit of Love; in Man, God's immortal Child, created in His image, educated by His Providence towards a final success; in that religion whose soul is a perpetual sacrifice of love and a constant service to man; in Christ, the Lord, the perfect Man, the incarnate love of God; in the Church of Christ, the Schoolmaster appointed to lead all nations upward to the open heights of the Kingdom of Heaven. Then let what will come and go, we have a foundation immovable, that shall endure through the life that now is, through every life that is to come.

At the close of Mr. Mayo's Address, the following letters from former pastors were read:

ALBANY, N. Y., October 7th, 1874.

MY DEAR MR. EDDY:— Your favor of the 1st inst. has just reached me, via Staten Island. Hence the seeming delay of this response.

It would give me great pleasure to be with you at the proposed celebration. At present, however, I do not see how I can promise to be so. Urgent duties here, as well as the length and expense of the journey, forbid me to anticipate the tender joy of greeting the friends in Gloucester whom I remember so vividly and tenderly. Please say to any who may wish to know the reason of my absence, that it is *not* forgetfulness of, or indifference to the friends of former years. If absent in body, I shall not be in spirit. May you have a solemnly joyful occasion.

While I will not definitely promise the *letter* for which you ask, I will *try* to answer your wishes in that respect. But should my poor word be wanting, you will hardly miss it in the multitude of good words that will hardly fail to get said on the occasion.

I know not what hints I can furnish you that almost any of the older members of the Society could not. The Society moved calmly — it *never* moved any other way — on its course during my ministry, having, as I think, a larger congregation then than it had had for many previous years, if not than ever before. This was owing to two causes — the growth of the town, and the subsidence of old disagreements. The Sunday School grew from 96 to about 250 members. The galleries in the old church, which were inconvenient, disagreeable, unused, were remodelled and made desirable for sittings. Gas fixtures were introduced into the church. My salary rose at one time to $1600 per annum, which was the largest the Society had then ever paid, and was always promptly paid. As to the religious life of the parish, God only knows how prosperous, or otherwise, that was. I have a feeling that if it were less — as it certainly was — than we all desired, there was yet a tolerable degree of earnestness and devotion. In some hearts I know the sacred flame burned very brightly.

Of things personal, either to myself or to any of the friends, you need not that I speak. Could I be with you, or if I am able to write you, I should, or shall indulge in some reminiscences of this sort.

Wishing you a very pleasant and profitable time, and with kindest regards to both yourself and all my old acquaintances, I beg leave to subscribe myself,

Faithfully yours,
W. R. G. MELLEN.

PROVIDENCE, Oct. 19, 1874.

REV. R. EDDY,

MY DEAR SIR:— I have received through you the invitation of the Committee of the First Independent Church of Gloucester, to attend the Centennial Celebration of their Society, on the 3d of November. On many accounts it would give me great pleasure to comply with their request. Indeed, I feel a very strong impulse drawing me to be present and participate in the exercises of that occasion. But there are other reasons, more powerful still, which impel me to decline. Owing to the many changes that have occurred in my life, the sorrowful experiences I have endured since I was last in Gloucester, the presence of so many of my former friends, and other memorials of things which lie in my mind like a beautiful dream, would awaken in me feelings which, as yet, I am but poorly fitted to sustain. I trust I am neither morbid nor sentimental, but these are the impressions which I find myself unable to overcome. Doubtless they are still further strengthened by the fact that my ministry in Gloucester was in every way so thoroughly delightful. I do not believe it is possible to find on this Continent a religious society more generous, thoughtful and sympathetic, or that treats its minister with a more dignified and courteous respect. This I attribute largely to the fact that its foundations were laid by the pious hands of Murray, and that its growth and development were watched over for forty years by a minister of such staunch integrity as Father Jones, who, in the spirit of St. Paul's injunction, magnified his office on all occasions, and was diligent and faithful in discharging every duty belonging to it.

I know of no items of fact or suggestion, during my ministry, which you do not already possess.

Trusting that the occasion may prove all that the friends anticipate or desire for it, and devoutly praying that there may be other centuries of prosperity in store for the Parish, I remain

Very truly yours,

E. H. CAPEN.

The pastor then announced that the Church Records show that, in 1825, a young man joined this church who intended to devote himself to the Christian Ministry. That intention having been fulfilled, the person alluded to will now address you. Rev. Joseph P. Atkinson responded, in substance as follows:

I love this town, for here I was born; my friends and kindred are here. Many whose memories I cherish are lying in your cemeteries. I have frequently spoken from your pulpit. I remember the first sermon I ever preached. It was by invitation of Father Jones. He didn't like to be called *Father*, he wanted to be called *Brother* Jones. He often used to say: "Call no man *father* upon the earth." I remember that for that first sermon I took for my text the whole of the 20th chapter of Revelations. Father Jones thanked me for such a *wonderful* sermon. How plainly I remember the tithing-man! His pew was in the gallery, about midway. There was a pole run up from the pew, seven or eight feet long, painted white, so that we boys might know where he was. The tithing-man's name was Newman. I have no doubt that he was a kind man, but he scowled so at the girls, and rapped the boys so hard, that I thought him the crossest-looking Universalist I ever saw. William Tucker, his successor, was more severe than he. He would leave his seat and go round the church, striking the noisy boys with the knob of the stick, and the refractory girls with the feather which was attached to one end of the stick. I remember how attentive we were in prayer-time, listening for the "amen," that we might slam the seats as soon as we heard it.

I well remember Father Pearce and Drs. Ferson and Dale, Brother Elwell and many others. I shall never forget them. I hope I shall never forget the beautiful faith that influenced them to do their many good works.

The Pastor then remarked that in the letters received, and also in the remarks made, testimony had been borne to the promptness with which the financial concerns of the Society had been managed. The treasurers of the Society have been but few in number. One who has been so frequently alluded to — Benjamin K. Hough — held the office forty years. We will now listen to his successor, who also bears a portion of his name — Benjamin Hough Corliss. Mr. Corliss responded:

The hour is late, and it will not do for me to speak at any great length on this occasion. So much has already been said that we have literally been filled with a feast of good things. This has been a season of great pleasure to me.

The very able Address of our Pastor, to which we have listened to-day, reviewing, as it has, the history of this Church and of Universalism on the Cape for a period of One Hundred Years, has shown us how many circumstances connected with our progress may truly be regarded as providential. Planted in weakness, we have grown to be a powerful denomination, exerting a mighty influence on religious thought throughout the world. I am deeply impressed with a sense of the devotion and fidelity of the Founders of this Church to their convictions of duty. True to the work to which they were called, and although they could not foresee the result of their labors, they patiently wrought, believing that they were sowing the seeds of divine truth. Many sacrifices were required of them; they were obliged to break away from old associations, and ties of affection and friendship were severed. They firmly believed in the great doctrine of God's Fatherhood, and the Brotherhood of Man, and were determined to lay the foundation of a Church to be built on this doctrine; for which they suffered persecution and reproach, were subjected to calumny, misrepresentation, and the terrors of the law. Their steadfast and brave example has brought inspiration and hope to thousands of believing hearts.

We stand here to-night at the beginning of a new century, and have reason to be thankful for, and proud of the lessons they have taught us. Let us be faithful to duty in our day and generation, as they have been true and devoted in the past; and may the glorious record which they bequeath to us be regarded as a sacred legacy, to stimulate and quicken our faith, and consecrate us more earnestly to the work of life, and the obligations it imposes.

I was but a boy, six years old only, at the time of the Semi-Centennial Celebration, and consequently have no clear recollection of that event in our history. But I remember well many of the men whose names have been so often spoken this day, and I ever think of them as good, true, faithful disciples, whose bright example has always been to me a strong incentive to duty.

A complimentary allusion has been made to the Treasurership of the Society. In April, 1818, six months before I was born, my grandfather became the Treasurer. In 1853 I succeeded him to the office. I was justly proud of the honor of being considered worthy to succeed the devoted men who have served the Society in this capacity, and to have my own name placed on the record in connection with those of Somes, Pearce and Hough. It has been my aim and desire so to conduct the finances of the Society as not to be deemed unworthy of the mantle that has fallen upon my shoulders; and if in this respect I have measurably succeeded, I can truly say I am content.

In conclusion, permit me to say that I am grateful for the privilege of being present at this anniversary, and of participating in the services of this interesting occasion. I wish also to express the confident belief that there is in the future for our denomination, much to encourage and hope for. If we are true to ourselves, and live up to the teachings of our glorious faith, we shall abundantly prosper, and our light will so shine, that all men, we trust, will eventually come to the knowledge of the truth, and be blessed with the assurance of God's all-embracing love.

When Mr. Corliss had concluded, allusion was made to the fact that the Old World having sent us Rev. John Murray, it was a pleasant circumstance at this time to know that we are favored with a representative of the Universalism across the waters, in the person of Rev. James Ure Mitchell, of Scotland, who would favor us with a few words. Mr. Mitchell responded with a song which he had improvised for the occasion, and then said:

I am an old-fashioned preacher. I believe in the old-fashioned heaven and hell. My idea of hell is much older than that of Calvin. Our doctrines are older than any church organization. Let us, like Murray, abide by the Word of God; let us show forth in our lives the simplicity of the Gospel; make Christ and Him crucified the central truth we present. While I am strengthened by intercourse with the people of our faith here, some things are painful to me. I find on the part of some preachers a desire to be wise above what is written. I am satisfied that five years of Murray's life did more good for the cause of truth and humanity than five times five spent in the study of philosophical essays. When the Universalists of Scotland go to the church, it is with the Bible in their hands. I know the letter is not the spirit, but the spirit cannot be found independent of the letter; the chaff is necessary to the wheat. The pews should speak to the pulpit, as well as the pulpit to the pews; the Bible should be personally studied by all. The pioneers of our faith went to the people with the Bible in their hands and in their hearts. If we would advance in the work to which God has called us, let us be students of the Word. The work is progressing in Scotland. Many are rejoicing in the truth of the Gospel who, twelve years ago, thought the Bible a bundle of riddles. Five years ago I entered Dunfermline. Our doctrines were strange, and I a stranger. The Sunday before I left, I found there 573 who received the hand of fellowship and had passed from darkness into light; 300 of these had previously been in a state of practical infidelity. Work is going on in the old towns of Scotland. Through the help of the Woman's Centenary Association, the society at Edinburg has been reorganized. If the people of to-day are as happy in reaping as your fathers were in sowing, then shall be rejoicing. Persecution has been said to be the seed of the church. Little did the Old World think that in persecuting Murray they were planting the seed which would bring forth such a great and glorious harvest. Be ye steadfast; stand fast in the liberty wherewith God has made you free, and be not weary in well doing.

The services having now been protracted until half-past ten o'clock, were brought to a close by singing the Doxology: " Praise God from whom all blessings flow," and the Benediction was pronounced by the Pastor.

REV. AMORY D. MAYO.
Sixth Pastor, 1846-1854.

APPENDIX A.

LETTER TO REV. ELI FORBES.

GLOCESTER, April 4th, 1776.

REV'D SIR:—You will have laid before you the Votes of the Parish relating to your Settlement, and as it may be of great importance to you as well as to us, we think it our duty to address you on the subject. For many years past, our trade, and particularly the fishery, by which our chief dependence is, has greatly declin'd, that, except a very few persons, we have been carrying on both trade and fishery to a very great loss; that many of us have sunk thousands; that we have large debts outstanding which will be entirely lost. Our fishery at present is at an end, and merchandize abroad very dangerous and precarious; several of our vessels taken, others missing; our tradesmen and labourers dependent mostly on the trade for their subsistence. Should the Publick dispute continue much longer, our fishery must be entirely ruined, and then, of course, all other business of any consequence here, must fail, as we are at such a distance from ye country that it will be in vain to expect anything therefrom in our trade. We are greatly in arrears in our taxes of every kind for two years past: new and heavy ones increasing daily; most of our people gone: not the least expectation but we shall be put to ye flight again. Two or three of our principal traders left ye parish; more intend it.

Some of us remember the Spanish and French Wars at different periods, with other sore calamities; but never did our eyes behold such a Gloomy Aspect as our Affairs wear at this season. In short, time would fail us to enumerate the many difficulties that attend us. We are desirous that that Harmony that has existed for these many years in this Parish, may continue. But if you should think proper to give your voice in the affirmative, it must entirely be at an end, as we shall be obliged to take such steps as would by no means be agreeable to you or our brethren. Therefore we thought it our duty to apprize you of this, and hope your Wisdom will direct you to that which will be to your Honour.

We are your most Humb'l Serv'ts,

WINTHROP SARGENT,	EBENEZER PARSONS,
JOSEPH FOSTER,	ABRAHAM SAWYER,
SAM'L SAYWARD	BENJAMIN WEBBER,
BRAD'Y SANDERS,	JOHN DAVIS,
WILLIAM SARGENT,	WILLIAM MORGAN,
WM. CARD,	PHILEMON PARSONS,
JNO. BABSON,	GEORGE CREIGHTON,
IGNATIUS WORTH, SR.,	EPES SARGENT,
DAVID PEARCE,	JAMES JORDAN,
JOHN MCKEAN,	PHILEMON HASKELL,
JAMES ODELL,	NATHANIEL ELLERY,
JOHN STEVENS ELLERY,	JOHN STEVENS, JR.

APPENDIX B.

MR. MURRAY BEFORE THE COMMITTEE OF SAFETY.

A witness of this interview has left the following account of it: "The chairman of the committee opened the business. 'We have sent for you, to know who you are, and from whence you came?' 'Your question is rather difficult, sir; I hardly know how to answer you. Do you mean where did I come from last?' 'I say where did you come from?' 'I have been in various places in this country, sir.' 'I say where did you come from when you came into this country?' 'From England.' 'From what part of England?' 'London.' 'What business had you to come to this country?' 'Business, sir! I felt disposed to come, and came —' 'What business have you in this town?' 'The same as I have in every town where I happen to sojourn.' Here one of the committee arose, and requesting leave to speak, which was granted, said: 'I conceive we have sent for this man to know from whence he came, who he is, and what business he has here: this is a time of difficulty, we are at variance with England, he calls himself an Englishman, we do not know what he is. He associates with a great many whom we look upon as enemies to this country, and they go to hear him, converse — I think — I cannot call it *preaching*.' Here Mr. Murray would have spoken, but he was imperiously, not to say impudently commanded to be silent, and his accuser proceeded, until at length the chairman again resumed: 'Where did you come from? We want to know where you were born, and brought up?' Mr. Murray answered, 'Gentlemen, it is not my wish to give you unnecessary trouble. I was born in England. Shortly after I had attained my eleventh year I accompanied my father to Ireland, where I continued many years under his care. When I was between 19 and 20, I returned to England, where I abode, living generally in London, until I quitted it for this country. Since I came into this country my residence has been in Maryland, Pennsylvania, the Jerseys, New York, Connecticut, Rhode Island, Massachusetts and New Hampshire.' 'What did you come into this country for?' 'In pursuit of retirement, but concurrent circumstances rendered me a preacher.' 'Have you any credentials?' 'Yes, sir.' 'Show them.' 'I have none present; there are many in this town who have heard me, and received my testimony: they are my credentials.' 'Ay, that is nothing — you see he has no authority. How could you think of preaching without authority?' 'When I came into this country there was no war; I believed it to be a land of civil and religious liberty — every charter and every law made among yourselves breathed a spirit of toleration. I felt assured I should be allowed liberty of conscience; my intentions were upright. A conviction that God has ordained me to proclaim the Gospel has been powerfully impressed upon my mind, and I am still convinced that I ought to preach the Gospel.' 'How long do you intend to stay in this town?' 'I do not precisely know; but certainly until the weather and roads shall be good.' 'The weather will do, and it is pretty good travelling now.' [At this time, the weather having been extremely severe, the roads were nearly impassable.] 'I do not believe I shall quit Gloucester until April; about that time I expect to commence a journey to Philadelphia.' 'The town is very uneasy at your continuance here, and we are a committee of safety. We are to take up all strangers and send them out of town.' 'Sir, I have already been warned out of town, and if you be apprehensive of my becoming a charge, I can procure bonds.' One of the committee addressed the chair for liberty to speak, which having obtained, he said: 'Your stay in this town is cause of uneasiness to many: you hurt the morals of the people, and a great many who hear you are enemies to the country.' 'Those who hear me, and believe what I deliver, can never be injured in their morals.' 'I do not believe you.' 'You have not heard all I have said in defence of my persuasion.' 'I have heard enough; I neither *believe, nor like it.*' 'Well, sir, there is no act of assembly to compel you to hear; but you should remember your neighbor is entitled to equal liberty with yourself.' 'You deliver very erroneous principles.' 'My principles are all to be found in the sacred records of divine truth.'

'Ay, so you say.' 'I was not apprized that I was cited before a spiritual court. Sir,' addressing the chair, 'this gentleman asserts that I associate with a great many enemies of this country. I demand that they be pointed out. If I associate with an individual of this description, it is unknown to me.' A gentleman at the chairman's elbow observed: 'Mr. Chairman, I think we have no business to answer this man a single question; We did not send for him to answer his questions, but to ask questions of him.' The chairman then repeated that the town were very uneasy, and advised Mr. Murray to depart to prevent further trouble, to which he answered: 'Sir, I have been nearly seven years in this country; perhaps no one has a more extensive acquaintance. I have many friends, and many enemies. I feel that I am a friend to all mankind, and I am happy that no circumstance of my life can prove the contrary. I was invited to this town, and I have been cordially received; but it seems I am suspected, because I associate with many who are enemies to this country. I associate with Captain Winthrop Sargent, pray is he an enemy? During my residence in this place I have never heard a syllable uttered which this committee ought to consider as reprehensible. I am not acquainted with a single individual who appears to me an enemy to this country; two or three worthy characters I know, who do not perfectly approve every measure which has been adopted. I have recently endeavored to recollect how many gentlemen the circle of my connexions from Maryland to New Hampshire contained, who were suspected of being unfriendly to the presest order of things, and I could number but five persons, not an individual of whom has ever been proved inimical to American prosperity. For myself, I rejoice in the reflection that I am a staunch friend to liberty, genuine liberty. It is well known that I have labored to promote the cause of this country, and I rejoice that I have not labored in vain. I am so well known, and I have the happiness to be so well respected, that his Excellency, General Washington, appointed me to officiate as Chaplain to several Regiments. I should have imagined this fact would have been *sufficient Credentials here.* I have injured no person in this town. I am invited to meet my friends, in the house of a friend, where they desire me to read the Bible, to comment thereon, and to unite with them in solemn prayer to Almighty God, for the continuance of His mercies to us as a people, and not unto us only, but to a once lost, and now redeemed world.' A member of the committee observed that they could not be answerable for anything that might be done by a Mob, and it was not in their power to prevent it, if he did not, without delay, leave the town. Mr. Murray, laying his spread hand upon his breast, answered: 'Sir, I feel such a consciousness of innocence here, that I know not what it is to fear. It is with perfect composure that I commit myself to God, and the Laws of this Commonwealth. If I have broken any law, let me be punished by law; but I bless God I am not a lawless person. Sir, I am a stranger to fear; I have committed no action worthy of punishment. Sir, I know not what it is to fear. No man can have any power over me except it be given to him from above: no injury can be done me but by the permission of my God. But I am not afraid. The worst this Mob can do, is to deprive me of a life which I have been many years quite willing to resign. Sir, I commit myself and my cause to the Ruler of Heaven and of Earth.' One gentleman observed that the rule upon Earth was delegated to them, or words to that effect; when Mr. Murray replied: 'Sir, I conceive the God of Heaven is the only Ruler in Heaven above, and in Earth beneath,' and, addressing the chair, he added: 'Sir, I have answered every question you have thought proper to ask, and as I find it difficult to speak, I am so very ill, I will take leave to wish you a good evening. Gentlemen, good night,'" when, without interruption, he departed.

The following named gentlemen were Members of the Committee of Safety; any five of the seventeen made a quorum: John Stevens, Capt. Jacob Allen, Maj. Sam'l Whittemore, Capt. William Coas, Capt. Winthrop Sargent, Capt. Jacob Parsons, Capt. William Ellery, Samuel Plumer, Esq., Col. John Low, Mr. Daniel Thurston, Capt. John Row, Mr. John Hale, Col. Peter Coffin, Deacon Nathaniel Haskell, Mr. James Porter, Capt. John Smith, Deacon Hubbard Haskell.

APPENDIX C.

ACTION OF THE FIRST PARISH CHURCH.

The following from the Records of the First Parish Church, gives a full account of the dealings of that body with its absenting members. The records are literally copied:

Feby. 11, 1777. the Chh met by appoint^t.

Voted. That Epes Sargent and wife, Winthrop Sargent and wife, Eben^r. Parsons and wife, David Pearce, James Millet, Lydia Prentiss, Rebecca Smith, Judith Stevens, Anna Babson, Jemi^a. Cook, Han^h. Tucker, Nancy Saunders, and Jemima Parsons be called upon to give reasons, if any they had, why they absented themselves from the Worship and ordinances of God in his House.

Voted 2^{ly}. That the following letter be sent to each of the above said members—viz—We have observed with concern that you have absented yourselves from the Worship and ordinances of God in his House notwithstanding your Covenant engagements to the contrary, and as we are mutually bound as a Chh to watch over one another, in ye Lord and to admonish one another, as occasion may require, we think it our Duty to call upon you to give us reasons, if any you have, why you have thus absented yourselves that we may judge of the same, for which purpose we shall meet again in the Meeting House, on Wednesday, the 19th Instant, at 3 o'clock in the afternoon; when we pray you personally to appear and give your reasons for such absence, either in writing or verbally as you shall chuse.

We are with tender concern most affectionately your Brethren,

ELI FORBES, Pastor.

In church meeting, Feby. 11, 1777.

Voted 3^{ly}. That Deacons Haskel & Kinsman be desired to carry the above letter to each of the aforesaid delinquent members.

Then the meeting was adjourned to Wednesday, the 19th Instant, then to meet again at the Meeting House at 3 o'clock afternoon.

Feby. 19, 1777. Met by adjournment and received a paper delivered by Eber. Parsons which was in answer to the Letter wrote the absenting members on the 11th Instant, and which was as follows—

We have considered the Substance of your *Note*, and not being fond of contention, lest anything should pass tending thereto, we think it best thus to inform you, that our reasons for our absenting ourselves from your society are purely of a religious nature, which is wholly between God and our own souls. We trust we have a good conscience and are happy in ye consideration yt Jesus only is appointed our Judge.

Feby. 19, 1777. To the Chh.

EPES SARGENT	CATHne SARGENT
WINTHROP SARGENT	JUD. SARGENT
EBENr PARSONS	PHEBE PARSONS
DAVID PEARCE	HANh. TUCKER
REBECCA SMITH	LYDIA. PRENTISS
JUDh STEVENS	JEMI. COOK
ANNE BABSON	JEMi. PARSONS
NANCY SAUNDERS	

which paper was read and duly considered and

Voted 1. That it was by no means Satisfactory to the Chh, or as containing any reasons at all why the above named shd absent themselves from the worship and ordinances of God.

Vot. 2ly. That an answer should be sent to the absenting members in which proper notice should be taken of ye contemptuous manr in which they treated the Chhs Letter, and as they have given no reasons at all for their absence, that they be further called upon to give those reasons if any they have.

Vot. 3. That Messieurs Whittemore & Porter assist ye pastor in forming the above sd answer—then the meeting was adjourned till next Sabbath after meeting then to be detained to hear the answer.

Feb. 23. The Chh was Stayed after the public services, and the answer to the absenting members was read and accepted, and is as Follows—

The 1st Church of Christ in Gloucester send again to their absenting members.

Beloved in ye Lord

Tho we are not fond of contention, and would carefully avoid anything tending thereunto, yet is our right to ask, and your duty to give reasons (if any you have) why you have so long absented yourselves from our communion in the worship and ordinances of God in his House.

We did not expect yt you would treat our friendly Letter which was wrote in the Bowels of christian meekness, as a contemptuous *Note*, and we did not ask you why you absented yourselves from our Society, for we have not done it, nor do we ask for those reasons which are wholly between God and your Souls, for they don't belong to us.

But for those reasons which has induced you to absent yourselves from our communion in ye worship and ordinances of God in his House and those reasons being purely of a religious nature as you intimate cant be any argument why we shd not be favoured with ye knowledge of them. And that we may keep a good conscience in obede to our Lord and master, who is our supreme Judge as well as yours, we call upon you again for your Reasons, assuring you that what you have ordered we cant receive as any reasons at all for your conduct or as anyway Satisfactory to us.

Tho' you may treat us with contempt we mean to treat you with christian tenderness. We pity and pray for you and would not neglect anything in our power to recover you from those paths in which you have Strayed and to bring you back to the fold of Christ, yt in attendance upon divine ordinances you may be nourished up unto eternal life. Please to read

    Matew XVIII, 15, 16.
    1 Cor. X, 32.
    1 Thes. X, 14.
    1 Pet. III, 13, 14, 15, 16, 17.

ELI FORBES, Pasr. in ye name and at the desire of ye Chh.

GLOUCESTER, Feb. 23, 1777.

Then the meeting was adjourned to the 13th of next March then to meet at 3 o'clock, p. m.

March 13. Met according to the above adjourmt and as the absenting members did not see fit to make or send us any answer to ours of the 23ᵈ of Feby we adjourned again to the 3ᵈ of April next then to meet at 3 o'Clo p. m. In the meantime the Deacons were desired to Discourse with them.

March 30. the Chh was Stayed, and the Deacons informed that they were not ready to make report. The meeting was further adjourned to the 10th Inst.

April 10. the Chh met according to yᵉ last adjournᵗ when the Decons reported that they had seen and conversed wite sevel of the delinquent members, but could not receive any satisfactory answers or reasons why they absented themselves—the Chh voted to send them the following letter.

The 1 Chh of Christ in Glocester send again to their absent members—

Beloved in the Lord—
We are very sorry that you refuse to give us any sufficient reasons why you absent yourselves from the House and ordinances of God, contry to your most solemn Covenant engagements. We think by this refusal you give us new and just matter of offence; and you constrain us to bear our joint and public Testimony against your proceedings.

1. That you have Separated yourselves from our worship and communion without any just Cause on our part.
2. That you refuse to meet with us, or to give us any reasons either verbally or by writing why you have thus Separated yourselves from our worship and Communᵑ by this you cast contempt upon the Chh of Christ and refuse to Submit to yᵗ discipline & Govermᵗ wʰ he has ordained in his Chh. We pray you to Consider of the matter well, and if there is any matter of grievance on your part, pray propose some method by wʰ it may be removed or an accommodation may take place, and if you have any matters which you are not willing shd be heard and judged of by the first Chh of Christ in Glocester, we are ready to submit the matter to yᵉ Judgement of a Council of Chhs mutually chosen for that very purpose and will subject the whole of your conduct to yᵉ inspection and Judgement of the impartial, and shall for the present wait your answer, as we above all things

would seek and pursue the things that make for peace and whereby we may edifie one another.
   and subscribe your offended Brethren
   ELI FORBES Pastor in ye name of ye Chh.
GLOCESTER 10 April 1777 in Chh meeting.

May 1. Chh met by adjourn^t after the Exercises of the Public Fast to hear what our delinquent Brethren had to offer in defence of y^r Separation and absenting from us but as none of them were present nor sent anything in answer to our last letter the Chh adjourned to the 19 of June next.

June 19 the Chh met after Lecture but we heard nothing from our delinquent members we adjourned to the next Lecture wⁿ we proposed to meet to hear what said delinquent members have to offer and to chuse one or more ruling Elders as they should think proper—the day to which the meeting stands adjourned is the 31 of next July.

Octr 16 the Chh met by several adjourn^t and hearing nothing from their Separating members vote unanimously the Following
 To the Separating members of the first Chh of Christ in Glocester.
Christian Friends
 We the first Chh of Christ in Glocester, have for a long time beheld with concern your Separation from our worship and communion. We have compassionately called after you and upon you to return to your Duty, or to favor us with those reasons by which you mean to Support or Justifie your Separation. We have remonstrated against your unreasonable, unscriptural, unconstitutional Behavior. In short we have prayed you if you have any matters of grievance or objection to lay them before us, or propose some method of Removing them—or that you w^d join with us, and Submit the matter of Grievance or objection to a Council of Chhs mutually chosen—so that we have done every thing we can think of, on our Part all w^h you have treated with a silent Neglect yet we feel the Bowels of Christian compassion & tenderness, and are constrained from the love we bear to our common Lord and you to admonish you, and in the Name of our Lord Jesus and by the authority w^h he has com-

mitted to his Chh, we call upon you again to return to our worship and communion that there may be no Schism in the Body, but in all lowliness of mind forbearing one another in love Endeavoring to keep the unity of the Spirit in the Bond of peace, as there is but one God and Father of us all, one Lord Jesus, one Baptism and one hope of our calling—for, by making and keeping up this unreasonable and unchristian Separation you counteract the Designs of Christianity itself, Dishonor the Christian Name, offend God and grieve his People therefore as you love God and Jesus Christ as you love the people of God and the Peace of Society and mean to support the order and Discipline of the Chh of Christ return to our Worship and Communion or else Shew before impartial Judges that you have good and sufficient reason for your Separation.

E. FORBES Pastor
in ye Name of ye Brethren.

GLOCESTER 16 Octr 1777.

then the above was unanimously voted to be communicated to Epes Sargent & wife Winthrop Sargent & wife Eben^r Parsons & wife David Pearce Lydia Prentiss Judith Stevens Rebec^a Smith Anna Babson Jemima Cooke Hannah Tucker Nancy Saunders Jemima Parsons—

the same to be committed to the Care of Eben^r Parsons who is desired to communicate the above Admonitory Letter to the above named Separating members—then the meeting was adjourned to our next Lecture.

Glocester 9 1778 at a Chh meeting voted that ye follows letter shd be sent to the Separating and absenting members of the Chh, viz —

We must remind you again y^t we have repeatedly called upon you for your reasons why you Separate from us, and absent yourselves from the worship and ordinances of God in his House, but could obtain none, You said "your reasons were purely of a religious nature and belonged to God and your own Souls." We then let you know that your answer was no ways satisfactory and in the most friendly man^r we remonstrated to you which you treated with silent neglect. We then desired the Deacons to discourse you upon the subject. But they could obtain no sufficient answer.

We then plainly told you as a Chh that we were offended and bore our joint and public testimony agst your proceedings as being unscriptural, unconstitutional and contrary to your most solemn Covenant Engagements.

We then proposed if you had any matter of Grievance, you would propose some method of removal or accommodation; or if you had any matters which you were not willing shd be Judged upon by the Chh, that you would join us in a mutual Council, and that we were willing to submit all matters in dispute to the inspection & Judgement of said Council all which you treated with contemptuous Silence. We then in ye Bowels of Christ did admonish and intreat you pointing out your Error, and shewed you wherein thro the whole of your Separation you had counteracted ye very Spirit and design of Christianity but we could obtain no answer.

We have waited long in hope that the rules of common decency and good Breeding (if no higher Motive) would at length have induced you to make some reply, but we have waited to no purpose. Ergo are obliged from a Sense of Duty to our great Lord and Master, to you and to ourselves to Suspend you from our communion and you are accordingly Suspended.

But we declare at ye same time y^t we are ready to receive you to our public Charity and Communion again upon your return from your Error in sentiment and practice and offering such Satisfaction, as the Laws of Christianity recognize or ye discipline of the Chh demands and subscribe most affectionately your offended Brethren

ELI FORBES Pastor.

APPENDIX D.

MINISTERIAL HELPERS.

In the "Answer to an Appeal," it is said, p. 20, that Mr. Murray has in "his train a *Tyler*, who (by report) is a Tory Episcopalian; a *Wright*, who is a German Moravian; with an illiterate *Townsend, Streeter, Parker, a duplicate of Winchesters*, etc., etc." A brief notice of these early preachers, and also of those who supplied the pulpit in Gloucester from 1793 to 1804, may not be devoid of interest to those who are desirous of knowing something of the contemporaries of Rev. John Murray.

REV. JOHN TYLER became Rector of Christ's Church in Norwich, Conn., in 1769, and so remained till his death in 1823. Mr. Murray preached in Norwich as early as 1773, and was from the first received with friendship by Mr. Tyler, who became at last a believer in Universalism, on the Rellyan plan. He wrote in its defence, and one of his works, entitled, "Universal Damnation and Salvation clearly proved by the Scriptures of the Old and New Testament," was anonymously published in Boston, in 1798. There were other editions of later dates. In consequence of his making the distinction which Mr. Murray did, between salvation and redemption, he was often misunderstood, and was frequently accused of denying the sentiments taught in his writings. But he retained his Universalist views to the last. Mr. Tyler frequently preached in Gloucester, and occasionally to the Universalists in Oxford, Mass.

REV. MATTHEW WRIGHT was not a German, but a Dane. His name was written in his native tongue, Reuz, and was by himself anglicized into Rights, as it is now by families of that name living in South Carolina; but his contemporaries spelled it Wright. "He was educated," said the late Rev. Edward

Turner, "at the University of Copenhagen, was a man of eminent literary attainments, able to converse, pray or preach as well in Latin as in his mother tongue. He was a Universalist in his early youth, and used to speak of the affectionate remonstrances of his mother against his heresy. He was Calvinistic, and continued Moravian in all respects excepting the idea of the universality of salvation. He was 'pure in heart,' and in life of the most sweet and amiable disposition. He lived in uncomplaining, cheerful poverty: frequently teaching school in the country towns, and preaching when requested. I know not when, nor where he died. These items of information I had from an aged member of Mr. Murray's Society, when I was a young man."[69]

Mr. Wright was in Gloucester before 1785. He was here also in 1790 while Mr. Murray was attending the Convention, and again in 1793, after Mr. Murray's removal to Boston. In 1754 Matthew Reuz was at the Moravian Station at Bethlehem, Pennsylvania, whence he was occasionally sent out to preach to the Swedish settlers on the Delaware. He frequently preached at Cohansey, Penn's Neck, Piles' Grove, and Maurice River, New Jersey.[70] If this was our Matthew Wright, which is probable, we have an insight into some of the causes which led to the formation of Universalist Societies at all these places, except the last, as early as 1789.

SHIPPIE TOWNSEND was a Block maker, in Boston. He was a man of fair education, a terse writer, and occasionally preached in Boston, and on two or three occasions in Gloucester. He was probably the first layman to wield the pen in exposition and defence of Universalism, in New England. From about 1785 to 1793, he published ten or eleven pamphlets, which in 1794 he gathered into a volume of 376 pp., publishing the compilation under the title of "Gospel News." He died in 1800, at an advanced age.

---

[69] Universalist Quarterly, Vol. vi: p. 11. I have in my possession a letter written by Mr. Rights in 1783. At this time he was teaching school in Taunton, Mass.

[70] See Vol. xi. *Memoirs of the Historical Society of Pennsylvania*, pp. 410, 440, 442.

Rev. Adams Streeter became a Universalist in 1777 or 1778, prior to which date he had been for several years a Baptist Clergyman. His first preaching to Universalists was at Oxford, Mass., the records of that Society showing that for a number of years prior to 1785 they had "supported him by free contributions." In 1785 he divided his time between Oxford and Providence, R. I. In 1786 he was at Boston once in two weeks until about the time of his death, which occurred suddenly at Smithfield, R. I., in August of that year. He is represented as having been "a man of good natural powers, which had not been much, or well, cultivated; a very free, easy, eloquent speaker. The Calvinistic elements entered largely into his discourses." His visits to Gloucester were probably for the purpose of exchange with Mr. Murray, enabling the latter to visit Providence and Boston.

Rev. Noah Parker probably never received Ordination. He was, prior to 1777, a mechanic, a blacksmith, known as an honest and upright man, "with a fair education, a large thinking brain, an easy gift of utterance, and a soul all aglow with love for the gospel." He became a Universalist under the preaching of Mr. Murray during his frequent visits to Portsmouth, N. H., and after several years of study, with such assistance as Mr. Murray could give him, he commenced on the year above mentioned, his ministry to a Society of believers who had begun to hold meetings in a school-house in that town. Seven years later, the cause having prospered under his ministry, his people erected a House of Worship, in which he continued to be their minister until his death in 1787. Mrs. Murray gives him the reputation of an "Exemplary Philanthropist." He was a decided Rellyan, much beloved and respected by Mr. Murray, with whom he frequently exchanged.

Rev. Elhanan Winchester was by far the most eminent of all the early Universalist preachers, in theological learning and intellectual power. He entered the Baptist Ministry in 1769, and avowed himself a Universalist in 1781, after a severe conflict, for nearly three years, with his doubts and hopes on the subject. Originally a staunch Calvinist, he became, on embracing Universalism, an Arminian, and so of course advocated

REV. W. R. G. MELLEN.
SEVENTH PASTOR, 1855-1861.

the final salvation of the race on very different principles from those held by Mr. Murray. Their personal relations, however, were exceedingly pleasant and affectionate. Mr. Winchester preached in Philadelphia four years after becoming a Universalist, and spent the winter of 1785-6 in New England, and was in Gloucester a few times during that season. The next year he went to England, where he remained seven years, constantly busy with his pen and voice. Returning to America in 1794, he preached in various parts of the country until midwinter of 1796, when he was prostrated by hemorrhage of the lungs, which left him in a condition of debility from which he never recovered. His death occurred April 18, 1797, when he was in his 46th year. His published books and pamphlets number about forty titles, and he wrote much besides, for various Magazines. A Memoir of Winchester was published in London shortly after his death, by Rev. William Vidler; and another from the pen of Rev. E. M. Stone, in Boston, in 1836. Both of these have long been out of print.

REV. MOSES WINCHESTER was a half-brother of Elhanan, and commenced preaching after his more distinguished brother had become a Universalist. But little is known of him. Most of his preaching was in New Jersey. He came to Gloucester in the winter of 1785, and remained in New England, frequently visiting this place, about a year. I think it probable that he was a Rellyan, as Mr. Murray speaks of him as having "clearer views of the Gospel preached unto Abraham, than his brother has." He died in Philadelphia in 1793.

REV. HOSEA BALLOU. I cannot give any just idea of this remarkable man, who in so many respects recast the Universalist theology, in the brief space contemplated for these notes. Reference must be had to his Biography, published by his son, Maturin M. Ballou, in 1852, or to the more extended Memoir by Rev. Thomas Whittemore, in 1854.

REV. THOMAS BARNS. The family now write the name Barnes, but I have retained the spelling used by himself. Mr. Barns was born in Merrimac, N. H., Oct. 4th, 1749. Early in life he joined the Baptist Church, of which he continued to be a member till 1782, when, under the preaching of Rev. Caleb Rich, he became a believer in Universalism, and soon after began to preach. His first settlement was at New Fane, Vt., afterwards in Oxford, Mass., and for about two years, dating from 1792, he itinerated in Connecticut, Rhode Island and Massachusetts, having his home at Woodstock, Ct. His first preaching in Gloucester was May 25th, 1794, from which time till the fall of 1798 he was the principal minister of the Society.

Capt. Joseph Pearce, who had been an attendant on Mr. Murray's ministry here, received from his brother William a gift of two hundred and fifty acres of land located in New Gloucester, Maine, and removed there, probably before Mr. Murray left Gloucester. For several years, as there was no preaching near enough for them to attend, he met with his neighbors at each other's houses, on Sundays, for religious worship and conversation. It fell to his lot to take the lead in these services, and before long it was found that a large number of the settlers of that and the adjoining towns were Universalists, who empowered him to obtain a minister of that faith to take up his abode with them. At once he wrote to his brother William for information and advice; who proposed to Mr. Barns to visit the District, and made generous offers of assistance if he would settle there.

After making them a visit in 1798, Mr. Barns concluded to remove to Maine, which he did the following winter, taking only a portion of his family with him, his wife and younger children remaining at Woodstock till a more favorable season for what was then a long and difficult journey. The following extract from a letter written during his journey will show the tediousness of travel in those days.

"PORTLAND, Feb. 16, 1799.

MY DEAR WIFE AND CHILDREN:— If I had time I would write you a long letter, but I am now in Portland, engaged in business among my friends. Expect to preach in this neighborhood to-morrow. We have arrived safely at Poland, where we are kindly received. Our journey was longer than I expected. We were hindered some by an ox falling sick the third day of our journey. Lucy had a short turn of the asthma, which hindered us part of two days.⁷¹ We were also hindered some by a storm, which altogether, made our journey eighteen days, and our expenses twenty-three dollars. If the Spring is forward with us, I shall come for you before planting, but you will excuse my not coming in planting time. The scarcity of hay for 120 miles of the journey, will make our journey costly before planting. If I stay till after planting, the grass will be plenty, the days long, and the riding good."

Mr. Barns' friends assisted him in the purchase of a farm in the town of Poland, on which he continued to reside till his removal from earth. A few Societies were immediately formed, which in October, 1799, organized the Eastern Association, now the Maine Convention. The circuit in which he preached for several years was extensive; "the travel necessary for his Sabbath engagements amounted to about forty miles on an average, which he performed on horseback in the summer and in a sleigh in the winter; and storms were seldom so violent as to detain him from fulfilling his appointments." In 1814 he was attacked with heart disease, which, not long after its commencement, was pronounced incurable by his physicians. The intelligence was received with composure, and after familiar conversation with his family concerning the near approach of death, he proceeded to regulate his temporal affairs, and to preach farewell discourses to the several societies that had been blessed with his ministry for seventeen years. Thursday, Oct. 3d, 1816, he died suddenly, in his barn, while engaged in threshing wheat, aged 67 years.

As a man, Mr. Barns was respected by all who knew him, and held in high repute for sound judgment and unimpeachable habits. He represented the District of Maine, in the Legislature of Massachusetts, several sessions, in which position he did himself honor, and faithfully served the State. As a preacher he was sound and instructive, eminently successful as a controversialist, and a Son of Consolation to the sorrowing. Concerning him, the late Hosea Ballou wrote: "In the *little* circle of the preachers of Universalism, at the early date

---

⁷¹ Lucy Barns, his daughter, was a zealous and devoted Universalist. She was the author of a pamphlet entitled, "Serious and Important Questions, with Scripture Answers;" of which many thousand copies have been put in circulation. She died in 1839.

to which I refer, Br. Barnes was esteemed as one of the first for strength of mind, for extensive acquaintance with the Scriptures, for ease in speaking and force in argument. In the *wider* circle of believers in the impartial Gospel of the Lord Jesus, Br. Barnes' labors were much sought and highly prized; nor was he less esteemed for his integrity, honesty, and general moral character, than for his ministerial talents."

REV. ZEPHANIAH LATHE was originally a Baptist preacher, at Grafton, Mass. He became a Universalist about 1785. In becoming a Universalist he dropped the Calvinistic doctrine of necessity. He is represented as having been well read in Theology, Metaphysics and History, and as being held in high esteem by all who knew him, as a deep and patient thinker, and a man of eminently Christian spirit. He preached stately for several years, in Hardwick, Petersham, and Grafton, Mass., and also in Lebanon, N. H., and was besides a self-constituted missionary in all the New England States. He was one of the Committee to draft the Winchester Profession of Belief. His first preaching in Gloucester was June 15th, 1794. He came at the solicitation of Rev. George Richards, who wrote to the committee: "As he has undertaken this journey on my recommendation of you, I entreat that he may be received as a brother well beloved: and if you should not wish to employ him in future, I beg that he may be forwarded towards his home in the blessings of Love, for I have a great affection for him and his." He died April 29th, 1828, aged 74.

REV. ISAAC MANSFIELD, born at Marblehead, in 1750, graduated at Harvard College in 1767. He was Ordained as a Congregationalist Clergyman in 1776, and settled over the First Church, in Exeter, N. H., where he remained till 1787, when he was dismissed by a Council called for that purpose, "according to his agreement with the parish." What the circumstances were which produced "such a crisis as to render a separation eligible on both parts" cannot be ascertained; but the Council say, as put on the records of the Exeter Church, "We feel ourselves constrained by duty and love to testify the sense we have of the valuable ministerial gifts and qualifications with which God hath furnished Mr. Mansfield, and which have been well approved not only among his own people, but by the churches in this vicinity." He removed from Exeter to Marblehead, where he became a magistrate, and was afterwards known as Isaac Mansfield, Esq., succeeding in office, his father, Isaac Mansfield, Esq., who died in 1792. Whether he had become a Universalist before leaving Exeter, is unknown; but his reputation as a Universalist, seven years later, caused the following letter to be sent to him:

GLOUCESTER, March 18th, 1794.

DEAR SIR:—The Rev'd Mr. John Murray, who has long ministered to us in preaching the glad tidings of salvation, greatly to our satisfaction, has thought it his duty to preach ye same to a much larger congregation in Boston; which we should greatly regret if we did not hope that he would be the means of advancing the knowledge of the great salvation of Jesus Christ to ye great joy of many of our fellow-heirs of salvation.

The Society in this place are at this time destitute of a publick preacher. They wish to meet together as often as they can, and have the same Gospel preached to them that the disciples of our Blessed Lord and Saviour preached. Having tasted of ye good word of God, they rejoice therein. From what they have heard of you, that you have been taught by the Spirit of Jesus, they wish you to come and see them and speak to them, a few Lord's days, at least, if you can find your mind clear; they not doubting but the Great Lord of the Harvest will dispose your mind and theirs, to His Glory.

For this purpose, Mr. Wm. Card, one of the committee, waits on you to invite you to preach with us one or two days in the present month, if you can make it convenient.

We are, Dear Sir, with great esteem, your Friends and Brethren at command.

DAVID PLUMER,
ISAAC ELWELL,
WILLIAM CARD.

Committee of the Christian Independent Society of Gloucester.

To this request Mr. Mansfield responded by preaching in Gloucester the following Sunday. I find no account of any subsequent visit. Mr. Mansfield died in Boston, September, 1826, aged 76.

Rev. Michael Coffin was the son of John Coffein, — as the name was originally written, — who was the first settler of Cavendish, Vt., in 1769. In the fall of 1790, which is the first mention I find of Mr. Coffin, he visited Mr. Murray, and was then "preaching on the confines of Canada," probably in Vermont. Three years later he was at Oxford, Mass., where he remained till 1797. He was always noted for eccentricities, and was finally silenced as an unprofitable preacher.

Rev. John Foster was originally a Congregationalist preacher. While serving in this capacity in Taunton, Mass., he became a Universalist. Subsequently he joined Thomas Paine and Elihu Palmer, in New York, in avowed infidelity, and was indicted in the Courts for blasphemy. He then gave himself, for several years, to fitting young men for college; and finally became very much degraded in morals. He died in the winter of 1844, at the advanced age of 90. A gifted and talented man, but never reliable, he was no honor to any sect, and was discountenanced and silenced as soon as his character became known.

Rev. George Richards was born in or near Newport, R. I., about 1755, and was educated in the higher branches of learning under the care of a clergyman in Newport, who gave him, as he often remarked, "as extensive advantages as he could have enjoyed under Dr. Manning, President of Brown University." During a portion of the Revolutionary War he was Chaplain and Purser under Commodore Manly; after which he taught school in Boston. In 1786, while teaching in Boston, he officiated as Reader in the North Episcopal Church in that city, and the next year began to preach Universalism. From that time until Mr. Murray's removal to Boston, he continued to teach school, and to preach in that city and vicinity. In 1793 he removed to Portsmouth, N. H., and was pastor of the Universalist Society there until 1809, when he went to Philadelphia as pastor of the Lombard St. Church. He was one of the committee to draft the Winchester Profession of Belief, and was for many years one of the most active and respected ministers in our denomination. Recently, by Mr. Haven of the American Antiquarian Society, and by Rev. E. E. Hale, his fame as a patriotic poet has been celebrated in the pages of the "Transactions" of the Antiquarian Society, and in the "Old and New." Several of his hymns are still in use. He was also an eminent Free Mason, and for a while edited the "Free Masons' Magazine." Possessed of keen sensibilities, he never failed to go to the full extent of his means in relieving the poor, he sorrowed most deeply with those who were in trouble, and was sorely pained whenever the thoughtless or disorderly brought reproach on the cause which he loved. The death of his wife, at a time when secular troubles, growing out of political differences, were dividing his church, so keenly affected him as to produce a dangerous sickness, in the midst of which he became insane. Recovering from this sickness sufficiently to attend to some trifling business, but not becoming wholly sane, he soon became the victim of fixed insanity, and on the night of March 1st, 1814, he closed his mortal career.

REV. EBENEZER PAINE was in Gloucester not more than twice. He was not a man of learning, nor of stability; and was disfellowshipped by the Convention in 1812.

REV. EDWARD TURNER had been preaching three years when he came to Gloucester. He was active in all denominational matters, a constant attendant on and worker in the Convention for over twenty years; and then one of the number who felt compelled to withdraw and to enter the new organization of Restorationists. His name ranks high in our early history, on account of his abilities, his character, and the almost constant demand for his services in the general cause. He was one of the first and best writers in defence of our faith, a popular preacher, a hymnologist of no small merit, and an acknowledged Christian in life and spirit. After 1828 his ministry was spent in the Unitarian denomination, but without any change of his views as to Universal salvation. He died in 1853, in the seventy-third year of his age. Rev. E. G. Brooks, D. D., published a Biographical sketch of Mr. Turner in the "Universalist Quarterly" for 1871, which contains valuable information with regard to the man, and also with reference to the Restorationist controversy.

Rev. Joshua Flagg was a man of more than ordinary talents, of a ready address, and especially gifted in prayer. He was a strong controversialist, but so eccentric in his early life that his services lacked uniformity, and at times he was not equal to the demands of the occasion, or the expectations of his friends. In later life his devout spirit predominated, and his soul was cheered by intelligence of the religious growth of any Christian sect. He lived in the enjoyment and comfort of his faith until Nov. 10th, 1859, when he passed away, in the 87th year of his age.

Rev. Isaac Root was "a man of strong talents, clear views, and great personal worth." He had been a Baptist preacher. He was in Gloucester but one Sunday. In 1815 he moved to Western New York, where he died about 1818.

Rev. Noah Murray was a native of Litchfield County, Conn., where he was born in 1745. He was a soldier in the War for Independence; at the close of which he removed to Lanesboro', Mass., where he commenced preaching as a Baptist. In a few years, as early as 1785, he became a Universalist, and after preaching a short time in Duchess Co., N. Y., settled near Tioga Point, Penn'a, in a township which was called after him, "Murraysfield." He had a short settlement in Philadelphia, beginning in 1807, after which he returned to his farm. He died, after a brief illness, May 16th, 1811. Officious religious opponents hung around his death-bed, trying to shake his faith, and as he was unable to talk, they whispered among themselves that his belief in Universalism was growing weaker. Motioning to his son for a piece of chalk, he wrote, "stronger." Resting for a moment, he wrote again, *"stronger."* Then after a brief interval, he wrote, "STRONGER." And thus, with growing strength, he passed on to the fruition of his Christian hopes.

Mr. Gleason. Of this man I find no mention, except in a letter from George Richards to the Gloucester Society, Aug. 5, 1803, in which he says: "Brother Gleason, I am told, has been with you;" and the Society's answer: "We have, as you have been informed, had Mr. Gleason with us, and are much pleased with his performances; and are in hopes, as he is so near us, we shall be able to have him frequently with us. And our Society are so well satisfied with him that they would not seek further while it is in his power to preach among us." I find by the sexton's record that he was here six Sundays in 1803, and one in 1804. In 1846, a Benjamin Gleason, of Concord, Mass., furnished Rev. Thomas Whittemore with a large collection of letters addressed to himself by Rev. George Richards, with whom he was intimate during Mr. Richards' residence in Boston, and for many years after. Possibly this man may have been a lay-preacher for a brief period.

APPENDIX E.

THE RELLY HYMN BOOK.

The title of this book is: "Christian Hymns, Poems, and Spiritual Songs, Sacred to the Praise of God our Saviour. By James and John Relly." It was originally published in London in 1770. Mr. Murray republished it at Burlington, N. J., in 1776; and another edition was published by Rev. Noah Parker, at Portsmouth, N. H., in 1782. In Mr. Murray's edition there is a list of the subscribers, amounting in all to 223 persons, who took 468 copies. Providence, R. I., had the largest number of subscribers, being 47, but Gloucester, with 38 subscribers, took the largest number of copies, 93.

The names of the Gloucester subscribers, with the number taken by each, were:

Winthrop Allen	1	Joseph Lufkin	1
Isaac Bennett	2	Zebulon Lufkin	2
Isaac Ball	1	Aaron Lufkin	2
Solomon Babson	3	James Millen	1
James Babson	2	Ebenezer Parsons	3
James Broom	2	David Pearce	6
William Card	1	David Plumer	5
Capt. Peter Dolliver	2	William Sargent	1
William Dolliver	3	Miss Nancy Sanders	2
John Stevens Ellery	2	John Stevens	3
Isaac Ellwell. Jr.	1	Winthrop Sargent	6
Nathaniel Foster	1	Samuel Sayward	2
Daniel Giddings	1	Daniel Sargent	6
Joseph Herrick	2	John Somes	2
Philemon Haskell	2	Abraham Sawyer	2
Barnett Harkin	1	Bradbury Sanders	6
Jourdan James	2	Epes Sargent	6
Isaac Lane	2	Winthrop Sargent, Jr	3
Theophilus Lane	2	Jonathan Trask	1

APPENDIX F.

SUIT AGAINST THE FIRST PARISH.

After Mr. Murray's consent to have the suit brought in his own name had been obtained, the following agreement in regard to the expenses, was put into his hands:

"For the more effectual carrying on a certain process at Law between John Murray, Clerk, and the inhabitants of the First Parish of Glocester, or whatever other form in Law may be assumed for procuring and establishing our Religious Liberties, Know all men that we, Winthrop Sargent, David Pearce, Joseph Foster, David Plumer, John Somes, Joshua Plumer, and Epes Sargent, all of Glocester, County of Essex and State of Massachusetts whose names and seals are hereunto subscribed and affixed, Do associate, mutually pledge, covenant, agree and bind ourselves jointly the one to the other, as well for ourselves as our Heirs, Executors and Administrators, to advance and pay such sum or sums as shall be necessary and adequate to the well conducting of said Process, the whole of which costs of suit and other expenses when terminated to be respectively by us borne in such proportions as we are taxed in the different rate lists delivered to the Collectors by the Assessors of the first Parish of Glocester, for 1781, 1782, 1783.

"And it is further agreed, that David Plumer and Joseph Foster above named be a committee to transact and conduct the causes before mentioned, to receive all monies; They or any one of them giving receipts for such sums as shall be paid them, and to be accountable to this association for the expenditure of the same.

"And it is further agreed as the interest and meaning of this association, to comprehend all or any expenses that have arisen in conducting the cause aforesaid heretofore as well as what may arise at this present or in future.

"It is further agreed that the said David Plumer and Joseph Foster, committee, shall have power of assembling this association at such times and place as shall be most expedient.

"And it is further Covenanted and agreed that this association will aid, strengthen, counsell, and countenance each other in the prosecution and vindication of their rights against a species of usurpation and tyranny which tho' sanctified by the greatest number, has for its object, not the good order of civil society, but the subversion of humanity and religious freedom.

"In witness of the foregoing we the associating and contracting parties have hereunto subscribed our names and affixed our seals in Glocester this third day of February, one thousand seven hundred and eighty four.

      WINTHROP SARGENT,
      JOHN STEVENS ELLERY
       in behalf of Capⁿ. David Pearce,
      JOSEPH FOSTER,
      DAVID PLUMER,
      JOHN SOMES,
      JOSHUA PLUMER,
      EPES SARGENT."

Mr. Babson, in his History of Gloucester, has preserved the following anecdotes of the trial of this suit: " Mr. Giddings, a Quaker, was on the stand to testify that Mr. Murray's supporters had a house of worship. It had been objected against them that they had a secret, which, in the state of public affairs at that time, might be dangerous to the liberties of the people. Mr. Giddings, being questioned on this point and pressed rather closely, at length answered, " Yes, they have a secret; and it is this (quoting Ps. xxv: 14,): 'The secret of the Lord is with them that fear him, and he will show them his covenant.' They have no other secret to my knowledge."

After the case had been submitted to the Jury, they were out several hours, and then returned to Court, saying they could not agree. The Judge then addressed them, and they retired once more. The foreman made an earnest appeal for Mr. Murray, urging that his supporters had as good a right to worship God according to the dictates of conscience as others had, and that he was prepared to render a verdict accordingly. He then composed himself to sleep, with the remark, that they might arouse him as soon as they could agree. During the night they came to an agreement; and in the morning went into Court with their verdict."—*History of Gloucester, p. 435.*

APPENDIX G.

AN APPEAL TO THE IMPARTIAL PUBLIC BY THE SOCIETY OF CHRISTIAN INDEPENDENTS, CONGREGATING IN GLOCESTER.

FRIENDS AND COUNTRYMEN,

In our appeal to you, we feel a confidence, which in an address to the rulers of a tyrannical government, we could never possess.

While the people have the power of forming their own government, of enacting their own laws; and while they hold in their own hands the sovereignty of their Commonwealth, justly deeming their highest officers their servants, and are attentive to every measure, which may in its consequences, affect their liberty, they cannot fail to be free and happy.

We should be far from giving our countrymen the trouble of attending to an appeal from a society, so small and inconsiderable as ours, had we not been drawn before a civil tribunal, in defence of what we suppose to be our just, invaluable and constitutional rights. A question has been agitated respecting us, the decision of which, ultimately regards every citizen of the Commonwealth, and instantly affects the several religious orders of Episcopalians, Baptists, Presbyterians, Sandemanians, Quakers, and every other denomination of Christians, who in this State have been called Sectaries.

Had we ever done anything in opposition to the freedom or independence of our Country, nay, had we ever shewn a backwardness in the late war, to assist in the preservation of those privileges, for which we now are called to contend in courts of justice, we should feel a diffidence in laying our cause before the impartial public ; but feeling ourselves deservedly vested with the privileges and immunities of free citizens of this Commonwealth, and entitled to those liberties with which Heaven has made us free, and which we believe to be secured to us, by a constitution of government happily established by the people, and which we never mean to part with, while we can defend or retain them, we proceed to lay our cause before you.

When Mr. John Murray, our present teacher in religious matters, had been invited to preach in the Meeting-House of the first Parish in Glocester, we heard him with an increasing pleasure, and a growing satisfaction. On the settlement of Mr. Forbes, the present minister there, we being obliged to withhold our assent to the doctrines he taught, disagreed to his settlement. In the year 1779, we associated for the purpose of public worship, by a covenant, a copy whereof we have caused to be herewith submitted to the public eye.

Though we are united in a mode of worship, and a form of discipline, yet in our association, we have carefully avoided the establishment of it, because we are fully convinced that our blessed Redeemer left no particular form to his followers, but submitted all to their own wisdom and prudence. We conceive that a voluntary agreement, in religious matters, ought to be departed from, the moment the individual who is party to it, conceives that he has done wrong; and where those religious forms have been established by laws, we find by the best history of Ecclesiastical matters, that they have only tended to fetter the human understanding, and have been the unhappy means of substituting the form for the substance of religion.

We did not in our agreement, associate for the belief of any particular tenets, or peculiar doctrines, because we conceived that all conviction must rise from evidence rationally applied to the understanding; and we could not suppose that the same evidence would strike every mind in the society with the same force. We therefore concluded that confessions of faith with us, might do what we believe they have done in other societies, where those of human invention have been introduced, oblige men, either to submit their faith to the controul of others, and believe without examining, or to profess to believe that which they have never fully considered or understood. With that humility which we find inculcated in every part of the Gospel, we humbly hoped, that it would be sufficient for us to believe the Holy Scriptures, and to adopt the system of morals therein contained, *as the rule of our Conduct, and the man of our Counsel.* We readily conceived, that when our mode of worship, or the doctrines taught us by our teaching Brother, should become disagreeable to any one of our brethren, he would dissent from us and join himself to some other society.

Upon examining the matter for ourselves, we are fully convinced, that by establishing articles of faith, we should only injure the cause of religion, and possibly might lay a foundation for persecution in a future day. Very soon after the glorious doctrine of salvation by Jesus Christ, was proclaimed to a sinful world, contentions, annimosities, hatred, and envy, were introduced by uncharitable and incanded men, who, proudly feeling their own imaginary infallibility, could not bear that any one should dissent from their opinion. So bigotted are men generally to their own religious opinions, that they have rarely failed to procure, where it could be done, the civil authority, to compel others to profess a belief of their tenets.

Upon the conversion of Constantine, the first Roman Emperor who embraced Christianity, the civil arm was extended to establish the faith which he supposed all must hold, because he believed. One of his predecessors, though an heathen, had by the edict of Milan established a universal toleration to Christians, and to every denomination of religionists: but this Christian Emperor at once violated it. And to use the language of Mr. Gibbons, in his history of that Prince, " The grateful applause of the Clergy has consecrated the memory of a Prince who indulged their passions, and promoted their interest, Constantine gave them security, wealth, honours and revenge: and the support of the Orthodox faith was considered as the most sacred and important duty of the Civil Magistrate. The edict of Milan, the great charter of toleration, had confirmed to each individual of the Roman world, the privilege of choosing and professing their own religion. But this inestimable priviledge was soon violated. With the knowledge of truth, the Emperor imbibed the maxims of persecution; and the sects which dissented from the Catholic church, were afflicted and oppressed by the triumph of Christianity. Constantine easily believed that the Hereticks, who presumed to dispute his opinions, or to oppose his commands, were guilty of the most absurd and criminal obstinacy; and that a seasonable application of moderate severities might save those unhappy men from danger of everlasting condemnation. Not a moment was lost in excluding ministers and teachers of the separated congregations from any share of the rewards and immunities which the Emperor had so liberally bestowed on the Orthodox clergy. But as the Sectaries might still exist under the cloud of royal disgrace, the conquest of the East was immediately followed by an edict which announced their total destruction. After a preamble filled with passion and reproach, Constantine absolutely prohibits the assemblies of the Heretics, and confiscates their public property to the use either of the revenue, or of the Catholic church."

The Jewish Christians of Alexandria, applied the ideas taught in the school of Plato, respecting the *Logos*, to our blessed Redeemer; whereupon the Arian Christians exerted themselves against what they called a dangerous error, and accused their opponents with adopting the polytheism of the Pagans. Hence upon a mystery above the comprehension of the human understanding, arose a controversy which time itself can never settle. Constantius, a Roman Emperor, had by a decree ordained, that "those who refused to communicate with the Arian Bishops, and particularly with Macedonius, should be deprived of the immunities of Ecclesiastics, and the rights of Christians; they were compelled to relinquish the possessions of Churches: and were strictly prohibited from holding their assemblies within the walls of the city. The execution of this unjust law, in the provinces of Thrace, and Asia Minor, was committed to the zeal of Macedonius. The civil and military power were directed to obey his commands, and the cruelties exercised by this Semi-Arian tyrant, in the support of the *Homoiousion*, exceeded the commission, and disgraced the reign of Constantius. The sacraments of the church were administered to the reluctant victims, who denied the vocation, and abhorred the principles of Macedonius. The rights of baptism were conferred on women and children, who, for that purpose, had been torn from the arms of their friends and parents; the mouths of the Communicants were held open by a wooden engine, while the consecrated bread was forced down their throats; the breasts of tender Virgins were either burnt with red-hot egg shells, or inhumanly compressed between sharp and heavy boards."

Theodosius, one of the successors of Constantius, declared himself on the side of the Athannians; he was baptized, and

REV. GEORGE W. SKINNER.
Eighth Pastor, 1862–1865.

as he ascended from the water, he promulgated his decree: "It is our pleasure, that all nations which are governed by our *clemency* and *moderation* should steadfastly adhere to the religion which was taught by Saint Peter to the Romans, which faithful tradition has preserved; and which is now professed by the pontiff Damasus, and by Peter, Bishop of Alexandria, a man of apostolic holiness; according to the discipline of the apostles, and the doctrine of the gospel, let us believe the sole deity of the father, the son, and the holy ghost; under an equal majesty, and a pious trinity. *We authorize* the followers of *this* doctrine to assume the title of *Catholic christians;* and as *we judge* that all others are extravagant madmen, *we* brand them with the infamous name of Heretics; and declare, that their *Conventicles* shall no longer usurp the respectable appellation of churches; besides the condemnation of divine justice, they must expect to suffer the severe penalties which *our* authority, guided by *heavenly wisdom*, shall think proper to inflict upon them." It can be no wonder that the council of Nice, by a majority of votes, settled the question in favor of the Emperor's decree. From this time, blood and slaughter, persecutions and murders, stained every decree of the cabinet, and served still to increase the hatred, and widen the sentiments of the parties; until a remedy more dreadful than the disease itself took place. In consequence of the decree of Theodosius, the Roman church assumed the appellations of Holy and Catholic, and arrogating to herself the power of infallibility, being also a *national church*, and having procured within her controul, the whole vengance of civil government, she wrapt the whole world in a cloud of impenetrable darkness, debilitated the mind of man, by closing the door of free enquiry, and gave birth to eight hundred years of ignorance, and barbarism, unequalled by any preceding time; hence arose an awful chasm in the history of the world, and men ceased to think because thinking was a crime.

In the fifteenth century the sons of inquiry began to think for themselves; they thought, they examined and decided for themselves upon these matters which rested only between their God and their own consciences; but this could not fail to awaken that horrid monster, persecution, for the church aided by the civil magistrate held the standard of orthodoxy, and the only measure of faith. Then commenced that horrid scene of bloodshed and devastation with which Europe was afflicted until the year 1688.

It would have been very happy for the *British* nation, of which we were then a part, if they had excluded from their laws all establishment of forms of worship; and had been as tolerant with regard to articles of faith, as they were respecting Church-government; but the magistrate still considering himself the guardian of the church, and the *defender of the faith*, not only established a national church, but by act of parliament settled articles of faith, and made it a crime not to believe the national creed. Amongst other things alike exceptionable, it was enacted at that time, that "If any person educated in the christian religion should, by writing, printing, teaching, or advised speaking, deny any *one of the persons* in the holy trinity to *be God*, or should maintain that there are more *Gods than one*, he should for the first offence be rendered incapable of holding any office, and for the second, be rendered incapable of bringing any action, or buying any lands."

Though the first settlers of this State fled from persecution, yet the light they had received was by no means sufficient to prevent their embracing those principles, which casts a shade over some of the best characters known in that age, and gives their history a complexion of intolerance which will ever be lamented by their more enlightened posterity. But when the Charter of William and Mary had tolerated all sorts of Christians except Papists, the Baptists and Quakers had security from persecution.

The articles of faith commonly called the Platform, and made in the year 1646, has ever shackled the freedom of the people in New England; but blessed be God, the liberty now happily established by our Constitution has given a fatal stab to all religious oppression in this state.

The evil which we find to have accrued from the establishment of creeds of human invention, we hope will make us sufficiently cautious, and prevent our forming any other mode of expression for articles of faith than the gospel, in its own language, and in its own form; for we consider them as mere deductions from facts which do appear to some, but may not appear to others upon the evidence offered in their support; and while we are assured that the same evidence which fully convinces one mind, may leave another in doubt and uncertainty; and are obliged to acknowledge from every day's experience, that those deductions and conclusions which appear in the highest propriety to one, may strike the mind of another as a gross absurdity, we are humbly contented to take the Gospel as the rule of our lives, and to profess to believe whatever is therein taught, as a divine revelation, looking for deliverance from sin, and punishment, in the manner therein graciously provided.

We find that the Sects of Christians in New England have ever been distinguished from each other by their form of church discipline, and their mode of administering of the ordinances; the doctrines, or articles of faith, held by all being as nearly similar as that of individuals in the same church has generally been. We distinguish ourselves from the church under the instruction of Mr. Forbes, by our not using baptism as an external rite. Though this may appear to some to be imcompatible with the religion we profess, yet it being a matter resting in opinion only, we know not why we should be condemned, while the Quakers meet the smiles of government, and while many others who omit the ordinance through inattention, or a total disregard to all religion, have the favours of the state. We differ from that church also in our mode of discipline, being *Independents*, holding as the first church in Boston, and many other churches in the state originally held, that "all ecclesiastical jurisdiction is committed by Christ to each organical church, from which there is no appeal: visible saintship being the matter, and express covenanting the form." *

"Ordination we account nothing else but the solemn putting a man into his place and office in the church, whereunto he hath a right before by election, the essence and substance of the outward calling of an ordinary officer in the church, doth not consist in ordination, but in his voluntary and free election by the church, and his accepting of that election; whereupon is founded that relation between pastor and flock, between such a minister and such a people. Ordination doth not constitute an officer, nor give him the credentials of his office: the apos-

---

* Governor Bellingham's Will made in 1672.

tles were elders without imposition of hands by men." Platform, chap. 9.

This was the sense of the country at that time, and it was so prevalent, that although the Platform was obtained, yet it could not be done without observing these sentiments. But as the word Ordain signifies no more than to appoint, we conceive that the election, and not the laying on of hands, makes the Ordination compleat. See sixth and thirteenth chapters of Acts.

Notwithstanding this, we have been, and yet are taxed to the support of Mr. Forbes, and our property is taken and exposed at auction to raise money for the support of a form of worship in which we can never join, and for the support of teaching by which we can have no instruction. Were we not thus oppressed, we should have been very contented to have enjoyed in silence that liberty which we feel ourselves entitled to as Free Citizens of this Commonwealth, always resolving to yield that obedience to government which is due from good subjects to a state that protects them in the enjoyment of their dearest rights.

We were advised that our situation was such as precluded all other relief from the oppression we complain of, otherwise than by an action brought in the name of our teacher to recover the money taken from us for the support of a public teacher of religion, piety and morality. He was very unwilling to have an action brought in his name; but upon our representing the cruelty of those who took this advantage of us, and the hardship of his not consenting to the only relief we could have, he gave his consent.

The action which we instituted was tried at the Supreme Judicial Court, held at Ipswich in June, 1785, when a verdict was given in our favour.* Had we no other motive than the saving of our money, we should have been more in our own interest by paying quietly to the support of Mr. Forbes, than we have been in building a house for public worship, supporting a teacher amongst ourselves, and by engaging in a troublesome and expensive lawsuit. But holding the rights of conscience as superior to every other consideration, we have per-

* The Counsel for the Plantifs, Mr. Sullivan, Mr. Tudor: for the Defend'ts, Mr. Bradbury, Mr. Parsons.

severed, and still intend to persevere, not doubting that our countrymen will do us the justice of securing to us that freedom wherein we have reason to rejoice under the present government.

As the principles agitated in the trial of the cause above mentioned, and the objections made against us, apply themselves equally to Episcopalians, Baptists, Quakers, Sandemanians, and Independents, and to every denomination of Christians whose society is not described and known by town or parish lines, or by a particular act of incorporation, we think it our duty to give the public our remarks and observation upon them. In doing this, though we should show a dissent from the opinion of some gentlemen of great learning and ability, and perhaps from some gentlemen of high civil rank in the state; and though we shall speak with the confidence becoming men who realize their constitutional freedom; yet we shall do it with all that deference and respect which we owe to the characters of great and good men who may have been opposed to our opinion. Whether they or we are right, we submit to the public.

The third article in the declaration of rights, provides, that "all monies paid by the subject to the support of public worship, and of the public teachers aforesaid, shall, if he require it, be uniformly applied to the support of the public teacher or teachers of his own religious sect or denomination, provided there be any on whose instructions he attends; otherwise it may be paid towards the support of the teacher or teachers of the parish in which the money is raised." For the reasons before mentioned, we consider ourselves a *Sect* different from those who attend upon the ministry of Mr. Forbes; and we therefore are of opinion that the money raised upon us ought to be applied to the support of the teacher of our own religious sect, there being one on whose instructions we attend. But it was objected that the teacher who is entitled to receive the money paid by his hearers, must be a teacher of piety, religion and morality; this we concede, but we are not convinced that the question, whether he is a teacher of piety, religion and morality, can be determined from a revision of the motives he offers as to the rewards and the punishments which are to be bestowed or inflicted in another world. We believe that the question must be decided by the evidence of his urging the people to piety and morality, as the foundation of the greatest good which their natures are capable of, and as a compliance with the will of their almighty Creator and preserver, without going into an inquiry of his opinion respecting the quantity of punishment in a future state.

That God will punish men for sin in such a manner as will far overbalance the pleasures which can be derived from vice in this world, is so clearly pointed out in the gospel that we are compelled to believe it; but whether the opinion of some learned and good men, who imagine that the wicked will be annihilated; or whether that of the learned Doctor Chauncy, Doctor Priestly, and many others, who believe that there is a temporary hell prepared for the ungodly, which is another state of probation, or any other opinion respecting that subject is best, every one must determine for himself. Neither statutes, penalties or rewards, can force or allure a man to consent to the truth of a proposition, without sufficient evidence received by a mind capable of examining and applying of it.

The idea that it is necessary to the good order of civil government, that the Teachers of Religion should thunder out the doctrine of everlasting punishment to deter men from atrocious crimes, which they may otherwise commit in secret, has long been hackneyed in the hands of men in power; but without any warrant from reason or revelation for doing of it; for reason itself, without the aid of revelation, gave no intimation of a state of retribution; it was the Gospel which brought life and immortality to light. God, in the civil constitution which he was pleased to form for the Jews, strongly prohibited murder, perjury, adultery, and many other crimes which men might then commit in secret; but never, in any one instance, gave an intimation that the Jews should be punished in another world for their crimes in this. Had a threatning of that nature been necessary to the support of civil government, we might with great propriety look for it there. It was not till the Christian Church was illegally weded to state policy, that men in power dared to hurl the Thunders of the Most High at those who offended against government; and even then, modesty forbid it, only as they arrogantly pretended to do it for the honor of God and the advantage of religion.

But should the point be maintained, that courts and juries

are authorized to determine whether the teacher of a religious sect is a teacher of morality, from his opinion either of the cause, mode, or state of men's happiness or misery in another world, or from his opinion of the nature or proportion of the rewards for virtue, or the punishment for vice there, no sect or denomination could be safe; it being a matter resting in opinion only, without any earthly tribunal having the ability or authority to settle the question. Suppose an Episcopalian teacher should have an action in his name to recover the money paid by his hearers; perhaps he might be one who had subscribed and sworn to the thirty-nine articles, *the truth of which is well supported by act of parliament:* an objection might be made from one of the articles, that tells us God from all eternity elected a certain number to happiness, and predestinated all the rest of the human race to everlasting misery; and this of his own sovereign will, without any regard to the merit of the one, or the demerit of the others. A jury might be found who would decide at once that this doctrine is subversive of all morality and good order; for if the state of every man is unalterably fixed from all eternity, and nothing done by him can in any wise change the divine decree, he had better eat, drink, and be merry, and indulge himself in all that can give him sensual pleasure. The argument is equally strong against all Calvinists, and in appearance stronger against Hopkintonians, Edwardians, and all other Fatalists. But should a sober Arminian be in trial, and it appeared that he taught his people that it was within their own power to procure future happiness by their virtue and goodness, and that God would punish them in another world for those crimes which they were under no necessity to commit in this; that this is a state of probation wherein it is in their power to lay the foundation of everlasting happiness; a jury might not be able to distinguish between the prescience and the fore-ordination of God; and it might be called impiety to alledge that the infinitely wise Being did not from all eternity know the ultimate fate and final end of all his creatures; it would at least be called derogatory to the honor of the Most High, to suppose anything to be contingent with him; and therefore a Teacher of such principles might, in the eye of some persons, be viewed as a Teacher of impiety and immorality.

We neither undertake to support or condemn any of the tenets we have alluded to, for we suppose that every good man, let his involuntary errors be multiplied as they may, will be in the favour of God. But we reason in this manner to shew the impracticability of deciding upon the morality of a teacher from his opinion of those matters; when all opinions must depend upon men's construction of the most holy word of God, as revealed in the scriptures. We will only add here, that if the courts of law in this State are to go into an inquiry of this kind, the conscience of the judges will be the standard of religious sentiment, and the only inquiry upon matters of faith will be, What was the opinion of the court in the last trial? It would more certainly be better to have the articles of faith settled by an act of the legislature at once.

Another objection raised against us in the above-mentioned trial was as unexpected as it was alarming to us. It was that no teacher of religion, piety and morality, could have a right to recover the money paid by his sect in the support of public teaching, and to the support of public worship, unless the person demanding of it is the teacher of a town, parish, precinct, or a society legally organized, and vested with civil and corporate powers. Or, in other words, that the people of no sect of Protestant christians can have the money paid by them in support of public teaching of piety, religion and morality, applied to the support of the teacher of their own sect, on whose teachings and instructions they attend, unless their teacher is the settled minister of a parish; or unless they are a society vested by the legislature with corporate powers. This we take to be a fair state of the objection as made in the trial of our cause; and we feel ourselves obliged, not only for our own, but for the security of every denomination of christians not known and described by parish lines, to examine the question with fairness and candour. That our reasoning may be subject to a fair investigation, we cause the two articles whereon we rely to be printed in the appendix. Though we can easily conceive, that through the malicious misrepresentations of our enemies, such prejudices are raised against us that even some good men may be ready to exchange their own religious liberty for our destruction; yet when we consider that the good sense of this people will show them clearly, that a wrong judgment now given against us may end in the persecution of those who now feel the greatest security, we have reason to hope we shall be heard with patience and candour.

The small and trifling objection, that we "have no name or appellation of Protestant Christians," hardly deserves notice. Yet thus much we say, that we call ourselves *Independents* — an appellation which was very honorable in the country until the Civil Government had begotten, and the Church had brought forth the idea of synods and consociations of churches; thereby making an unsavory mixture of politics and religion, for the purpose, as they affected to believe, of keeping religion pure and undefiled;* there has been no denomination of religionists but who have had the honor of receiving their appellation from their enemies; having it at first applied by way of reproach, but becoming honorable as their sect grew numerous and important; amongst these are the Gallileans, Christians, Lutherans, Calvinists, Protestants, Quakers, Baptists, and Dissenters. And we are humbly contented that our enemies, if they do not like the name of *Independents*, shall call us what they please. But we proceed to consider the objection.

If the objection above stated has a foundation which can support it against a careful examination, then all that security to the rights of conscience, all that equality in the several sects and denominations of Christians, and that strong barrier against oppression in religious matters which the people thought they had established by their constitution of civil government, has upon the very first juridical examination been found to be visionary and delusive; the language used by the compilers of the Form of Government is not accompanied with those ideas which have been associated with it in all other cases; but the people have been amused by the chicane of doubtful expression, and instead of something permanent and substantial, have believed a dream and embraced a shadow. But if the words used in the third article in the Declaration of Rights have the same meaning there as they have in other places, we have no difficulty arising from the objection under consideration.

---

* See the Platform, where the magistrate is to see the decrees of the council carried into execution.

The construction of these words will depend much upon the meaning of the word *Sect;* the money is to be applied to the support of the teacher of his own *Sect.* Therefore it will be necessary to have a precise meaning to that word.

Secta, from the verb seco, to cut off or assunder, to rend apart, or divide, was used by the Romans to express a kind of people of a different profession, a party or faction. In all countries where there is a church established by law as the national church, those who dissent from it are called *Sectaries;* as all in England who are not Episcopalians are called Schismatics and Sectaries. In this State there has been no church established since the charter of 1692, and therefore the word *Sect* must have a meaning here in some way different from what it has in those countries where churches are established by law. With us it undoubtedly includes and describes those persons who dissent from legal establishments which are instituted for religious purposes.

The laws of the State provide that each town not divided into parishes, and each precinct and parish, shall be obliged to settle and support a gospel minister, to whose settlement, support and maintenance all the persons and estates within the parish shall contribute by taxes duly and legally assessed ; and all those within the town or parish, whether they are Episcopalians, Baptists or Quakers, or whatever else they may be called, who dissent from the minister thus legally settled, and the mode of worship agreed upon by the majority, are *Sectaries.* Nay, even congregationalists, when the majority of the parish chuses a Presbyterian form of worship, may be a *Sect.* That this has been the idea of a Sect in this State from the time of the first legal establishment of local religious societies by parish and precinct lines, we submit to our countrymen. And we cannot but believe that it was used in this sense by the compilers of the Constitution, and conveyed this idea to the people when they established their Form of Government. It could not be confined in its meaning to the Sects only which existed at that time, as some intolerant and bigoted men have supposed, but extended to all which might arise thereafter; for the Convention could not be vain enough to suppose that all inquiry upon religious matters were at an end, nor ill-natured enough to wish to exclude the further investigation of truth. This does not, however, so much concern us, for we had associated before the Constitution was formed.

Taking the word *Sect* to mean as we have above explained it, we shall take it with us in that meaning, while we give our construction of the third article in the declaration of rights. And we find it necessary, as the history of this important article is fresh in the minds of our fellow-citizens, to go a little into it; indeed, ages yet to come may, and undoubtedly will, collect the same history from the arrangement of ideas and the mode of expression used in the article, which the people are now able to give from their memory.

The second article in the above-mentioned declaration provides, that, as it is as well the duty as the right of all men in civil society, to worship the supreme Being, no subject shall be hurt, molested, or restrained in his liberty or estate, for worshipping God in the manner and season most agreeable to the dictates of his own conscience, or for his religious profession or sentiments, provided he doth not disturb the public peace, or obstruct others in their religious worship. The ideas in this article were taken from Mr. Locke's letters on toleration, wherein that great man proves, from reason and scripture, that religion is at all times a matter between each individual and his God; and that no man has a right to dictate a mode of worship to another, nor can derive any authority to obstruct another in his way of worship. That each man may, and ought to enjoy his own mode, but may not sacrifice the life of another, because this is an injury to a person who stands on a perfect equality with himself. He cannot offer to his God the calf of another, because it would be robbing him of his property; but he may sacrifice his own calf or lamb in his own way, and no one has authority to prohibit it.

It was, on the one hand, thought necessary to make provision for the support of public worship, and of the public teachers of piety, religion and morality, for the sake of making men better citizens, and better members of the Commonwealth; while on the other, it was strenuously insisted upon that provision should be made for liberty of conscience, and express and ample security given against oppression in matters of religion. In this all agreed, for the Baptists, Quakers, &c., had depended for security from persecution upon a charter which was by the

New Constitution done away, and upon laws to secure them from oppression which might be repealed by the legislature at pleasure.

This article was a mere matter of negociation between parties; and unless some permanent measure could be contrived which could secure the sectaries against being compelled to contribute to the support of teachers whom they could never hear, and to the building of houses for public worship which they could never visit, there was but little hope of having the new form of government established; for the number of sectaries in the state, joined in the opposition with those who would oppose all forms of government predicated upon republican principles, would have turned a large majority against the constitution. It was urged, however, that there was not one society amongst the sectaries which had corporate powers, or were capable of making or compelling a tax; and therefore, to provide that they should not be taxed by the parish where they lived would be bidding a premium upon becoming sectaries, and offering a reward for the neglect of public worship. As the measure under consideration was intended only for civil purposes, and all religious ideas respecting the state of the individual in another world were disclaimed, the force of the reasoning was felt; and it was agreed that "all monies paid by the subject to the support of public worship, and *of the public teachers aforesaid*, should, if he require it, be uniformly applied to the support of the public teacher, or teachers, of his own religious sect or denomination; provided there be any on whose instructions he attends; otherwise it may be paid to the support of the teacher, or teachers, of the parish, or precinct, in which said monies are raised."

By this provision, all sectaries were obliged to contribute their proportion to the support of public worship, as an institution designed to establish the interest, and procure the safety of the Commonwealth. But "every christian demeaning himself peaceably was to be equally under the protection of the laws, and no subordination of any one *Sect*, or denomination, to another, was ever to be established by law." Therefore it was but just that the money "*paid by the subject*" *should be* uniformly applied to the teacher of his own religious sect or denomination, if he had such a teacher on whose instructions he attended; let him be either a teacher of a corporate society, vested by the legislature with civil powers, as a company holding a common estate, and then in a legal idea a denomination, or of a number of persons not described by parish lines, nor holding property in common as proprietors, and empowered by law to manage and dispose of it, but made up of a collection from parishes and precincts, and therefore called a *Sect*.

But it is said that the teacher to whose support the money is to be applied must be a teacher of a society vested with corporate powers, because that "all monies paid by the subject for the support of the *teachers aforesaid* is to be applied, &c." That this expression, *teachers aforesaid*, refers to teachers of parishes and societies with corporate powers, we grant. But still it does not support the objection. The article under consideration provides that the legislature shall have the power to authorize and require the several towns, parishes, precincts, and other bodies politick, and religious societies, to make provision, at their own expence, for the support of public worship; and we concede that there is no way for a legislature to compel a mere sect to make such provision; for they are neither capable of acting, nor can they be discerned by the legislative eye; and yet they have a right individually to protection from religious oppression. Here we grant all the facts which our opponents have asserted, but we totally deny the conclusions which they pretend to make; for tho' the parish has a right to tax the sectary towards the support of a public teacher, and thereby to compel him to contribute of his substance toward a measure intended for the benefit of the state; yet we say that the money is to be applied to the support of the teacher of his own *Sect*, who is supposed by the Constitution to teach those things which tend to piety and morality as much as the teacher of the parish; otherwise there would be a subordination of one sect or denomination to another. The word *Sect* can never mean a body with legal corporate powers; for the moment a society has an act of the legislature for their establishment they cease to be a sect, and become a legal body as much as a town or a parish is. There is a wide distinction between an establishment and a toleration. The dissenters in England, and the Hugonots in France, are tolerated; that is, they are freed from persecution, but not capable of acting as a legal body. But the idea of toleration at all times arises from a subordination of one sect to another; unless there may be an instance where the Civil Government makes no religious establishment, but tolerates all religions; where all sorts of *professions* of the Christian Religion are on a perfect equality, as they are by our Constitution: the idea of a toleration is inadmissible. But if the clause in the article was intended only for the benefit of Corporate Bodies, it was wholly unnecessary; for surely the law which gives them corporate powers, gives them at the same moment complete exemption, as far as the legislature can give it, from all taxes assessed by any other corporation. We conceive that the several parishes carved out of a town were never, by any language used in the country, considered as sects, because they were bodies established by law.

Moreover, as in matters of the support of teachers, the legislature can act only upon a consideration of the society which is the object of their law, holding and possessing property in common, or a common estate, as is not the case with us, the Baptists, and others who build their places of publick worship by a voluntary contribution, without contract, or an account of the expence. Those sects cannot be, by any law, put upon that footing, which they suppose the Constitution places them on.

All money raised for any purpose, by legal assessment, must indeed be raised by a corporate body; and therefore as a parish can raise no money by tax for the support of *public* teachers, but what is ostensibly raised for the support of a *parish* teacher, we suppose the expression, "*teacher or teachers aforesaid*," is used to express, the teacher or teachers of a parish or body politic. But when we come to the appropriation of the money, the expression is varied, and it is not to the "*teachers aforesaid*," but "*to the public teacher of his own religious Sect.*" Which clearly gives the priviledge of applying the money raised of the subject by legal authority, to the support of his own teacher, if he has one, of a *Sect* separated from the parish, on account of a difference in sentiment with respect to church discipline and the administration of religious rites.

We do not mean to suggest that every man who has a dislike to the minister of his parish, but still adheres to the same form of worship and mode of church discipline, has a right to have his money paid to one of the same denomination because he goes out of the parish to hear him; for in such case there is no difference of sects, and the constitution has made no provision about it.

If the construction we contend for is not the true one, then the Episcopalians, Baptists, Quakers, nor any other Sectary has any possible security against oppression in religious matters from the Constitution. For (as we believe) there is not one of them vested with corporate powers; the laws now in existence for their security can be repealed whenever the legislature shall see fit to do it, and they can all be placed in a day on the same ground which we now stand upon.

We have been told that we ought to apply to the legislature for an act of Incorporation, as the only remedy against the oppression we complain of; but could we be assured that our petition would be most readily granted, yet we should feel ourselves highly criminal in making the application.* Providence has so ordered it that we should, in the first instance, be called upon to contend for those religious liberties preserved by our excellent Constitution. The inconsiderableness of our party, and the prejudices raised by our enemies in the minds of our fellow-citizens, point us out as the proper objects of the first essay for religious tyranny; and should we fly to the lawmakers instead of that great law made by the people to govern the legislature itself, we should, in our apprehension, betray our country's freedom, and act a cowardly part. We should feel ourselves very unhappy if there was no other security in these matters than acts of legislation, which might be repealed at any time when a particular party should prevail.

We do not complain of persecution, but only of an oppression which we are convinced was intended by the Constitution to be prevented. For, blessed be God, there is no one sect or denomination at this time so prevalent in the State as to be able to introduce that horrid monster which for such a number of centuries has made havoc & destruction in the christian world.

Fellow-Citizens, When you shall be pleased to consider the vast variety of pursuits which the human race have been engaged in to procure that happiness which all are in search after; that what would canonize a man as a saint in one country would bring him to infamy in another; that though men

---

* If we did it with a view only to save our being taxed.

may have very different principles, yet they may be alike engaged in their researches after the truth. In short, when you extend your charity according to the dictates of reason and the instructions of the Christian religion, We believe that you will be contented to have our Sect treated as you wish to be treated yourselves. And that it will be your endeavor that we shall possess ourselves in peace and security.

We wish you to do in this case unto us, as you would reasonably expect us to do unto you in similar circumstances. That those who are Congregationalists may bring the matter home to themselves, we beg them to consider how they would stand affected if a majority of their parish should become Baptists, Presbyterians, Independents, or Sandemanians; and should elect a teacher whom they could not hear, and set up a form of worship in which they could not join, and compel the minority who were Congregationalists to pay to the support of it. If that be wrong, then we are abused, unless one sect is in subordination to another, and religion is no longer a matter between the heart of each individual and his God, but a matter submitted to, and under the controul of a majority in society.

"Judge not that ye be not judged; for with what judgment ye judge, ye shall be judged; and with what measure ye mete, it shall be measured to you again."

APPENDIX.

ARTICLES *in the Declaration of RIGHTS.*

II. It is the right as well as the duty of all men in society, publickly, and at stated seasons, to worship the SUPREME BEING, the great creator and preserver of the universe. And no subject shall be hurt, molested, or restrained, in his person, liberty or estate, for worshipping GOD in the manner and season most agreeable to the dictates of his own conscience; or for his religious profession or sentiments; provided he doth not disturb the public peace, or obstruct others in their religious worship.

ELMER H. CAPEN, D.D.,
NINTH PASTOR, 1865-1869.

III. As the happiness of a people, and the good order and preservation of civil government, essentially depend upon piety, religion and morality; and as these cannot be generally diffused through a community, but by the institution of the public worship of GOD, and of public instructions in piety, religion and morality: Therefore, to promote their happiness, and to secure the good order and preservation of their government, the people of this Commonwealth have a right to invest their legislature with power to authorize and require, and the legislature shall, from time to time, authorize and require, the several towns, parishes, precincts, and other bodies politic, or religious societies, to make suitable provision, at their own expence, for the institution of the public worship of GOD, and for the support and maintenance of public protestant teachers of piety, religion and morality, in all cases where such provision shall not be made voluntarily.

AND the people of this Commonwealth have also a right to, and do, invest their legislature with authority to enjoin upon all the subjects, an attendance upon the instructions of the public teachers aforesaid, at stated times and seasons; if there be any on whose instructions they can conscientiously and conveniently attend.

PROVIDED notwithstanding, that the several towns, parishes, precincts, and other bodies-politic, or religious societies, shall, at all times, have the exclusive right of electing their public teachers, and of contracting with them for their support and maintenance.

AND all monies paid by the subject to the support of public worship, and of the public teachers aforesaid, shall, if he require it, be uniformly applied to the support of the public teacher or teachers of his own religious sect or denomination, provided there be any on whose instructions he attends; otherwise it may be paid towards the support of the teacher or teachers of the parish or precinct in which the said monies are raised.

AND every denomination of Christians, demeaning themselves peaceably, and as good subjects of the Commonwealth, shall be equally under the protection of the law: And no subordination of any one sect or denomination to another shall ever be established by law.

ASSOCIATION of the Independent Church in GLOCESTER.

INASMUCH as it hath pleased God of his great mercy, in every age of the world, to choose a people for himself; giving them his fear, and revealing to them his secret; and as this great Lord of heaven and earth, the Father of our Lord Jesus Christ, hath been pleased to reveal to babes, what he has hid from the wise and prudent: We the subscribers, gratefully affected with a sense of the divine goodness, in thus distinguishing us, who had nothing in us to merit his notice; think it our interest and bounden duty, to let our light shine before men, that they may see our good works, and glorify our Father which is in heaven. As therefore it has pleased God to make us acquainted with the voice of the good shepherd, the Lord Jesus Christ, the great shepherd and bishop of souls; we cannot from henceforward follow the voice of a stranger; nor ever give attention to such who are unacquainted with the Saviour of the world. But though we cannot have fellowship with them whose fellowship is not with the Father, and with his Son Jesus Christ; yet we are determined, by the grace of God, never to forsake the assembling of ourselves together, as the manner of some is; but as a church of Christ, meet together in his name, being persuaded, wherever, or whenever two or three are thus met together, the invisible God will be present with them.

As Christians, we acknowledge no master but Christ Jesus, and as disciples of this divine master, we profess to follow no guide in spiritual matters, but his word, and his spirit.

As dwellers in this world, though not of it, we hold ourselves bound to yield obedience to every ordinance of man, for God's sake; and we will be peaceable and obedient subjects to the powers that are ordained of God, in all civil cases: But as subjects of that King, whose kingdom is not of this world—we cannot acknowledge the right of any human authority to make laws for the regulating of our conscience in any spiritual matters.

THUS, as a true independent church of Christ, looking unto Jesus the author and finisher of our faith, we mutually agree to walk together in christian fellowship, building up each other in our most holy faith, rejoicing in the liberty wherewith Christ hath made us free, and determining by his grace, no more to be entangled by any yoke of bondage.

As disciples of the meek and lowly Jesus, we resolve as far as in us lieth, to live peaceably with all men; yet as believers living godly in Christ Jesus, we expect to suffer as much persecution as the laws of the country we live in, will admit of: But we resolve by the grace of God, none of these things shall move us to act inconsistent with our character as christians. We will as much as possible avoid vain jangling, and unnecessary disputation; and should we be reviled, endeavor in patience to possess our souls.

As an independent church of Christ thus bound together by the cords of his love, and meeting together in his name; we mutually agree to receive as our Minister, that is our Servant, sent to labour among us in the work of the gospel by the great Lord of the vineyard, our friend and christian brother JOHN MURRAY: This we do from a full conviction that the same God that sent the first preachers of Jesus Christ, sent him; and that the same gospel they preached, we have from time to time received from him: Thus, believing him a minister of the New Testament, constantly declaring the whole counsel of God; proclaiming the same divine truth that all God's holy Prophets from the beginning of the world hath declared: WE cordially receive him as a Messenger from God.—And as it hath pleased God to open a great and effectual door for the preaching of his gospel by this his servant in sundry parts of this great continent, whenever it shall please his and our divine master to call him to preach the everlasting gospel elsewhere, we wish him God-speed; and pray that the good-will of him that dwelt in the bush may acccompany him, and make his way clear before him: But should he at any time preach any other gospel, than that we have received, we *will not* wish him God-speed, but consider him as a stranger.—And as the great Lord of the harvest has taught us to pray that he would send labourers into his harvest; and as he never taught us to pray in vain, but has assured us, every one that asketh receiveth, though he has not told us when, whenever he shall see fit to send us a messenger of glad tidings, a publisher of peace, we will with grateful hearts receive him.—And as the promise of the divine presence is to any two or three that meet together in the Saviour's name; we are resolved by God's grace, whether we are blessed with the publick preaching of the word or not, as often as we find convenient, to meet together, to supplicate the divine favour, to praise our redeeming God, to hear his most holy word, and freely to communicate whatever God shall please to manifest to us for our mutual edification.

AND that we may the more effectually shew forth his praise, who hath called us out of darkness into his marvellous light; we resolve to pay a serious regard to the exhortations, admonitions and instructions given to us by the Spirit of God, in the epistles dictated to our holy apostles. We will, as far as in us lieth, do good unto all men; but especially unto them who are of the household of faith.

WE will, by the grace of God, in word and in deed, endeavour to adorn the doctrine of God our Saviour. And as children of one father, as members of one head, who are united together in christian-fellowship, will, once every month meet together, to hold conference, and to deliberate on whatever may tend to our mutual profit.

Signed by all the Society.

[The names of the signers were:

John Murray, Winthrop Sargent, Catherine Sargent, Judith Sargent, Bradbury Sanders, Anna Sanders, Joseph Foster, Lydia Foster, David Pearce, David Plumer, Elizabeth Plumer, Jonathan Trask, Abigail Trask, John Somes, George Creighton, John Stevens, Jr., Judith Stevens, Philemon Haskell, Elizabeth Haskell, John Stevens Ellery, Esther Ellery, James Prentiss, Lydia Prentiss, William Pearce, Moses Bennett, Winthrop Allen, Sam'l. Sayward, Susa Sayward, Abraham Sawyer, Ann Ollive, Eben'r. Hough, Mary Hough, Joseph Everden, Aaron Lufkin, Robert Weston, Thos. Sparling, Isaac Bennett, Nabby Palfrey, Jemima Cook, Jerusha Jordan, Lydia Parsons, Israel Trask, Wm. Dolliver, Abigail Dolliver, Solomon Babson, Rebekah Babson, Benjamin Lufkin, Sarah Lufkin, Rebecca Smith, Hannah Tucker, Isaac Ball, Hannah Ball, Mary Sargent, Edw'd. Crossman, Rebecca Parsons, Jemima Parsons, Susanna Lane, Susanna Mellings, Mary Steele, Rebekah Ingersoll, Joseph Lufkin.]

APPENDIX H.

AN ANSWER TO A PIECE, ENTITLED, "AN APPEAL TO THE IMPARTIAL PUBLICK, BY AN ASSOCIATION" CALLING THEMSELVES "CHRISTIAN INDEPENDENTS, IN GLOCESTER."

FELLOW-CITIZENS —

We should not have troubled the publick, or taken any farther notice of the Appeal of those who call themselves *Christian Independents* in *Glocester*, than to have read it with an eye of candour, had they not grossly misrepresented the truth, and in several instances asserted things really false, with a design (we fear) of imposing upon the publick, and prejudicing their minds against the truth. We shall therefore,

1st, Give a fair and impartial relation of facts, as they took place, and gave rise to that Association who now stile themselves Christian Independents.

2dly, We shall make a few remarks upon their Appeal.

3dly, Close with a short address to the publick.

THE RELATION OF FACTS.

Sometime in the year 1774, the Rev. Mr. Samuel Chandler, the then pastor of the first church and parish in Glocester, fell into a decline, and was not able to carry on the work of the ministry. The committee for supplying the pulpit was informed that there was one Mr. Murray, in Boston, who came from the southward, and that he was a wonderful preacher, and urged them to send for him; but the committee thought it not prudent to send for a stranger, without something more to recommend him than what they learnt from their informers. However, he soon came; we suppose, by the invitation of his private friends; and being introduced by them to Mr. Chandler, he went into a free, candid and friendly conversation with him upon the subject of his education, and the manner of his being introduced into the work of the ministry; and he freely told him, though he had not been favoured with a liberal education, yet this was more than made up by an extraordinary *call from Heaven;* and went on to convince Mr. Chandler of the justness of his claim to this *extraordinary call.* However, Mr. Chandler was by no means satisfied; yet, as there was a sacramental lecture already appointed, the people in general very desirous of hearing this stranger, and Mr. Chandler not being able to preach himself, consented that he should preach in his pulpit. Soon after he named his text, he told us that as he was a stranger he was at a loss what to entertain us with; but, desirous of being directed, both his text and subject were revealed to him as he came along; so he gave us a sacramental discourse (as he called it) warm from the fountain of inspiration, and, in his way, recommended to us frequent communion at the Lord's table. In his whole preachment he was very incoherent, and threw out some dark and mystical things, which had a very different effect upon the hearers; some admired him, and swallowed all he said with great avidity; others doubted, and returned and searched the Scriptures, "to see if the things which had been spoken were so;" others were filled with indignation, and said they had been imposed upon; but the majority were for hearing him farther. At length he opened his whole sentiments, and roundly exploded the doctrine of future rewards and punishments, asserting the doctrine of universal salvation, without exception or distinction of characters, openly ridiculing the distinguishing doctrines of the gospel, as generally preached by the regular ministers of this land, whom he spoke of in the most contemptuous manner, as being a group of poor ignorant creatures, who knew nothing of the gospel of Christ, and said, "they were, like the horse in the mill, confined to a narrow circle, from whence they could not depart." This, with many other things he said in publick, in the run of his discourse, satisfied the doubtful, and for a while stumbled even his admirers; and the meeting-house doors were shut against him. Soon after this, Mr. Chandler, viewing himself approaching fast to the close of life, sent for him, and entered fully with him on the subject of universal salvation, when he asserted it in the strongest terms; and being asked whether there was no exception, he said, no. Upon Judas, the traitor, being mentioned, he said "he doubted not but he was now on a throne of glory, and that he shone as bright as any of the apostles." And when the tares among the wheat in the field were mentioned, (represented by our Saviour in a parable as being gathered together in bundles to be burned, implying future punishment), he said, those tares were the sins and evil dispositions of the human heart, which were punished in their principal, the Devil, separate from the subject who committed them; and many other such like strange and incoherent things were advanced by him in this conference. Mr. Chandler said but little, for he had but little strength; yet gave him, in most affecting and melting strains, his dying admonition, endeavoring to dissuade him from those strange and absurd tenets; but, if he should continue to advance them, not to do it here, to corrupt and mislead the dear people of his charge. After this, Mr. Chandler, for the last time, got, with much difficulty, into his own desk, where he took an affecting leave of his people, solemnly warning them not to hear this false and dangerous man, in the following words:

"MY BRETHREN AND FRIENDS:—I have much sorrow of heart, considering the state of affairs among us. I am far advanced in life, and labour under threatening maladies, and know not how soon I may be taken from you and from this world. As one drawing near the eternal world—*take heed what you hear.* The seeds of heresy are sowing and sprouting up among us, and souls are in danger of being seduced into errours. There is one, who calls himself John Murray, who has declared the following things to be his settled opinion: That the whole human race, every one of Adam's posterity, have an interest in Christ, and are God's beloved ones; That the whole human race, every individual of mankind, shall finally be saved; That Judas shall sit upon a throne in the kingdom of Heaven; That at death the good go into a state of happiness, and the bad into an intermediate state, to abide there for a certain season, but shall finally be saved; which, however dressed up in soft terms and smooth expressions, is the very popish purgatory.

"The substance of these things and many other errours he hath openly avowed, and declared to be his sentiments, at my house, in the hearing of many witnesses. These are unscriptural tenets; and notwithstanding all his perverting the holy Scriptures, and wresting and torturing the word of God, he was not able to produce one plausible proof, nor one rational argument, for the support of these pernicious principles. They naturally lead to many other gross errours and popish absurdities, and they are extremely dangerous to the souls of men; they encourage the wicked in their wickedness; for, upon these principles, a man may live and die in sin, and yet go to Heaven at last; he may get drunk, commit fornication and adultery; he may cheat, and steal, and lie, and indulge all manner of carnal gratifications, and be saved nothwithstanding. But you may say you do not discover any of these errors in his preaching. Why, others, who have been accounted serious, discerning, judicious men, and whose judgment would heretofore have had some weight in your minds, have discovered them in his public discourses. But however he seems artfully to hide them, your minds are not prepared to receive them; your affections must first be broken off from your ministers, and your minds filled with prejudices against them, by their being reviled and vilified, and your affections set upon *himself*, and you brought to receive the words of his mouth with implicit faith; then, doubtless, these dangerous doctrines, and many others will be inculcated. My brethren and friends, I must caution you to take heed and beware of false teachers. Beware, lest ye be led away by errours, and fall from your steadfastness. Beware of false prophets, concerning whom our blessed Saviour hath warned us that if it were possible they shall deceive the very elect. SAMUEL CHANDLER."

Glocester, February 3d, 1775.

And after this, Mr. Murray continued his preachments in a private house, and used every method to touch the passions and sooth the vices of mankind, to gain proselytes to his party, till Mr. Chandler died, which was on the 16th of March, 1775. The town, from a tender concern for the morals of the people, and that they might, if possible, preserve peace and good order in the place, took the matter up, and sent for this stranger, and inquired of him, who he was? what were his credentials? and for what purpose he tarried in this place? The town thought they were illy treated by him, and resolved pretty unanimously that he was a dangerous man, and should be desired to leave the town in a given time; but he positively told those who delivered the message to him from the town, that he would not; and, to prevent his being carried out by an officer, one of his friends made him a freeholder. And as we were then involved in a war with our mother state, and men's passions were agitated and fiery, we thought it not best to carry matters to extremity, and so he continued; and the separation remained much the same, till we gave Mr. Forbes an invitation to settle with us in the work of the ministry, when the separation made a formal opposition, as appears by their letter to him, which is as follows:

Glocester, April 4th, 1776.

"REVEREND SIR:— You will have laid before you the votes of the parish, relative to your settlement; and as it may be of great importance to you as well as us, we think it our duty to address you on the subject. For many years past, our trade, and particularly the fishery, by which our chief dependence is, has greatly declined; that except a very few persons, we have been carrying on both trade and fishery to a very great loss; that many of us have sunk thousands; that we have large debts outstanding, which will be entirely lost; our fishery at present is at an end, and merchandize very dangerous and precarious; several of our vessels taken, others missing; our tradesmen and labourers dependent mostly on the trade for their subsistence. Should the publick dispute continue much longer, our fishery must be entirely ruined, and then of course all other business must fail here, of any consequence, as we are such a distance from the country that it will be in vain to expect anything therefrom in our trade. We are greatly in arrears in our taxes of every kind for two years past; new and heavy ones increasing daily; most of our people gone; not the least expectation but we shall be put to the flight again; two or three of our principal traders left the parish, and more intend it. Some of us remember the Spanish and French wars at different periods, with other sore calamities; but never did our eyes behold such a gloomy aspect as our affairs wear at this season. In short, time would fail us to enumerate the many difficulties that attend us. We are desirous that that harmony that has subsisted these many years in this parish may continue. If you think proper to give your voice in the affirmative, it must entirely be at an end, as we shall be obliged to take such steps as would by no means be agreeable to you or our brethren; therefore we thought it our duty to apprize you of this, and hope your wisdom will direct you to that which will be to your honour. We are your most humble servants."

This letter was signed by ten of those that now form the Association. As it did not appear by this letter that the opposition was against him (Mr. Forbes), or that they had any objection to his doctrines or character, but against a re-settlement in general, therefore we thought, and the installing council thought, it would be no bar to his settlement; accordingly, being chosen by a large majority both in the church and parish, and a council being convened by letters missive for that purpose, he was installed on the fifth of June, 1776, without any opposition, and in as much peace and harmony as could be expected. After this, Mr. Forbes had several conferences with Mr. Murray, and wished to know his true character; but he could not learn it from him or his adherents; and being informed that Dr. Stiles, of Newport, then residing at Portsmouth, and now President of New-Haven college, had the best intelligence, he wrote him on the subject, and had in answer the following:

Portsmouth, Dec. 24, 1777.

"REV. SIR : — Mr. Murray, of whom you ask some account, is one of those ostentatious, obstinate, but subtle, delusory characters, with which it is best to have little to do. I do not know that his moral character is directly reprehensible, but I believe him to be one of the most unprincipled of all men. The most of the little I know of him I received from his own mouth, and from that little I judge him a consummate hypocrite; at best, he is a man of duplicity and dubiousness of conduct. He is a man of no education, though he spent a few months with, I think, a Romanist, who had set up a little academy in Ireland, when he quarrelled, or seemed to quarrel, with his master, and left him abruptly. He was connected with the Westleans till he was 18; then he quarrelled with and left them. He so far went over to the Baptists, that he was rebaptized by immersion, in Ireland, among the Baptists. From the time he left the Westleans, till just before he came to America, he connected himself with no religious society, but followed the trade of a silk weaver, in London, about 12 years. This business failing, he meditated coming to America, though with no thoughts of preaching. Though unused to attend the Tabernacle, yet he applied to Mr. Whitefield, just before his last voyage to America, and with his leave he partook of the Sacrament once at the Tabernacle. This was religious hypocrisy, for, whatever he was, he was neither a Whitefieldean, nor a Westlean, nor a Baptist.

"He told me he did not communicate to Mr. Whitefield his intentions of coming to America; but the plan he had projected, he said, was this: to come here as a follower of Mr. Whitefield, and here to make himself known to him by reminding him of his communicating at the Tabernacle, and then request of Mr. Whitefield to put him into some secular employment at the Orphan House in Georgia; for, he said, he never had preached in England, and had no thoughts of it here, except that he had sometimes spoken or exhorted in some of the small Westlean societies before he was 18 years old. Upon coming here, his plan was broken up, as Mr. Whitefield died a few weeks before or after his arrival. I have been informed of some of his ludicrous and jocund conversation, while on the passage, respecting what business he should follow here, intimating his readiness to go upon the stage, or, &c. &c., indicating an undetermined and an unprincipled adventurer, ready, indifferently, to turn himself to any course. Being shipwrecked on the Jersey shore, he was received with hospitality by an opulent Presbyterian, who had built a meeting-house there for travelling ministers, especially those sent by the Synods. Mr. Murray here offered himself first to preach. From that time to this he has been preaching in different parts, as you know.

There was a society set up in London, about 1765, which held the principles that Mr. Murray does. I suppose that when Mr. Murray determined to profane the sacred desk, he recollected and took this society for his model; resolving to strike, like Sandeman, at all ministers and churches, and thus render himself noticed; and then choose out a palatable religion for corrupt nature, and so go forth preaching, as he has done, with an unpolite and unparalleled effrontery. He adopts the principles of *universal salvation*, but is no ways versed in the writings and arguments upon it, except a pamphlet writer or two, of very small and slender talents. His scheme is short: All are lost without possibility of self-recovery; and all are saved by Christ's righteousness and divine love. All texts of Scripture speaking of love and mercy, he takes literally; those that speak of punishment, both the parables and express declarations of Christ, he allegorizes, till he loses his hearers in clouds and delusions of universal happiness. But he is unstudied and undigested in his own scheme. At first he laughed at a literal hell, and denied all future misery. Afterwards he allowed some future punishment, but denies the eternity of it, and goes into the popish doctrine of purgatory. In short, he is to this day unsettled in his scheme — a scheme infinitely dangerous to morality. When he visited me, I asked his opinion respecting his supposed tenet of universal salvation. But he positively denied it to me, and asserted both the reality and perpetuity of the future misery and damnation of those of the human race who should be found on the left hand of Jesus; and he said a number of mankind would be found on the left hand of Jesus, at the great day. I believed him for once, though I never asked him to preach in my pulpit, where he had preached repeatedly in my absence. But he went no further than Narraganset, and preached directly contrary; and at East Greenwich, in conversation, he denied a hell — not only a local hell, but that there was any state of misery after death. And it is said that once, after supper, he talked ludicrously of the Lord's supper, as being only like drinking a health unto the memory of an absent friend; and profanely said, Here is bread, and here is wine; what forbids but we should have it now? One of the company replied, Several things forbid it: in order to a due partaking or administering of that holy ordinance, there are two things necessary, viz., proper subjects, and a proper person to administer it; neither of which, says he, do I know to be here. Murray replied, They were fit subjects, and he, or any other person, had power, &c., and so it ended. Mr. Murray denies all this, with certain artful duplicity or coverings; but I had it from the mouth of one of the gentlemen present, and do not doubt the fact. Indeed, it is said by others, that now he talks lightly about outward ordinances. When he was at Newport, he went to the Quakers' meeting there, when he rose and spoke, and personated the Quaker preacher, to the universal disgust of the

Friends and all others, even his best admirers, sundry of whom I heard pronounce it *hypocrisy*. Some men of his sentiments may be reasoned with, some cannot; he is one of those with whom it is vain to reason. I rather consider him a Romanist in disguise, endeavoring to excite confusion in our churches. But I can easily see he is the meteor of the night only; like S—d—n or G—r—n, he and his disciples will soon vanish; though we must expect others to rise up, till the second coming of Christ. Let us not be distressed. Let us testify the truth with firmness, and leave the church to the care of Jesus.

I am, sir, your brother,

EZRA STILES.

"P. S. In his politicks he has been at first an Anti-American, then for us, and now against us, and for reconciliation, &c."

This letter Mr. Forbes communicated to Mr. Murray, and, by the Doctor's leave, gave him an attested copy, at which he appeared much offended, and said that he would prove to the world that it was a false and injurious aspersion, and made for a while a bustle, and did nothing; so his character with us remains just in that point of light in which the Doctor gave it.

In the Preface (dated Boston, Aug. 1782) to the Pamphlet entitled, "Salvation for all Men," is the following paragraph:

"The doctrine of *Universal Salvation* has, in this and some other towns, been held forth by a stranger, who has, of himself, assumed the character of a *preacher*, in direct contradiction not only to all the before mentioned writers, but to the *whole tenour of the New Testament books, from their beginning to their end*. According to this *preacher*, a man may go to Heaven, notwithstanding all the sins he has been guilty of in the course of his life. Such a doctrine looks very like an *encouragement* to *libertinism*, and falls in with the scheme of too many in this degenerate age, who, under pretence of *promoting religion, undermine it at the very root*. It is certainly fitted to this end, and has already had this effect upon many, especially of our younger people, who, by means of it, have lost all sense of religion, and given themselves up to the most criminal excesses! If this kind of preaching is encouraged, it may prove as hurtful to *civil society* as to *religion*."

As there were a number in this separation who were members of our church in full standing, who had forsaken our worship and communion to follow this stranger, without giving any reasons for their so doing, we thought it our duty to inquire into the reasons of their conduct; therefore appointed a church meeting for that purpose, but they did not attend. We then adjourned the meeting, and wrote to them severally, desiring them to give us their reasons, if any they had, why they absented themselves from the worship of God, and our communion; but they refused to meet with, or to give us any reasons for their conduct. We wrote them again, as a church, in the most pacifick manner, praying them, if they had any matters of grievance, they would make them known; or if they were of such a nature as that they were not willing that we should judge of them, that they would propose some method in which the grievance might be removed, or an accommodation take place; or we were ready to submit the matter to the judgment of a council of church members, mutually chosen for that purpose, and we would submit our whole conduct to the inspection and determination of the same; so we did everything in our power to satisfy or recover our deserting and separating members, as will abundantly appear by the church records.

But this, and every other method we could adopt, they treated with silent contempt. Yet we have ever treated them in the most lenient manner. But the outcry is, they are oppressed, because they are taxed in common for the payment of parish charges. But we think that as they never have been incorporated by any order or authority known in this commonwealth, nor at any time laid before us as a parish any reasons why they should be exempted, we cannot levy a lawful tax without including them. And we have borne with them from year to year; and when any of our collectors have called upon them for their proportion of taxes, they have treated them ill, and sometimes have threatened their lives; and we forebore still. At length they agreed that we should distrain on some of their party, and then they would try it out in the law; and as we saw no other way to have the matter issued, we agreed to the measure, however disagreeable it was for us to enter into the law; and we distrained on the goods of four of their number, named by them, and sold them at publick auction, and paid their tax, and tendered them the overplus; but they would not receive it, but cried out of oppression and injury, though it was a proposal of their own, to which we agreed only to bring the matter to an issue. They then endeavored to recover their goods by a writ of *Replevin*, but failed; then they sued the assessors, and harassed us in the law for several years, without suffering their case to come to a trial; then they withdrew their case, as not being tenable. And now their teacher, without a character, credentials or ordination, has assumed the character of a public teacher of piety, religion and morality, stiles himself *clerk*, and sued the parish for that money which had been taken from his friends by distraint; and after many unnecessary delays it came to a hearing before the Supreme Judicial Court, at their last session, in Ipswich, when a jury, in opposition to the whole court, and to the surprize of all parties, brought in a verdict partly in their favour; notwithstanding which, Mr. Murray has reviewed, and served us with his writ, though we had reviewed at the time of trial. Thus, while he affects to keep up an air of importance, he is determined to give us all the trouble he possibly can.

This is a concise and impartial relation of facts as they took place, and gave rise to that Association who now stile themselves Christian Independents.

We pass, SECONDLY, to make a few Remarks upon their Appeal.

1st. We cannot but remark upon the unheard-of name which they have assumed — *Christian Independents!* A solecism in nature! and when assumed by a society in confederate states, it implies treason! In a civil or political view, it is at best, imperium in imperio, which involves in it a contradiction; and if we consider it in a religious or ecclesiastical view, it is absurd; an independent church must either be the whole church of Christ, or it must be a particular part detached from the body catholick; but an independent part, or member of the body universal, is a contradiction; for one member "cannot say to the other, I have no need of thee." The Christian church is everywhere considered as consisting of confederating members, uniting in Christ the head, and holding communion with each other in the doctrines and institutions of Christ. But this Association holds no communion with any church on earth, in the doctrines and ordinances of Christ. They deny the morality of the Christian Sabbath, explode and ridicule the institutions of baptism and the Lord's supper. What claim can they have, then, to the Christian name, while they deny and disuse the distinguishing ordinances of Christianity?

Having remarked this upon the title page, we pass to take some notice of their Appeal.

And they introduce themselves with saying, "We should be far from giving our countrymen the trouble of attending to an appeal, had we not been drawn before a civil tribunal, in defence of what we suppose to be our just, invaluable and constitutional rights." To which we would only reply, It is not we, but they, who commenced and re-commenced the lawsuit, and are now first in serving us with their writ of review; so that it was not we who drew them, but they *us*, before a civil tribunal, in defence of what we call our just and constitutional rights. In their fourth page they seem to think they have some special claim to the favour of their country, from their not "shewing any backwardness in the late war." We are sorry that we are obliged to say this is a misrepresentation of real facts; for though some of them have shown a becoming zeal for the rights and safety of their country, yet it is a well-known fact that all who were unfriendly to the American cause here, were in this separation. It is also a known fact, that their teacher was admired most by those that were most unfriendly to the American cause, not only in this town, but through this commonwealth; and several who are of this Association would do nothing in defence of the cause but by constraint. Little reason, then, have they to boast on this head, or claim the favor of their country as her favorite sons; especially since they have a man for their leader who is himself a foreigner, and has ever been the idol of Tories, and often been closeted by the rankest of that tribe, in other places as well as in this.

They say, also, in the same page, "When Mr. Murray, our present teacher in religious matters, had been invited to preach in the meeting-house, we heard him with increasing pleasure and a glowing satisfaction." This also is a misrepresentation. Many of those who now form the Association were then his greatest opposers; and those who were his first admirers, and who were chiefly concerned in introducing him into the pulpit,

RICHARD EDDY, D.D.
TENTH PASTOR, 1870-1877.

soon discovered his jesuitical designs, and were the foremost in endeavoring his removal hence. In the same page, also, they say, "On the settlement of Mr. Forbes, being obliged to withhold our assent to the doctrines he taught, disagreed to his settlement." This is, we think, a falsehood; which sufficiently appears from their own letter sent to Mr. Forbes, and communicated by him to the parish.* This letter was sent as containing their objections; but there is not a word in it which intimated that they could not assent to his doctrines. The only ostensible ground of their objection then was, the then present war, and the circumstances of the parish. Nay, upon being asked, they said "they had no objection to Mr. Forbes; they were willing to be their proportion in hiring him for a supply; and if we must settle, they were as willing he should be the man as anybody." For them now to say that they could not assent to his doctrines, and therefore disagreed to his settlement, bears too great a resemblance to a falsehood. We wished then, and do now wish, to put the best construction upon this mystical part of conduct; and we appeal to the public to say whether this does not look as if they had formed a design to make a breach in this (till then peaceful) society, and made use of this stranger as a fit tool to carry into execution their malignant design.†

We leave now our dissenting brethren to contend with *Constantius*, *Theodosius*, and to define in the school of Plato the Homoiousion as they please; or to dispute with their old friend the *British monarch* for the title, *defender of the faith*, &c. and to make their own strictures upon the conduct of the first settlers of this commonwealth. Yet we cannot but observe, in their 13th page, how unfairly they speak of their distinguishing character. They say, "We distinguish ourselves from the church under the instruction of Mr. Forbes, in our not using baptism as an external rite, and also in our mode of discipline, being Independents." Whereas the truth is, they are totally distinguished from us, and from all the churches in this commonwealth, by their being no church at all, not being incorporated by any order or authority known in this commonwealth; but a mere jumble of detached members, some of which, in the

* Page 7.

† See the closing sentence of their letter to Mr. Forbes, p. 8.

most irregular manner, separated themselves, without cause, from the first church in Glocester, and who have obstinately continued in their separation, against all reasoning, remonstrating and persuasion, deaf to all the most pacifick proposals made on the part of the church from whom they separated; and their Association is made up partly from other parishes, and partly of foreigners, and some of the most abandoned characters; in short, any body and any thing whom they could by persuasion or pecuniary consideration hire into their service. We are sorry to say this, but are constrained to do it in our own defence, and in honour to the church; for we think it the highest dishonour to the church of Christ for such a heterogeneous body to call themselves a church, distinguished only from the other churches in this land by the external rite of baptism, and the mode of discipline. This would naturally lead the impartial publick to conclude that they were a set of sober Christians, of tender consciences, distinguished from their brethren only in a few non-essential modes that were merely external; whereas, they have not one single feature of a church of Christ, or any mode of discipline, that we can discern, among them. They resemble Nebuchadnezzar's image as much as any thing we can think of, which was made of gold, silver, brass, iron and clay, and was broken to pieces by a stone cast out of the mountain without hands, and all become like the chaff of the summer threshing floor; for some of their members sustain fair moral characters, yet not without a strong tinge of enthusiasm. But they ask "why the Quakers should meet with the smiles of government, and they not have the favours of the state?" We answer, they are a sect made up of peaceable, honest people, who speak the truth, and should, therefore, and will, meet the smiles of government, while those of a contrary character may expect their frowns. But they say, 14th page, "Notwithstanding this, we have been, and are still, taxed to the support of Mr. Forbes, and our property is taken and exposed at auction, to raise money for the support of a form of worship in which we can never join." There they have in part told the truth; but they hold the truth in unrighteousness, for they seem not to love the truth in her naked simplicity. The simple truth is this: They have been and are still taxed in common with the other members of our parish to raise money to defray parish charges, (some part of which is appropriated to the support of publick worship), all which they have constantly refused to pay: and though they pretend to ground that refusal upon the Constitution, yet they equally refuse to pay that which was levied before the Constitution took place, and have repeatedly sued us for taxes levied upon them to pay the necessary and contingent charges of the parish, as well as for that which is appropriated to the support of public worship — "a form in which (they say) they can never join." Why? When any have resided for a while in neighboring towns, they have attended and joined with the people where they resided; and some of those who were first in the separation, and now form the Association, being members of our church, have partook of the sacrament of the Lord's supper in other churches, joining with them not only in publick worship, but in the holy communion, though they had the same form of worship as ours, and in full communion with our church; so that their cannot must be their will not; and because they will not, conscience is not concerned here.

In page 16th they seem to be concerned for their minister, lest they should not be able to prove that he is a preacher of piety, religion and morality; they had rather the question should be waved, but if decided at all, they think it ought to be from his urging his hearers to the practice of morality. We beg leave to ask, Can a man who publickly discards the doctrine of God's moral government — of future rewards and punishments — urge, with a good face, or with any hope of success, the practice of morality? Can he confidently preach up morality, when he at the same time saps its very foundation, and cuts the nerves of Christian piety, by blending all characters together, and by making all equally holy because equally united to Christ in his incarnation? But here our brethren tremble for their minister, and would fain shelter him under the cloaks of the learned Doctors Chauncy and Priestley, who, they say, believe that there is a temporary hell for the ungodly — and why may not their unlearned teacher believe there is no hell prepared for any body but the poor devils, and yet be in law a good preacher of piety, religion and morality? But those learned men will shake him from their skirts as a corrupting leprosy, if we may believe Doctor Chauncy's own words in his preface to his book of extracts.

We do not know how our brethren come to blunder upon that gross mistake, "that God, in his civil constitution he was pleased to form for the Jews, never in any one instance gave intimation that the Jews should be punished in another world for their crimes committed in this"; we charitably believe that it was owing to their being implicitly led by one who is totally ignorant of the original languages, the nature and designs of the Sinai covenant. Without quoting those passages from Moses and the prophets which would evince the contrary, (for we are no textuaries), we refer them to the apostle to the Hebrews, who considered the rest of the early Canaan as typical of the rest of the heavenly; and as unbelief and disobedience excluded the Jews from the earthly, so they would from the heavenly. But we are not so much surprized at this as we are at the indignity which they obliquely cast upon Christ himself, when, in page 18th, they say, "It was not till the Christian church was illegally wedded to state policy, that men in power dared to hurl the thunders of the Most High at those who offended against government." We disapprove of the terms, (though borrowed without credit), yet more of the sentiments couched under those sonorous terms. We take it, both from this sentence and from what they said above, that it is their opinion that it was not till Christ came, a preacher of the everlasting gospel, that men were threatened with punishments in another world for crimes committed in this; that this is a doctrine peculiar to Christ and his apostles, and so from them has been preached up, and handed down, to this day, by those who knew no better. It is certain Christ opened his ministry by preaching up the doctrine of future rewards and punishments; but our brethren say "this was not done till the Christian church was illegally wedded to state policy." The Christian church was formed by Christ; she took her name from him, and was so far wedded to state policy as that he made "kings and queens nursing fathers and mothers," & made the "earth to help the woman." This marriage they call illegal, and implicitly charge it upon Christ; but they dare not speak it out. It was not till then, they say, that offences against government were threatened with future punishment. All immoralities are offences against government, against God's moral government, and every form which he has ordained for men; and all immoralities, without repentance and a believing application to Christ, have been, ever since the Christian era, threatened with future punishments. The truth of the matter is this — the doctrines of their teacher do not correspond with those of Christ and his apostles; yet they want to make it out that he is a teacher of piety, religion and morality.

We pass over all the arguments which they deduce from the various denominations which unhappily divide the Christian name, as being futile and inconclusive; yet cannot but observe how inconsistent they are with themselves, when they say, 20th page, that "we suppose every *good man*, let his involuntary errors be what they may, will be in the favour of God." So they suppose it consistent that every bad man, be his involuntary errors what they may, is and will be in favour with God. But where is the sense of talking of good men or bad men, when with them all characters are alike?

We cannot close our remarks without observing that towards the close of their Appeal they address the publick under the endearing character of *fellow-citizens*. This, we suppose, they adopt as a conciliating term, without meaning; for an independent *fellow-citizen* is an animal we have no name for, and involves so many contradictions as confounds all ideas.

We pass over to their Association, 36th page. And we suppose that we look on it as the impartial public does — *a mere farce*; for there they speak of an election — "God's choosing in every age a select number for himself"; whereas they deny all elections; and to this chosen body God reveals "his secret," of which all the world beside are ignorant; and then, in a kind of transport, they conceive themselves these favorites: "We, the subscribers, greatly affected with the divine goodness in thus distinguishing *us*, think it our interest and bounden duty to let our lights shine before men," &c., and we think so, too. But their good works are, like their revelations, a profound secret.

But they say, "it hath pleased God to make us acquainted with the voice of the good Shepherd, the Lord Jesus Christ." And we ask, Hath it not pleased God to make us, also, acquainted with his voice? His word of salvation is sent unto us, as well as unto them. But they say, We cannot follow a stranger, or give attention to those who are not acquainted with the

Saviour; and yet "they have loved strangers, and after them they will go"; while they forsake and desert those whose soundness of doctrines and piety of life have long demonstrated that they have been with Jesus, forming their sentiments from his doctrines, and their lives from his examples; for, besides their present teacher, who is a stranger in every sense of the word, they have in his train a *Tyler*, who (by report) is a Tory Episcopalian, a *Wright*, who is a German Moravian, with an illiterate *Townsend, Streeter, Parker, a duplicate of Winchesters*, &c., &c. A goodly band indeed! With such strolling mendicants this town has been infested ever since this Association has been formed; which has kept us in one continual hubbub, to the obstructing business, the corrupting the morals, of youth especially, and the total destruction of peace and harmony.

But they say, "We resolve, by the grace of God, we will avoid, as much as possible, vain jangling and unnecessary disputation, &c.;" and yet the very reverse has been their constant practice, especially with those who have the greatest influence. Such is their rage for proselyting, that they are forever disputing, and using every art of fascination; and upon those whom they cannot gain to their party by these means, they try the force of interest, promising those that come into town to seek employment that they will put them into business, promising them constant employment if they will go to their meeting; and threatening others, who are already in their employ, that they will turn them out unless they will be of their party; so that some, who have no affection for their system, attend their meeting sometimes, lest they and their families should want bread. And they say, "We mutually agree to receive as our minister, id est, as our servant, friend and Christian brother, Mr. John Murray, from a full conviction that the same God who sent the first ministers of Jesus Christ, sent him." So we say, the same God who sent the spirit of truth into the mouths of his prophets Elijah and Micaiah, whom Ahab hated because they did not sooth him in his vices, sent a lying spirit into the mouth of all his false prophets, for his punishment; and we believe the same Jesus who sent forth his seventy disciples to preach the gospel of truth, sent also a legion of devils into the herd of swine for the punishment of those who would not receive him and his gospel; and we believe this enemy of peace and righteousness was, by the permissive providence of God, sent among us, in sheep's clothing, for our trial if not for our punishment, for abusing the gospel which has been so clearly and faithfully preached among us for a century past. And they say, "we cordially receive him as a messenger sent from God;" and we have no right to dispute it, since some of the more sanguine among them make no scruple to say "that they believe all that he says and does is from the immediate inspiration of the Holy Ghost," and that "he has a commission to baptize with the Holy Ghost." And this association, they say, was signed by all the society. But that we deny.

We close with a short address to the impartial publick.

FELLOW-CITIZENS,

You may think yourselves less in danger, from the standard of impiety being erected in this small peninsula of Cape Ann, but the ill consequences may be sooner and more sensibly felt by you, than you are aware of. If this Association should be adopted, and this artful deceiver supported by law, we may expect that an hundred similar associations will soon be formed, and as many mushroom teachers spring up from the seculency of vice and laziness to take the lead of them, to the discouragement of all science and erudition, the destruction of peace and order, which will soon precipitate these infant free States into anarchy and confusion. We speak feelingly, from experience. This town, once the seat of peace and commerce, is now nodding on the brink of ruin, owing chiefly, if not entirely, to this Association, headed by this foreigner, who, through a too great indulgence, has acquired the effrontery to claim equal privileges with the learned, regular and ordained ministers of this commonwealth; assuming their title, he sues for support. If this Association should be supported by law, then any one, two or three families may form themselves into the same, and claim the same privileges. What then will become of our colleges, incorporated parishes and churches? All crumbled into parties, and buried in ignorance and superstition, we shall be left, too late, and with more reason to weep, with the Roman orator, O tempora! O mores! What can we expect, when a system is defended and supported by law, which destroys both the solemnity and validity of an oath, which are predicated upon the certain future punishment of perjury? What safety, either of our persons or our property, can we expect? Nay, may we not expect frequently to see Beadle's tragedy acted over again — suicide and murders committed from pure benevolence? And what will become of our youth? Their natures already viciated, their morals corrupted by this wretched system of licentiousness, their opening minds uncultivated with erudition, and unimpressed with virtuous principles, they will enter the stage, after us, ignorant and vicious; and under the direction of the wild-fire of enthusiasm, will soon be swallowed up in the vortex of superstition. You may say, this is only the uncertain flights of fancy. No, fellow-citizens, no. We feel it, we realize it every day; and it is the opinion of the most judicious and feeling hearts among us, that this man and his pernicious doctrines have been more damage to this town than the late war; for while this destroyed our interest, those have corrupted our morals in their first principles, broke up our peace, and deeply sowed the seeds of fell discord among us; our trade interrupted by a party spirit, our churches rent by divisions; nothing can be done in town-meeting but through strife and unfair dealings; and the offices of benevolence cease, or are confined to a party; and the contagious influence of this system has been sensibly felt in other towns through this and the neighboring states.

But we feel most sensibly for the rising generation. Therefore, fellow-citizens, call your children around you, fold them in your arms, and ask your own hearts, Are you willing that these pieces of yourselves should be formed into such an Association, and have such a teacher for their guide? Or, in other words, Are you willing that knowledge, virtue and religion should die in the hands of your children? And as ye would it should be done to and for you and them, so do ye for us and ours. Consider of it, take advice, and speak your minds.

PUBLISHED *by a Number of the Inhabitants of the first Parish in Glocester, October, 1785.*

APPENDIX I.

MR. MURRAY'S BROADSIDE.

[*The author of the following Piece intended it for publication in the Salem Gazette of November 1, 1785, but Circumstances rendering it expedient to publish it by itself, the Reader will consider this Half Sheet as a Supplement to that Paper, in order that the Introduction, and some other Parts of the Performance, may appear with Propriety.*]

BOSTON, October 29, 1785.

MR. PRINTER :— Presuming on your known liberality, I beg leave to offer to the impartial publick, through the channel of your paper, a few remarks on a piece published last Thursday, entitled "An Answer to a Piece entitled 'An Appeal to the Impartial Publick,' &c."

Had this collection of falsehoods been levelled at me only, how slanderous soever, I should not have troubled you, or the publick, with any reply thereto, or remarks thereon; but as it is calculated, cruelly calculated, to injure a considerable number of very respectable characters, both in their fame and fortune, a love of truth, a detestation of falsehood, and a well-earned affection for these respectable sufferers, compel me to reply.

The writers of this piece set out with informing their fellow-citizens that they will "give a fair and impartial relation of facts, as they took place."

Had what follows, under this head, been consistent with the title, it would have been more for the honour of the writers; then would they not have injured themselves, imposed on the publick, or troubled me; but, unhappily, the very reverse of this is the case.

Never, I believe, was the publick more grossly imposed on by a collection of falsehoods, under the title of facts, than in this ungenerous Answer to the Appeal. The falsity thereof is so *very* notorious, in almost every instance, that was the piece to go no further than Glocester, it would be folly in the extreme to take any notice of it.

If the limits of our time, and your paper, would admit of it, I could trace them step by step, and prove, to a demonstration, every single charge they have laid against me and my Christian friends as false as they are slanderous.

How very far from the truth the account they pretend to give of a conversation I had, years ago, with Mr. Chandler! Here they have left unsaid what they ought to have said, and delivered sayings I never heard of before. The account of this conversation is very far from the truth, both in matter and manner; they have not stated, to my knowledge, one single *fact* in that conversation; and there are living witnesses, whose characters will bear the strictest scrutiny, that are ready, whenever they are properly called on, to prove this.

The account of my first sermon is equally unfair and disingenuous. All who are accustomed to hear me well know I never speak to the people in the manner they inform the public I then addressed them. I believe, most sincerely, our Saviour sent me to preach the gospel; but I never told Mr. Chandler, "I had an extraordinary call from Heaven, to make up the want of a liberal education."

I never, either in that first sermon or any other, "roundly exploded the doctrine of rewards and punishments." I have constantly supported the doctrine — not, indeed, as some do, to the denying the Lord that bought us — but as far as I found it supported by divine revelation. I have therefore constantly affirmed that God will reward every man according to his works, and that neither here nor hereafter can any individual be *happy* till he is made *holy*.

I feel a secret satisfaction in the conscious assurance of never, in the whole of my labours, "in publick or private, openly or secretly, ridiculing the distinguishing doctrines of the gospel," be they preached by whomsoever they may. My soul feeds with inexpressible delight on the doctrines of the gospel; and whether they are preached through envy or through gain, I cannot fail of rejoicing.

It is not true that I "speak in a contemptuous manner of the Ministers of this land, calling them a group of ignorant creatures, who know nothing of the gospel." This is not the first time my adversaries have imposed on the publick, and endeavored to prejudice the minds of my fellow-citizens against me, by propagating this infamous falsehood. The truth is, that I believe the clerical character is as well supported in this as in any country under heaven; and many of them know a vast deal of the gospel; though, at the same time, it is a melancholy truth that many of them, by the meanness of their conduct, by their lies, deceit and hypocrisy, bring a reproach on the profession, and do more towards encouraging the growth of infidelity and immorality than any other characters in the country. It must have a disagreeable effect on the minds of common people, to hear a man preaching up holiness while he is continually bearing false witness against his neighbour, and, by lying and slandering, doing all in his power to rob a neighbour of what is infinitely better than life itself. But though some individuals are thus notoriously base, the *character* is certainly not the worse. There are not, I am persuaded, better men in this or any other country than I have the honour of being acquainted with, in the clerical character, in this state.

It is not true that I said "the Apostle Judas was on a throne of glory." Whenever I have been questioned respecting that poor, unhappy man, I have answered, in the language of divine revelation, God has not appointed me to be his judge. He is gone to his own place; I know not where that is.

It is not true that I ever said "the tares were punished in their principal, the Devil." I never gave any other exposition of that parable than our divine Master gave to his Disciples. I never taught that "sin was punished distinct from an agent;" indeed, I have taught that our ever blessed Saviour suffered for our sins, the just for the unjust, to bring us to God; and for this I am reprobated as an heretick. But if this be heresy, I dare to say that in the way which they call heresy, worship I the God of my fathers.

Mr. Chandler's address to his people, respecting me, was both unchristian, ungentlemanlike and uncharitable, and gives us a melancholy proof of the weakness of human nature. But he is gone, and, I humbly hope, has found mercy with Him who is exalted as a Prince and a Saviour to give repentance and remission of sins. But, poor man! he laid many sayings to my charge he never heard from me.

How very disingenuous and ungenerous what follows! You are informed the town was illy treated by me; that they sent for me, as a *stranger*, to make inquiries who I was, etc. But how must the publick be astonished when (after having read this account) they find that this stranger had been an inhabitant of the town from the year 1774; that he was invited by some of the first characters in our army to give his assistance as a Chaplain; that he did this with all his heart, without fee or reward save the satisfaction he found from the approbation of his own heart and the honourable friends he had the honour of associating with; that when some of his enemies strove to prejudice the Commander-in-Chief against him, the only answer they found was in General Orders, where his Excellency appointed him Chaplain of the Rhode Island Regiments, ordering that he may be treated accordingly; that he continued labouring with the army, in this character, as long as his health would admit; and when his honourable friend, General Greene, in whose family he had the honour to reside, sent him home to Glocester sick, on his recovery, being a spectator of the sufferings of the poor, compassion compelled him to set out, late in the Fall, with a subscription paper, in order to raise some support for these unhappy sufferers; and that through the goodness of God, and the generosity of his honourable friends, his Excellency at the head of them, he collected a very large sum of money, his Excellency subscribing £10, each of the Major Generals £5, each of the Brigadiers £3, besides generous donations from many other respectable characters, in and out of the army, each subscriber setting down the sum subscribed; that on his return to Glocester he called the Selectmen together, made them count the money, and though he was determined, as a trustee for the generous donors, to see their donations disposed of himself, yet he never let any person receive of it till ther had obtained a recommendation from some one or other of the Selectmen; that having laid out the money to the best advantage, he relieved, at sundry times, (to the best of his knowledge) upwards of a thousand individuals, who, in consequence of this very providential and seasonable support, were enabled to get through the worst winter they ever experienced through the war; that he never had any advantage of a pecuniary nature for himself, but, on the contrary, was thirty dollars out of pocket, happy that he had it so to dispose of; that soon after this, a few individuals had indeed the effrontery to treat him as they inform you they did; and that Mr. Lowell wrote them a very severe letter on the occasion, setting their conduct before them in its true light, and giving them to understand that if they did not make him *satisfaction* for the injury they had done him, he should be obliged to deal with them as the law in such cases directs. How, I say, must the publick be astonished to find this is the stranger they speak of, who has treated the town so very ill! And yet this stranger dares any man to the proof of his ever giving the town any treatment worse than this. This stranger, as they are pleased to call him, is very happy in a conscience void of offence toward this, or any other town. He is happy in the assurance that it is not in the power of his worst enemy to prove that he has ever injured any man, in his person, property or reputation, except, indeed, where, in defence of himself, and in a fair and candid manner, he has been reduced to the necessity of exposing the wickedness of any of his inveterate persecutors.

Again — The publick will be very much surprised when they find that on the Rev. Doctor Stiles's writing to the Rev. Mr. Forbes, I repeatedly requested a copy of the libel; and not being able to obtain it, I set out for Portsmouth. I there demanded a meeting with the Doctor, insisting on his either proving or retracting the false and scandalous reports he sent his reverend correspondent in that letter; but though under the influence of prejudice, that bane of society, he was able to propagate falsehoods, yet (to his honour be it spoken) he had not courage enough to defend them. No arguments made use of by his best friends could bring him to my face. He told them, indeed, that he was sure he said no *harm* of me; and that if he had said anything to my disadvantage, he was ready to ask my pardon; that he wrote to Mr. Forbes in confidence, not expecting that I would ever hear of it. All this, and much more to the same purpose, can be attested by the most respectable characters who waited on him on the occasion.

The publick will be astonished, almost as much as I was, when they find the story the Doctor has furnished his reverend friend with, respecting my treating the sacrament irreverently, was ten years ago proved to him, by the best and most respectable authorities, a gross and palpable falsehood. One of the Doctor's best friends, a Mr. Belcher, made it his business to inquire into the affair; and when he had found me fully justified, on the respectable authority of General Greene, a letter from the present Governor's lady of Rhode Island, Mr. Gordon, a Minister in East Greenwich, and General Varnum, who were all present on the occasion where it was said I thus burlesqued the sacrament, he informed Dr. Stiles of it; but though the Doctor had this information, he still, in private, to help a good cause, continued to propagate the lie. And many years after this, when he wrote it to Mr. Forbes, this same Mr. Belcher, impelled by a love of truth and justice, wrote a letter to Mr. Forbes, to convince him of the falsehood of this slander. This letter Mr. Forbes did not think proper to publish; a copy of it, however, can be produced at a moment's warning.

But the limits of your paper will not admit my tracing my calumniators through the whole of the dirty path they have taken. The publick may form some judgment of the credit which ought to be given to the rest of their vile calumnies, from the specimen now laid before them; and I can in this way only declare that I am able and willing, at any time, when properly called on, to prove the rest of the charges they have exhibited equally false and slanderous.

When we ventured to lodge our Appeal before the bar of the impartial publick, we did not call on them to attend the sacrifice of any individual's reputation; we made use of no personal invectives; we did not aim at poisoning the minds of our fellow-citizens with prejudice, imposing on them by vile misrepresentations; we were prevented from thus acting, by motives which, we trust, will always have weight with us, (viz.) the fear of God, a respect for the publick, and a regard for ourselves.

On our giving ourselves the character of Independent Christians, our implacable enemies inhumanly insinuate a charge of treason against us. Merciful God, defend us! What will not an inordinate love of money lead some of the fallen race to do! O! if these good men could but obtain a law to erect a stake and collect faggots, how cheerfully their pious souls would join in doing God and themselves service by killing us! But the publick will not be imposed on. They well know the character, Independent, among the religious, is not an unheard-of name, and that all we intend by it is, that, as *Christians*, we know no master to whom we look for aid or direction in spiritual matters, but Christ Jesus. It is well known to be an article of our church, that we will alway be *obedient subjects*, &c.

The same bad spirit that prompts our adversaries to do all in their power to rob us of the privilege of citizens and subjects of the state, has led them to aim at cutting us off from the Kingdom of Heaven. They will not allow us to be a church, nor entitled to the name Christian. They are afraid, if we are allowed the character of Christians, our happy CONSTITUTION will save us from their power. But honest, unprejudiced men well know that wherever two or three meet together, in the name of Jesus, he is with them; and this, according to the definition of their own Divines, is a *Church*.

They say we have brought them into the law. Amazing! I wonder they are not ashamed to impose on the publick in so gross a manner. They took the people's property, and by that means reduced them to the disagreeable necessity of going into the law for redress. When a Jury of faithful, honest men gave a verdict in our favour, they, not content with the first decision of their country, demanded a review. Our people, not contending for damages, but for their constitutional liberties, were willing to set down with their liberties, contented. They made this proposal; it was rejected; we *must* follow them into the thorny maze of law again. We *therefore* took the liberty to avail ourselves of our right; yet they complain of our bringing them into the law. So may any one by whom you are robbed of your property, complain (when you have brought him to justice) that you have drawn him into the law.

These good people complain of being grieved and worried by our having preachers to visit us; but they have had as many visiting teachers as we have had; yet we have never been distressed on this account; it has not broke our peace, though they have been very liberal of their abuse and anathemas on these occasions. We were not, however, obliged to hear them, and know our neighbors had a right to hear whoever they pleased.

I pray God the persecuted and slandered may have patience

to bear, and, now all manner of evil is said of them falsely, attend to their character, and revile not again.

On the whole, it is plain what our enemies aim at. They hope that personal abuse, and a collection of infamous falsehoods, will so far operate on the minds of the Court and Jury, (under God the only defenders of our natural and constitutional rights and liberties), as to gain a verdict in their favour. And the plain intent of their address is this:

"*Our fellow-citizens, we call on you to assist us in reprobating those wicked wretches, who, not having the fear of God, will not quietly part with their property to us. We desire you not to look on such wretches as fellow-citizens. God hates them, we hate them, and we hope you will hate them. We are holy, righteous, just and good; they are the reverse of all this. We are God's own dear children; they are children of the Devil. You ought, therefore, to believe all we say, but nothing that they say. We have a right to choose our own teacher; they have not. No law ought to oblige us to support any other than we hear; but the law ought to oblige them to support the Minister they do not hear. You ought to give us their money for nothing; and when they are base enough to refuse to part with it freely, and we send a Constable to take away their property, you ought never to afford them any redress; for if you do not oblige them to pay our teacher, what will become of your colleges! your parishes! your country! The rising generation all, all will go to destruction if you do not oblige them to support our teacher.*"

However, had these gentlemen confined themselves to argument, and endeavored to prove that a Doctor had a right to demand a fee from another Doctor's patient, a Lawyer from another Lawyer's client, a Minister from another Minister's hearers, the press was free — they had a right to offer their reasons; but when, as defenders of the faith, they strive by bitter invectives to rob us, first of our reputation, in order to influence a jury to enable them to rob us of our property, and

REV. COSTELLO WESTON,
Eleventh Pastor, 1879-1883.

thus, in a pretended zeal for piety and morality, bear false witness against their neighbour, surely every thinking, unprejudiced person must see their conduct in its true light, and detest it.

Their piece, I find, is published by a number of the inhabitants of the first parish in Glocester; and it is but common justice to inform the publick that there are a considerable number of that parish whose honest hearts despise and detest the base conduct of their mistaken brethren; there are many very respectable characters in that parish who will be sufficiently mortified on account of the conduct of their brethren in this last instance.

Though the limits of my time and your paper oblige me to pass unnoticed many of the slanderous invectives thrown out against my friends and myself, in the publication adverted to, yet if in future it is thought necessary, a full refutation of *every* slander in this piece shall be given to the publick by their and your most obedient, humble servant,

JOHN MURRAY.

APPENDIX J.

THE CHARTER OF COMPACT.

"WHEREAS, The greatest benefits arise to a Society from assuming a form best suited to answer the purposes of its design; and considering the necessity there is of speedily taking such salutary measures as are pointed out by the Constitution; we, therefore, the underwritten, convinced by Reason and prompted by inclination, do mutually pledge ourselves each to the other, and enter into the following

Charter of Compact.

"First. That there shall be a stated annual meeting of the subscribers on CHRISTMAS DAY, except when it happens on a Sunday, in that case to be on the day following, for the purposes of choosing a Select Committee, whose powers shall be as hereafter defined. And at the same time a Secretary shall be chosen.

"Secondly. That Funds shall be provided by voluntary subscription, for the purposes of supporting a teacher or teachers, of PIETY, RELIGION and MORALITY; the repairing of the public edifice; and the relief of poor and distressed brethren.

"Thirdly. The powers of the Select Committee are to be extended to calling a meeting of the subscribers, when they see proper, or on the request of nine of them; Notifications to be posted up at least nine days previous to the meeting. They shall constitute the TREASURY, and shall distribute the monies lodged in their hands according to the order of the subscribers; of which monies they shall make regular report, both of receipt and distribution. They shall have power to admit new subscribers.

"Fourth. The Secretary shall record the transactions of the subscribers, and likewise of the Select Committee, in a book open to the inspection of any one.

"Fifth. Persons who shall subscribe, and not pay with punctuality, shall be exempt from the benefits of the Compact, and the Select Committee shall erase their names, the Committee having discretionary power to remit subscriptions on reasonable representation made to them. The subscriptions are to be paid into the hands of the Committee, which will render useless the office of a Collector. The Committee shall give public testimonial of payment, on its being made; which shall be produced at the general annual meeting.

"Sixth. Subscriptions shall be opened at the general annual meetings, and continued at those periods, unless any exigence should require them to be more frequent.

"Seventh. All subscribers shall have an equal vote.

"Eighth. Questions shall be decided by two-thirds of the present members. And nine shall constitute a meeting.

"Ninth. Whereas the priviledge of choosing and professing

one's own RELIGION is inestimable: And in order to maintain that priviledge unimpaired, in case any person associating with us should suffer persecution from the undue exercise of power, we do agree and resolve to afford him all legal means of extricating him from difficulty, and of enjoying that freedom which is held forth by the CONSTITUTION.

"Tenth. Subscribers shall be at liberty to withdraw their names from this CHARTER at the annual meeting.

"Eleventh. The foregoing shall continue permanent, and shall not undergo any alteration except by two-thirds of the subscribers. The absent subscribers shall have right, in this case, to vote by proxy. Six months' notice being given before any alteration can take place.

"AND BE IT KNOWN UNIVERSALLY, That we who have signed our names to this CHARTER OF COMPACT for the purposes heretofore cited, compose and do belong to the INDEPENDENT CHRISTIAN SOCIETY OF GLOUCESTER.

GLOUCESTER, September 6th, 1785.

CALEB POOL,
JOSHUA GAMMAGE,
FRANCIS NORWOOD,
NATH'L SARGENT,
JOSEPH EVERDEN,
JEREMIAH FOSTER,
DOWNING LEE,
WILLIAM DOYLE,
MICHAEL GAFFNEY,
ABRAHAM ROW,
JONATHAN BROWN,
ABRAHAM BROWN,
STEPHEN NORWOOD,
DAVID POOL,
NATHAN POOL,
JOHN NORWOOD,
CALEB NORWOOD, JR.,
BENJAMIN TARR, JR.,
THOMAS BABBIT,
SAMUEL MORGAN,
EPHRAIM ROBERTS,
JOHN GOTT,
EBENEZER GOTT,

EBENEZER POOL,
WILLIAM HALES,
JONa. LOW,
FRANCIS LOW,
CALEB NORWOOD,
ISAAC ELWELL,
SAM'L SAYWARD,
WM. MURPHY,
JOB KNIGHT,
WILLIAM PEARCE,
JOHN LOW, THIRD,
ISRAEL TRASK,
THOMAS MASON,
JAS. HARRIS,
ISAAC TRASK,
JOHN ALLEN,
JAMES BLAKE,
THOMAS FOSTER,
NATHANIEL BENNETT,
DAVID SARGENT,
ABRAHAM SAWYER, JR.,
JOSEPH LUFKIN,
FRANCIS POOL,

JOSEPH BAKER,
JOSHUA WEBSTER,
JAMES SAUNDERS,
GLOSTER DALTON,
WM. CARD,
JAMES SAWYER, THIRD,
COAS GARDNER,
AARON LUFKIN,
SAMUEL MARSHALL,
SAMUEL MORHEAD,
WM. GEE,
ABRAHAM SAWYER,
RICHARD (X) PEW, his mark
JOSEPH MOORE,
DAVID PEARCE,
JOSEPH FOSTER, JR.,
JAMES BABSON,
PETER DOLLIVER,
JOHN POOL,

WINTHROP SARGENT,
JOSEPH FOSTER,
DAVID PLUMER,
EPES SARGENT,
JOHN SOMES,
JOHN STEVENS,
JOHN STEVENS ELLERY,
BARNETT HARKIN,
W. WIER,
PHILEMON HASKELL,
JOB WHIPPLE,
JESSE SAVILLE,
GIDEON CHALLIS,
BENJAMIN LUFKIN,
HUMPHREY MORSE,
JAMES STEELE,
JONATHAN TRASK,
JOSEPH SAUNDERS,
SAMUEL LANE,
BENJⁿ. HALE.

These were all men of good repute, and some of them were eminent in the town. Biographical sketches of several of them are given in Babson's "History of Gloucester." One humble colored man, the only one of his race whose name appears among these signers, deserves here — both on his own account, since he has no other earthly record, and also as showing the sympathetic company in which he found himself placed by joining the Universalist Society — the mention made by Mr. Jones in recording the fact of his death and burial:

"April 11th, 1813, Gloster Dalton, an African. In this country from a youth. Supposed to be 90 years old, or upwards. The said Gloster Dalton was an honest, industrious man. He had been infirm about two or three years. He was a believer in Jesus Christ, the Saviour of the world, and belonged to the independent Christian Society many years. He was a native of Africa, and brought away as a slave (so called). For there are no slaves! All men are born free!!!

T. JONES."

APPENDIX K.

MRS. JUDITH MURRAY.

Judith Sargent was born in Gloucester, May 5th, 1751, and was the oldest of eight children of Winthrop and Judith Sargent, *née* Saunders. She is described by the genealogist of her family as being "a most kind, affectionate and excellent lady." She is remembered as having uncommon beauty of person, and a superior mind, which was cultivated and enriched by the best education the times afforded to young women. She was married, October 3d, 1769, to John Stevens, also a native of Gloucester, who, after an unsuccessful career as a merchant and trader, became bankrupt, and to avoid arrest for debt, fled in a vessel belonging to his father-in-law, to St. Eustatia, in 1786, where he died. Two years later, his widow married Mr. Murray. Their union was an exceedingly happy one. She became, soon after her marriage to Mr. Murray, a writer for the "Massachusetts Magazine," contributing prose articles over the signature of "Constantia;" and furnished poetry for the "Boston Weekly Magazine," over the signature of "Honora Martesia." These writings gave her a popularity of which her husband was justly proud. She was as proud of his position and influence; and being a firm believer in the Rellyan theology, was very impatient of any advocacy of Universalism that was not based on that theory. Hence the following incident: During Mr. Murray's temporary absence from Boston, on one occasion, Rev. Hosea Ballou supplied his pulpit; and on the last Sunday of his engagement, gave his views of 1 Cor. xv : 26-28, and interpreted it to mean that the Son of God would deliver up the mediatorial kingdom to God, when he had brought all things into subjection to himself, and God should then be all in all. Mrs. Murray — who believed, as did her husband, that the

Son here referred to was the "Son of perdition," [72] and that God was to succeed in getting the kingdom out of his hands — called a neighbor to her pew before the services were concluded, and despatched him to the singing-seats, with a message to Mr. Balch, one of the singers, who, as Mr. Ballou arose to announce the closing hymn, stood up in the gallery and announced as follows: "I wish to give notice that the doctrine which has been preached here this afternoon is not the doctrine which is usually preached in this house." "The audience will please to take notice of what our brother has said,' was the calm reply of Mr. Ballou.

In 1795, Mrs. Murray concluded to make an addition to the number of the prose articles she had written for the Magazine, and to publish them in book form. "Till very lately," Mr. Murray wrote to a friend, "she never thought of turning her labors to any account in this way; but finding out that nothing can be saved out of my support, and that as I came into this world a considerable time before her, I may go out of it as much before her, and considering she has a little daughter, who, with herself, may be thrown on an unfeeling world, without the means of making friends of the Mammon of unrighteousness, I have, as well as some others of her friends, ventured to persuade her to make this trial."

The work appeared in duo-decimo form, in 1798, and bore this title: "The Gleaner. A Miscellaneous Production. In Three Volumes. By Constantia." These volumes were published by subscription, the names of the subscribers, somewhat exceeding eight hundred, appear in the last volume, and include

---

[72] I give this story as it is always told, but am confident that it does not correctly state Mr. Murray's views, whatever may have been the belief of his wife. Mr. Murray's interpretation of the passage is as follows:

"Then shall the Son also himself be *subject unto him that did put all things under him*. The offspring of God, the human family, was first exhibited in the singular character, in this character they sinned, and in this character they must be saved; accordingly we are admonished to have a *single* eye.—Matthew vi: 22. And hence Jesus Christ, as the head of every man, is called the light of the world, and when all things shall be *subdued* unto him, who is the light of the world, then shall the Son also, who was made subject to vanity, be subjected to vanity no more. Human nature in the aggregate shall be brought into subjection to him, who is able to subdue all things unto himself; until that period, partial reforms may take place, but the day of retribution will be the day of *final subjection*." Murray's Works, Vol. 3, p. 278.

some of the most notable people of the time. The Genealogist of the Sargent Family says, that Mr. Murray, "as an itinerary preacher, from Georgia to Maine, made the publication profitable, 'preaching universal salvation and universal subscription;'" a statement which could have had no foundation in fact, as Mr. Murray itinerated but little after moving to Boston, in 1793, and went no farther south than Philadelphia; nor did he visit that place till five years after the publication of this work.

The children of Mr. and Mrs. Murray were, a son, who died in infancy; a daughter, Julia Maria, born in Gloucester, Aug. 22, 1791, married in 1812, to Adam Lewis Bingaman, and died in 1822, leaving one son, named for his father, who married in New York.

Mrs. Murray died at Natchez, Miss., June 6, 1820. By her will she left Two Hundred Dollars in trust to Benjamin K. Hough, Esq., to be distributed according to his judgment, "for the benefit of the needy widows, and others who are poor, of my native place, who do not receive their chief support from the Town." There were 157 recipients of this gift, of whom 96 were widows.

APPENDIX L.

MR. MURRAY'S ORDINATION, CHRISTMAS, 1788.

The original account of Mr. Murray's Ordination, December 25th, 1788, as prepared at that time for the Society Records.

"Last Thursday (being Christmas Day) Mr. Murray was ordained to the pastoral charge of the Independent Church of Christ in Gloucester. The ceremony of his Ordination was conducted in a solemn, serious and Christian-like manner. The business of the day was introduced by an Anthem suitable to the occasion. Mr. Murray prayed, and after singing, the Church's committee (appointed for that purpose) introduced

the transactions of the ordination thus, one of them declaring —
"This Independent Church of Christ having years past, before the Constitution we now live under was formed, made choice of Mr. John Murray for our Minister, and having called him, and he accepting of our call, we then ordained and did set him apart to the office. But since the formation of our Constitution, the ordination of our Minister not being thought sufficiently made known, we now proceed in this publick manner to declare the Choice of this Church, their call of Mr. Murray, his acceptance of the call, with the resolve of the Church and Congregation respecting this public Ordination. We, therefore, the Committee appointed by the Church and Congregation, in behalf thereof, again present you with this call, to Continue to be our Minister."

To which Mr. Murray replied:

"Persuaded of the truth of the declaration made by the compilers of the Shorter Catechism, 'That God's works of Providence are his most holy, wise, and powerful, preserving and governing all his creatures and all their actions;' and from a full conviction that the affairs of His Church are in an especial manner under his immediate direction, and that you, my Christian friends and brethren, are now, as formerly, under the directing influence of that divine spirit, who, 'taking of the things of Jesus, and showing them unto me,' constrained me to become a preacher of the Everlasting Gospel, and directed you to set me apart, or ordain me to be your Minister, I now again, with humble gratitude to my Divine Master, and grateful affection for you, my long-tried, faithful Christian Friends and Brethren, most cordially accept of this call."

One of the Committee [73] then read the vote of the Church:

"Resolved, that we, the proprietors of the Independent meeting-house in Gloucester, the members of the church and congregation usually attending there for the purpose of divine worship, do, by virtue of that power vested in us by the great High Priest of our profession, the Bishop of our souls, and the great and only Head of the church; and according to the insti-

---

[73] In the Society Records, preceding this account of the Ordination, is the following: "At a meeting of the Independent Society of Christians held in Gloucester:

"Voted, that Capt. Winthrop Sargent, Mr. David Plummer and Barnett Harkin be a committee on the behalf of the Church and congregation to transact the Ceremonies of the Ordination, which is to be on Christmas day next.

"Voted, that Barnett Harkin present the call of the Church."

tutions of the first churches in New England, and in perfect conformity to the third article of the declaration of rights, in this public manner solemnly *elect* and *ordain*, constitute and appoint Mr. John Murray, of said Gloucester, clerk, to be our settled minister, pastor, and teaching elder; to preach the word of God, and to inculcate lessons and instructions of piety, religion and morality, on the congregation; and to do, perform and discharge all the duties and offices which of right belong to any other minister of the gospel, or public teacher of piety, religion and morality; and it is hereby intended and understood, that the authority and rights hereby given to the said Mr. John Murray, to be our settled ordained minister, and public teacher, are to remain in full force so long as he shall continue to preach the word of God, and dispense instructions of piety, religion and morality, conformable to our opinions, and no longer."

The committee then solemnly presented him the Bible, saying on its presentation: "We present you these Sacred Scriptures as a solemn seal of this your Ordination to the ministry of the New Testament, and the sole directory of your faith and practice."

His acceptance was affecting, as I believe what came from the heart went to the heart:

"With my full heart I thank our merciful God for this inestimable gift. I press it to my soul with grateful transport! I take it as the copy of our Father's will, as the decree of our incorruptible inheritance, as the unerring guide to our feet and lantern to our path. Dear precious treasure! thou hast been my constant support in every trying hour, and a never failing source of true consolation!

"I thank you, most sincerely I thank you, my Christian friends, for this confirming seal, this sure directory; and pray that the Spirit who dictated these sacred pages may enable me to make the best use thereof."

After which he preached a suitable sermon from Luke x : 2. The words, "The harvest truly is great, but the labourers are few; pray ye therefore, etc."

The solemnity, attention, and Christian demeanour that attended the whole of the transactions of Ordination, and every other occurrence of the day, gave universal satisfaction to a numerous audience."

APPENDIX M.

AGREEMENT TO BE TAXED FOR SALARY FOR MR. MURRAY.

Whereas the modes heretofore adopted for the support of publick teaching have been found burdensome and inefficient; and for the more fully carrying into execution the design of the Law, which enjoins the maintenance of Publick Worship, for the promotion of Piety, Religion, and Morality; and that the great ends of the Society may be answered in the best manner, the expense of the same equally borne, and proper and certain provision made for the Publick Teacher: In obedience to the law and to fulfill so pious and laudable a purpose, we whose names are underwritten, members of the Christian Independent Society of Gloucester, do agree and oblige ourselves, each for himself, to pay our parts of One Hundred Pounds a year, for the support of our dear brother in God, and Christian Teacher, John Murray, as long as he shall continue to minister unto, and we to hear him. Which sum we agree shall be paid by us in such a proportion as we pay in the Town or State tax the year immediately preceding the one the money we agree shall be raised for the aforesaid purpose; which Town or State Assessment shall be a Rule to govern us for the assessment of the aforesaid sum of One Hundred Pounds. And we further covenant and agree that the aforesaid sum of One Hundred Pounds shall be paid into the hands of certain persons as shall voluntarily become sureties for the said sum to the said John Murray, whose names shall be hereafter annexed. In witness whereof we have hereunto affixed our hands this ninth day of September, One thousand seven hundred and eighty-eight.

David Plumer, Winthrop Sargent, Epes Sargent, Philemon Haskell, Joseph Foster, John Somes, Nathaniel Sargent, William Murphy, John Stevens Ellery, Winthrop Allen, William Dolliver, Thomas Foster, Joseph Foster, jr., Francis Low, John Low, 3d, John Osborne Sargent, Joseph Herrick, Isaac Elwell,

Barnett Harkin, William Pearce, William Hales, Jonathan Trask, James Saunders, Robert Watson, Jonathan Low, William Pew, Humphrey Morse, Christr. Minot, Ebenr. Hough, John Allen, Jonathan Brown, Ephraim Brown, Wm. Gee, Aaron Lufkin, Samuel Lufkin, Solomon Babson, Benjamin Tarbox, Benjamin Lufkin, Thomas Mason, James Sawyer, 3d, Abram Sawyer, jr., Gideon Challis, James Blake, James Steele, Benjn. K. Hough, Daniel Trew, Samuel Morhead, Coas Gardner, Abraham Sawyer, Jeremiah Foster, Joseph Everden, Samuel Lane, Stephen Brown, Thomas Babbitt, David Sargent, Caleb Pool, Caleb Norwood, Francis Pool, Ebenezer Pool, William Card, Benjamin Hale, David Pool, William Tarr Andrews, Nathan Pool, Joseph Procter, William Hutchins, Thomas Moore, Joseph Saunders, Caleb Norwood, jr., John Norwood, Benjamin Tarr, jr., Joseph Lufkin, jr., Thomas Oakes, Sam'l Morgan, Stephen Norwood.

APPENDIX N.

THE REQUEST FROM BOSTON.

It was not an unusual thing in the early days for such requests to be made. Rev. Adams Streeter, to whom allusion is made in the following letter, had been released from Providence to preach more frequently in Boston; and as peculiar circumstances seemed to demand help, it was often asked, and as often granted.

BOSTON, Decr. 8, 1786.

BRETHREN:—Since the death of our worthy Teacher, Mr. Streeter,[74] who statedly visited us once a month, we are left destitute excepting when Mr. Murray is with us: and as a wide Door is opened for his preaching the Gospel to a very great congregation among us, we wish your consent that he might

[74] See Appendix E.

visit us one Lord's Day in three, untill He who received Gifts for Men, even for the Rebellious, is pleased to bestow one upon us, when, perhaps by their changing, neither of us may be left destitute.

"We are endeavouring to look out for such a Blessing, and are encouraged the more to prefer our request to you from that paragraph in your Association: "And as it hath pleased God to open a great and effectual Door for the preaching of his Gospel by this his servant in sundry parts of this great Continent; whenever it shall please his and our Divine Master to call him to preach the Gospel elsewhere, we wish him Godspeed, and pray that the good will of Him that dwelt in the Bush may accompany him and make his way clear before him." To which we add our Amen. May the Peace and glad tidings published by the Gospel have their influence upon us in promoting a Conversation becoming the same, expressed in Praise and Thanksgiving to Him that Loved us, and in Love one to another, and towards all Men.

SHIPPIE TOWNSEND,
JAMES PRENTISS,
JOSIAH SNELLING, } Committee in behalf of the Society.
JOHN PAGE,
JON^{a.} STODDET,

To Mr. Plummer
to be communicated to
the society of Christian
Independents in
      Glocester.

After Rev. George Richards had concluded to visit New York and Philadelphia, in 1806, a request for the services of Rev. Thomas Jones was sent to Gloucester, and a favorable response was returned.

PORTSMOUTH, New Hampshire, August 4, 1806.

The Wardens and Brethren of the Universal Society, Portsmouth, to their Brethren of the Christian Independent Church in Gloucester, Cape Ann:

DEARLY BELOVED: — The expected absence of Brother Richards leads us to ask it as a favour, that you will indulge us with the gifts of Brother Thomas Jones, for the *two first Sabbaths in the month of September;* and as Brother Richards has been attentive to your wants, when destitute of a preacher, by endeavoring to supply, we feel a sort of boldness in making this request; and being informed that Brother Jones has a wish to visit his Portsmouth friends, we also have a wish that he may be gratified and thereby edify us. Should you ever have need, we will cheerfully repay the obligation by a like act of brotherly kindness. Please to return us your answer by the 12th of the Month, if possible, as Brother Richards leaves the last week in August.

In the name and by request of the Wardens and Society at Portsmouth,

GEORGE RICHARDS, Minister.

Another peculiarity of the early day was the voting of an annual appropriation for defraying the expenses of the pastor in making exchanges. Among Mr. Jones' memoranda I find the following items:

"1809, August. A Letter was received from the Boston Society, wishing a change between the Ministers in union, as often as convenient; and it was concluded that a small sum should be appropriated out of the common treasury to defray this expense."

"May 17, 1810. It was voted at the last Annual Meeting that there should be a sum, not exceeding Twenty Dollars, appropriated to pay the Expenses of Exchange of the Minister. That is to say, to pay the Stage hire of the Pastor out and home, when he shall exchange with any of the Ministers in the same Connection of Friendship and Doctrine of Universal Grace."

This custom continued for thirty years, the annual appropriations varying from the sum named above to Seventy-five dollars.

In 1813, the Society voted their Minister a vacation of four Sundays; and continued it in subsequent annual arrangements, several years.

APPENDIX O.

THE ACT OF INCORPORATION.

"COMMONWEALTH OF MASSACHUSETTS.
In the year of our Lord One thousand seven hundred and ninety-two.

"AN ACT to incorporate certain persons by the name of the Independent Christian Church in Gloucester.

"WHEREAS sundry persons, inhabitants of the town of Gloucester, have for several years past associated for the purpose of Public Worship, and have at their own expense supported a public teacher in preaching the Gospel upon principles most agreeable to the dictates of their own consciences; and have petitioned this Court to be incorporated, that they may be better enabled to conduct their parochial affairs with ease and regularity:

"Be it Enacted by the Senate and House of Representatives in General Court assembled, and by the authority of the same, that David Pearce, Winthrop Sargent, Joseph Foster, Epes Sargent, John Somes, David Plumer, Barnet Harkin, John Low, 3d, William Pearce, Isaac Elwell, James Sawyer, Abraham Sawyer, jr., William Gee, Abraham Sawyer, Francis Low, Joseph Herrick, Lemuel Gates, William Card, Francis Norwood, Benjamin Hale, Daniel Marchant, jr., Aaron Sargent, Samuel Wonson, jr., Caleb Pool, John Stevens Ellery, Benjamin Lufkin, Benjamin K. Hough, William Murphy, Jonathan Low, Benjamin Tarbox, Henry Phelps, Moses Fitz, Thomas Foster, Joseph Procter, Solomon Babson, Daniel E. Procter, Aaron Hall, Joseph Allen, jr., Winthrop Allen, John Allen, David Sargent, William Baty, Caleb Norwood, Joseph Baker, John Gott, Ebenezer Gott, Samuel Wonson, Benjamin Marshall, Ebenezer Pool, John Norwood, Nathan Pool, together with all those who are, and those who shall become members of the same Church, or being of the same religious denomination shall unite with them in the same place of Worship, within said town of Gloucester, together with their several Estates, lying within said Town be, and they hereby are set apart and incorporated into a Society by the name of 'The Independent Christian Church in Gloucester,' and by that name may sue and be sued, plead and be impleaded, defend and be defended, in any Court or place whatever.

"And be it further Enacted by the authority aforesaid, that the Members of said Incorporation at any meeting of the Society, shall have a right by a majority of votes to ordain and establish all such rules and regulations and to appoint such Officers for the government of said Society as shall not be repugnant to the Laws and Constitution of the Commonwealth, and at such meetings to vote such taxes, and make such assessments thereof as shall be necessary for the support of said Church, and the public teacher thereof.

"And be it further Enacted by the authority aforesaid, that all male persons who usually assemble with the aforesaid Church and congregation for public worship, being of the same religious denomination and qualified by Law to vote in Town affairs, shall have a right to vote in all meetings in said Society.

"And be it further Enacted, by the authority aforesaid, that any five of the petitioners or other persons usually assembling with said Church and congregation may call a first meeting of said Society, at such time and such place within said town of Gloucester as they shall see fit, at which meeting the method of calling their future meetings shall be determined conformably to the Laws of the Commonwealth.

"And be it further Enacted, by the authority aforesaid, that the petitioners and all others their associates in said Church and Congregation, and their several Estates, lying in said Town of Gloucester, shall not be liable to any tax or assessment for the support of any other public teacher of Piety, Religion or Morality of whatever religious sect or denomination, but are hereby declared to be exempt therefrom.

"And be it further Enacted, that all those who hereafter shall be desirous of becoming members of said Church or Society, being inhabitants of said Town, shall leave their names with the Town Clerk of said Town, twenty days at least previous to the annual Meeting of the inhabitants of said Town in the month of March or April, otherwise they shall not be considered in law as members of said Church or Society.

In the House of Representatives, June 26th, 1792.

This Bill having had two several readings, passed to be Enacted.

SAM'L PHILLIPS, Presd't.

By the Governor approved, June 28th, 1792.

JOHN HANCOCK."

APPENDIX P.

MR. MURRAY'S COMMENDATION OF MR. JONES.

To Col. WILLIAM PEARCE.

BOSTON, August 23, 1803.

MR VERY DEAR FRIEND:—I beg leave to introduce to your kind notice our Brother, our Father's child, and the child of affliction. You recollect all I have told you of this dear faithful man, his sufferings and their causes, since he has been in this country. His school, which is his support, is now in vacation. He had six weeks' respite from toil; he ventured to set out on a visit to God's children, my Friends. He came unexpected to me. I wrote him, indeed, should the Fever be in his city, to leave it and come this way, and see what the Great Master may do for him. I requested him, in that case, to stop in New York and sundry other places. He never received my letter; he could not stop at N. Y., the Fever had shut it up. He came on here; he knew no one till he came here, and here *only* your humble servant. He preached in our House all Sunday. There never were two better sermons delivered in that pulpit; he gave universal satisfaction. He is anxious to see the place where the *first* House in this Country was built

REV. WILLIAM H. RIDER,
Twelfth Pastor, 1883.

for the reception of Paul's Gospel, or rather, God's everlasting Gospel embraced and preached by Paul. He has not much time to spare, but he will devote one week to my Gloucester Friends. *I write to you, my feeling Brother, as a lover of the Truth, as one blest by our common Parent with a feeling heart, and the means to gratify it*, by reaching forth the helping hand to as deserving a Brother as ever our Saviour gave you an opportunity of assisting. I write to you humbly requesting you to use your influence with your Brethren, your Friends, your neighbours, to do all in their power to relieve, and thus comfort the heart of this dear suffering Friend, who would not have suffered so much if he was less worthy. He is a timid, modest man, he is not fond of complaining, and so I am the more solicitous to lead the attention of you, and my other Friends of long standing, to this dear suffering man. I do not know a man in his character in this world that has suffered so much; yet the dear man has, with his little family, suffered in *silence*, and now he knows not that his Divine Master is using me as an humble instrument to introduce him to the notice of Friends so well able, and I am persuaded, so willing to help him. Will you, my dear Brother, I am sure you will, have the goodness to show this letter to our mutual Friends? Will you be so obliging as to present my regards to your Brother, to Captn. Elwell, to Captn. Somes, to Captn. Beach, and to request their attention to this letter. I am sure they all have feeling hearts. Of his Preaching I will say nothing, except to request of you to give him a chance of preaching as often as you can for the time he is in Gloucester. He cannot tarry longer than till next Monday. He may preach one Lecture, at least, before Sunday, to give the people a chance of knowing him, and expecting him on Sunday. I commend him to the good-will of Him that dwelt in the Bush, and to the kind notices of those that the *God of my life* made use of to comfort and support me when I was a stranger amongst you. Love to each of your dear Family. Believe me ever Yours, &c.,

J. MURRAY.

APPENDIX Q.

SUBSCRIBERS TO THE NEW MEETING-HOUSE.

The following are the names of the subscribers, with the number of shares taken by each:

William Pearce	15	Cyrus Stevens	1
John Somes	13	David P. Tarr	1
Israel Trask	4	Fitz W. Sargent	2
Joseph Foster	3	Isaac Elwell, jr	1
William Dolliver	1	Jonathan Low	2
Isaac Elwell	2	William Dexter	1
William Pearce, jr	4	John Low	1
Abraham Sawyer, jr	3	Sally Tarbox	1
Samuel Calder	3	Jacob Smith	1
Benjamin K. Hough	3	David Haraden	1
John Johnston	2	Andrew Mackay	1
David Haraden, jr	1	Jacob Hodgkins	1
William Saville	1	James Tappan	2
James Mansfield	1	Abraham Williams	1
John Dennis	1	Mary Plumer	2
John Close	1	James S. Sayward	1
Joseph Procter	1	John Somes, 3d	1
Jonathan Dodge	1	Henry Sayward	1
Stephen Brown	1	James Patrick	1
Eben Plumer	1	Daniel Rogers, jr	1
Joseph Everden	1	Joseph Moore	1
Daniel E. Procter	1	Michael Gaffney	1
John Somes, jr	1	David Babson	1
John Mason	1	Joseph Baker	2
William Rogers	1	Jonathan Brown, 3d	1
Eli Stacy	2	John Stacy	1

Total 100

APPENDIX R.

LAYING OF THE CORNER STONE.

The following is copied from the Records of Tyrian Lodge: "At a Meeting of the Master, Wardens and Brethren of Tyrian Lodge held at B'r Jonathan Lowe's, Sept. 5, 5805, at the special request of the Committee for superintending the Building of a New meeting house for the Christian Independent Society in Gloucester — to assist in Laying the Corner Stone of said building,

Present:

R. W. Bro. John Tucker,		Bro. Benj. K. Hough,
S. W. " Ebed Lincoln,		" Joseph Foster,
J. W. " Wm. Pearce, Jr.,		" Isaac Elwell,
P. M. " Nathl. Warner,		" Jonathan Lowe,
S. " Wm. Pearce,		" Benj. Tarr, 4th,
" Zenas Cushing,		" Robert Tarr,
" Eben H. Collins,		" Eli Stacy,
" Zach. Stevens,		" Charles Rogers,
" Wm. Rogers,		" John Rogers, Sec'y.
" Wm. Presson, Jr.,		
" Wm. Dolliver,		VISITORS.
" Joseph Babson,		Rev. Bro. Thomas Jones,
" Joshua Woodberry,		" John R. Hubbard,
" Elias Davis,		" Benj. Dodge,
" Daniel Collins,		" Wm. Ferson,
" Saml. Robinson,		" Jesse Wilson,
" Wm. Kingman,		" Jacob Smith,
" Josiah Herrick,		" Joseph Henderson,
" Daniel Rogers, Jr.,		" Nathan Park.

"The Lodge being opened in due form, the Procession was formed and went through Middle street to the appointed place, and placed the Corner Stone in Masonic Form, after which Rev. Bro. Thomas Jones made a pertinent and well-adapted prayer suited to the occasion. The Brethren then proceeded to

Bro. Wm. Pearce's, and partook of a cold collation. Being agreeably refreshed, they returned to the Lodge-room when the Lodge was closed in usual Form."

On the removal of the Corner Stone, July 20th, 1868, in making extensive alterations and repairs, the following was found in a sealed box in the cavity: a Twenty Dollar Gold piece coined in 1799, a cent of the coinage of 1803, and a parchment bearing this inscription, in the handwriting of William Saville, Esq., Clerk of the Society. "Anno Lucis 5805. On the fifth day of September, in the 29th year of American Independence, A. D. 1805, this corner stone of the first established Independent Christian Church in North America, was laid by the Officers and Brethren of the Tyrian Lodge of Gloucester."

The stone was re-laid August 3d, 1868, its former contents replaced, and in addition thereto, several other articles, accompanied by a parchment prepared by John Corliss, Esq., Clerk of the Society, containing a brief statement of the history of the Society.

APPENDIX S.

THE NEW HYMN BOOK.

Very few of the Hymns in Relly's Collection can be sung, the metre is so irregular; and it is quite surprising that the Congregation should have been contented with it so long. The Book which the Society published bore the following title: "Psalms, Hymns, and Spiritual Songs; Selected and designed for the use of the Independent Christian Church of Gloucester. Behold, God is my salvation. I will trust and not be afraid, for the Lord Jehovah is my strength and my song; he also is become my Salvation.—Isaiah. Boston, 1808." It was a 12mo. of 252 pp., containing 305 Hymns, and was prefaced with the following: "To the Members of the Independent Universal Christian Church and Society of Gloucester. Brethren,

The Committee to whom was entrusted the care of selecting a suitable number of Hymns, adapted to the public worship of God, for the use of the Independent Universal Christian Church in Gloucester, having to their best abilities performed the work committed to their hands, beg leave to present the following collection to the said Church and Society, humbly hoping that it may in some measure contribute to raise our devotion to the fountain of all good.

"They have been careful in omitting all hymns of a controversial nature, and have generally selected only those calculated to inspire the mind with sentiments of adoration, gratitude, and love to Him who first loved us.

"As the hymns are not original, they have been peculiarly mindful not to mutilate their genuine sense by the omission or addition of any word or verses, which would, if practised, leave room to incorporate or withhold sentiments injurious to the true spirit and meaning of their several authors.

"Gloucester (Mass.), March 25, 1808."

The compilers must have changed their minds after writing the last sentence in their report, since just one-half of the hymns from Relly's collection are greatly abridged.

APPENDIX T.

DEDICATION OF CHILDREN.

The following is Mr. Murray's account of the origin of this ceremony:

"You ask an account of the ceremony I have originated, instead of infant sprinkling. On my first appearance in this country, during my residence in the State of New Jersey, I was requested, as the phrase is, to christen the children of my hearers. I asked them what was their design in making such a proposal to me. They replied, they only wished to do their duty. 'How, my friends,' returned I, 'came you to believe infant sprinkling a duty?' 'Why, is it not a command of God to sprinkle infants?' 'If you will, from Scripture authority, produce any warrant sufficient to authorize me to baptize children, I will immediately, as in duty bound, submit thereto. Our Saviour sprinkled no infant with water; those who were baptized by his harbinger plunged into the River Jordan, which plunging was figurative of the ablution by which we are cleansed in the blood of our Saviour; but infants are not plunged in a river.

"'Paul declares he was not sent to baptize, and he thanks God that he had baptized so few; nor does it appear that among those few there were any infants. It is not a solitary instance to find a whole household without a babe. The eunuch conceived it necessary there should be much water for the performance of the rite of baptism; all this seems to preclude the idea of sprinkling and of infant baptism, and it is said that whole centuries passed by, after the commencement of the Christian era, before the sprinkling of a single infant. I am, however, commencing a long journey; many months will elapse before my return. I pray you to search the Scriptures during my absence, and if, when we meet again, you can point out the chapter and verse wherein my God has commanded his ministers to sprinkle infants, I will immediately prepare myself to yield an unhesitating obedience.' I pursued my journey. I returned to New Jersey, then my home, but no authority could be produced from the sacred writings for infant sprinkling. Still, however, religious parents were uneasy, and piously anxious to give testimony, public testimony, of their reliance upon and confidence in the God of their salvation. Many, perhaps, were influenced by the fashion of this world; but some, I trust, by considerations of a higher origin.

"I united with my friends in acknowledging that when God had blessed them by putting into their hands and under their care one of the members of his body which he had purchased with his precious blood, it seemed proper and reasonable that they should present the infant to the God who gave it, asking his aid in the important duty which had devolved upon them, and religiously confessing, by this act, their obligation to and dependence on the Father of all worlds. Yet we could not call an act of this kind baptism; we believe there is but *one baptism;* and this, because the Spirit of God asserts, by the Apostle Paul, that there is *but one baptism*, and the idea of this single baptism is corroborated by the class in which we find it placed. '*One Lord, one faith, one baptism, one God and Father of all, who is above all, and through all, and in you all.*'—Ephesians iv : 5, 6. After much deliberation, I proposed, and many of my hearers have adopted, the following mode : The parent or parents (I am always best pleased when both parents unite), bring their children into the great congregation, and stand in the broad aisle, in the presence of the worshippers of God. The father, receiving the babe from the arms of the mother, presents it to the servant of God who statedly ministers at his altar. The ambassador of Christ receives it in his arms, deriving his authority for this practice from the example of the Redeemer, who says, 'Suffer little children to come unto me, for of such is the kingdom of heaven.' The minister, therefore, taking the infant from its father, who gives him, as he presents it, the name of the child, proclaims aloud : 'John or Mary, we receive thee as a member of the mystical body of him who is the second Adam, the Redeemer of men, the Lord from heaven. We dedicate thee to him, to whom thou properly belongest, to be baptized with his own baptism, in the name of the Father, and of the Son, and of the Holy Ghost; and we pronounce upon thee that blessing which he commanded his ministers, Moses, Aaron, and his sons, to pronounce upon his people, saying :

"' The Lord bless thee and keep thee;

"' The Lord make his face to shine upon thee, and be gracious unto thee;

"' The Lord lift his countenance upon thee, and give thee peace.'

" For this procedure we have the command, the express command of God. Our reason and our religion concur to approve the solemnity, and our hearts are at peace." Murray's Works, Vol. 2, pp. 366-368.

APPENDIX U.

THE CHURCH ORGANIZATION.

Mr. Jones has recorded the steps taken in the Organization of the Church, and the various theories which he entertained from time to time in reference to its aims, and its management. I quote liberally from his memoranda:

"The following Church Covenant, introductory to the Communion of The Lord's Supper, was read publicly on the 19th of October, 1806.

It was, after some Revision, read a second time, to an assembly of the male members of the Society, on the 2d of November, 1806, When it was voted that a Committee of Seven should be nominated to inspect the Covenant and report upon it.

The committee: David Pearce, John Somes, Isaac Elwell, Abraham Sawyer, William Pearce, Paine Elwell, William Dolliver.

REPORT.

"We, the committee, having examined the foregoing articles, do approve of the same. Signed, William Pearce, President of the Committee."

On the twenty-third day of November, Anno Domini Christi one thousand eight hundred and six, the Covenant was again read to an assembly of the Male Members of the Society, when they voted,

"That this Covenant be the Covenant introductory to the Communion, in this parish."

Which Covenant is here transcribed.

I. The Address of the elder Brethren of the "Independent Christian Church of Gloucester", to their younger Brethren and Sisters in the same Society.

WHEREAS, we are an Independent Society of Christians, constituted by law, and we have by the good Providence of God built a new House of Worship; wishing to transmit our religious as well as civil rights honourably adorned unto our children and the rising generation; and wishing, as the remaining Fathers of the "Independent Christian Church of Gloucester," to impress upon your minds Love to God as good and merciful to all men as his offspring.

We introduce unto you this Covenant signed by us as our Church Covenant introductory to the Communion; to be signed by you also when you shall find yourselves so disposed. And we do hereby declare and ordain that the signing of this Covenant shall entitle the signers to sit down to our Communion, provided they are in their morals conformable to the rules of the church.

Those members who from scruple of any kind decline communing, shall not be censurable on that account.

[Let it be always understood that this Covenant shall not annul or any way set aside the powers and privileges of the Society denominated in the Constitution by Law of the State, "The Independent Christian Church of Gloucester;" nor shall the signers of this Covenant have any power or authority over the members of this Society, constituted by law, to curtail, or in any way infringe upon their priviledges as a legal incorporate body. And let it be understood that all the exclusive rights this Covenant shall give any one signing it, shall be only a right to the Communion, and a right to suffrage and legislation for communicants only. In all other respects they shall only be equal to other individuals in the parish according to law.]

And we ordain it as a Rule in our Church that any person wishing to become a Communicant, shall express the same to the Pastor of the Church, by writing or otherwise, and he shall notify the Wardens of the Church thereof; and at the end of one month from the notice, the Wardens shall give their answer to the Pastor of the Church, and he shall transmit the answer to the candidate; and to every accepted member the Covenant shall be read, and they consenting thereto, their names shall be inserted in the Church Book as members thereof.

We recommend that the Youth should have Two Lectures in the year devoted to them, on the first Rudiments of Religion and Virtue.

II. THE RELIGIOUS ARTICLES OF FAITH.

1. We believe that Jesus Christ is the Son of God, the Saviour of the World.

2. We receive the Bible as the Word and Revelation of God, and confess the authority of the New Testament as the Constitution and Law of the Christian Church.

3. We receive it as our Rule of Faith and Moral Conduct: and as we would Hope for Immortality by its gracious promises, we would conform ourselves to the morals which it inculcates, as both our priviledge and duty as believers of the Gospel of the Lord Jesus Christ, to glorify Him among men and in ourselves by a virtuous conduct — by Justice, Mercy, Industry, Temperance, Chastity, Sobriety; shunning all vice and immorality. And as we believe in and hope for the Redemption of All Men from the Bondage of Corruption, and their final Salvation from Sin and death by Jesus Christ our Lord, we would wish to feel and show unto all that this Grace teacheth us to deny all ungodliness, and to follow peace and holiness with all men.

4. Knowing our dependent state and imperfection in this state of learning, and being sensible of our dependence upon God, we hold it our duty and greatest priviledge to pray unto our Heavenly Father who seeth in secret, for his divine aid and influence to enlighten our understandings and sanctify our hearts by the means of the Gospel.

5. We esteem it our duty and priviledge to attend the ministry of the Gospel; to read or hear the Holy Scriptures, for our instruction and comfort; and to keep the first day of the week sacred to Religion.

6. We hold it our duty to instruct our Children and the youths under our care, in the first principles of the Christian Faith, and to inculcate and impress upon them moral virtue and industry, and the attendance of Public Worship on the Sabbath.

7. And as members of the Church we will consider ourselves under the authority of her laws subscribed by us.

8. Believing that Jesus Christ died for our Sins, and was raised again for our Justification, and that he is the Propitiation for the sin of the whole world,* as a medium of manifestation, we commemorate his death by the ordinance of the Supper, instituted by him, to be used by his disciples in Faith and Love, till his Second Advent. And we eat the bread and drink

---

* Christ's death I consider *not* as a Satisfaction to God for Sin; but as a manifestation of his Grace triumphing over Sin. T. Jones.

the wine as expressive Symbols of his Body and Blood, given for the manifestation of our redemption. And hereby, as by visible objects, we would impress our minds with the memory and import thereof.

And we hold it both a Duty and priviledge, to adorn our profession by a Life and Conversation conformable thereto.

THOMAS JONES,	HANNAH HARKIN,
Pastor of the Church,	DAVID DAY,
SOPHIA JONES,	LUCY DAY,
ABRAHAM SAWYER,	ABIGAIL DOLLIVER,
MRS. A. SAWYER,	LYDIA PRENTISS,
DAVID PEARCE,	TRIPHENE MASON,
ELIZABETH PEARCE,	ELIZABETH PROCTER,
ISAAC ELWELL,	ELIZABETH LOW,
TAMMY ELWELL,	ABIGAIL TRASK,
WILLIAM PEARCE,	LYDIA MORSE,
THOMAZINE PEARCE,	HANNAH INGERSOL,
HANNAH TUCKER,	SARAH RUST,
HANNAH BALL,	SARAH FOLSOM,
ANN HOUGH,	CALEB NORWOOD,
DAVID HARADEN,	MRS. C. NORWOOD,
HANNAH HARADEN,	JOSEPH MOORE,
SUSANNAH STANWOOD,	HANNAH MOORE.

All these foregoing names were signed while the Book stood open for the insertion of those in the parish who felt that liberty and desire in themselves, without standing proposed. After the space of four or five months, while the book was thus open, it was voted by the Church male Members assembled, that in future every Member should be proposed, and stand a Candidate one Month.

N. B. Though the "Independent Christian Church of Gloucester" was constituted by Law, as a Parish, many years ago, they had not the Ordinance of the Supper among them till now.

Facit per TH. JONES.

CHURCH AFFAIRS.

At a meeting of the Church Members in the Vestry, held May 25th, 1807, it was decided that there should be two Communions before Christmas next ensuing, after the Communion on the 31st of May, viz., on the last Sabbath in July, and on the last Sabbath in September. And the Communion following after, to be on the first Sabbath after Christmas Day; and afterwards regularly every two Months, and that on the first Sabbath in the Month.

A special meeting of the male Members of the Church was called September 24th, 1808, on some particular Business. Brothers Isaac Elwell and Paine Elwell were unanimously chosen Wardens of the Church.

May 4th, A. D. C. 1812.

Yesterday was our Communion day, and in the Sermon immediately before it I advanced the following theses, viz., That there should be no railing round the Communion Table. That all in a parish or congregation, of the age of discretion, should be considered as having a right to partake of the Lord's Supper, as they have a right to baptism, without ceremony. (For in my parish this is the case — every married couple have a right to present their children for baptism without any ceremony or process previous thereto.) That I conceived should such a mode be adopted, to admit whosoever willed, to the Communion, without ceremony, it would be no disadvantage to the Cause of Christianity, but rather an Advantage. That viscious characters would not be *inclined* to approach the table. That by free communion there would be no temptation to hypocrisy, as in that case all would be deemed equal. That it should be left entirely to the conscience of the individual; that there should be no force used to compel, or to restrain. That it should be optional — no umbrage taken at any time when certain did not partake — no questions asked. That it was the priviledge of all in a congregation who believed Christianity, to make this publick profession of it by the Communion. That doubtless our conduct ought to be conformable to our profession; that honour among men required this of us, and Christianity required no more than a uniform conformation to virtue in word and deed. And I here add, that if the members of a Society in general, celebrated the Communion, it would be the strength of that body or society.

WHEREFORE, I mean to introduce a proposition to the present Members of Communion, in the Society generally called the Church, in the following words, viz.:

WHEREAS, we hold universal grace in God towards all men, which is manifested in his Son, and preached by the Gospel, addressed to all indiscriminately; we think it right that each and every one in our Society, of age of discretion, possessing reason, and pure in morals, should have right and priviledge to partake of the Communion, without any previous ceremony of proposing themselves as members, being asked questions, &c.; as we would wish to make the Communion Table as free of access to all who feel liberty to partake of it, as we would our house of worship to all comers.*

Nov. 20th, 1814.

I did not introduce the above proposition till to-day, after afternoon service, when the Members of the Table stopped by request, on other business, which need not be written; and I took the opportunity to introduce the above proposition, in substance, for consideration, suggesting that we would have a meeting on the subject, and adopt or reject it.

Nov. 22d, 1814.

The preceding Proposition does not take with the leading persons who have the sway. So it must for the present be dropped. However, I think it would have done much good could it have been passed into a law; and would have destroyed envy, and the cause of it. Perhaps it may pass at some future day. I will here explain the Proposition more particularly, and say, it intends that all persons in the Parish, arrived at the age of 21, shall have a Right to Sit at the Communion Table, and partake thereof, without any Ceremony whatever. And lest any disorder should arise from this priviledge, by abuse, it was intended that there should be a committee of three appointed from among the Members of the Communion, to be called The Committee of Order. The Minister should be one of that Committee. The charge of the said Committee should be, to see that all things be done decently and in order; That no one stay to communion who is not a parishioner, ex-

* This proposition I mean to introduce to the present Church, for discussion, before the next Communion. And preparatory thereto, I mean to converse freely with the several members thereupon, and answer with candour any objections any of them may bring against such a proposition being adopted.—T. J.

cept by permission: to see that no one be present who is an immoral person and unreformed. Such shall be commanded to withdraw, by the said Committee, and if they refuse, shall be treated as disturbers of the peace. Moreover, it was intended that the said Committee should have it in charge to visit any Member of the Communion reported to walk disorderly, and to admonish such member, as the case may require; and if the case be flagrant, such as theft, adultery, fornication, profane swearing, fraud, lying, the said delinquent member shall be suspended three years, and after that term, if repentant and reformed, shall be received again into full fellowship.

But the Proposition has at present fallen through, and must lie dormant for awhile. But if ever revived in my day, the Right of Female Members to Suffrage shall be introduced and pleaded for.

Nov. 22d, 1814.

The Supper is postponed for this winter, and it is contemplated to celebrate it in March or April. After which, if the war continues, I mean to propose that it be postponed till after the war; and be had the next Sabbath after the Proclamation of Peace.

August 24th, 1816.

Made an attempt to add a supplementary article, on the mode of receiving members into the Church, viz., by vote of the whole church, of both male and female, on the Sabbath after they are proposed; but an aged Matron objected to females voting, as novel to us. So it falls through.

October, 1818.

A new Regulation in the admission of Church members. Instead of the mode hitherto used in admitting members in this Church, we adopt the following: A decisive answer shall be given the candidates for membership, the same week in which they propose themselves.

May, 1819.

A regulation agreed upon by the Communicants who govern: That this Summer and Fall the Communion shall be held the first Sabbath in every month."

After this several memoranda occur, to the effect that Mr. Jones contemplated proposing amendments with a view to make the Profession and Rules more simple; but it does not seem that any of these were brought to the notice of the church.

In 1840, while Mr. Smith was Junior Pastor; a committee consisting of Rev. Messrs. Smith and Jones and Mr. B. K. Hough, was appointed to revise the Articles of Faith, or present a new Constitution.

On their recommendation, the Church adopted, Jan. 20th, 1840, the following "Declaration of Faith. We believe in one God, the Father of all mankind; in Jesus Christ, the Son of God and Saviour of the whole world; and in the Holy Scriptures as the Word of God, and the revelation of the duty and the final destination of all mankind."

In 1863 a slight change was made in the laws and rules of the church; and in 1869 the Church adopted the "Articles of Religion and Rules of Government" proposed by the Roxbury Conference.

A Silver Service, of nine pieces, was presented to the Church in 1806, by Col. William Pearce, and is still in use.

APPENDIX V.

FUNERAL OF REV. JOHN MURRAY.

Mr. Murray's funeral took place September 4th, 1815. Mr. Jones' sermon on that occasion was prefaced by the following remarks:

"My friends, I am called this day to perform a solemn duty, — solemn to you and solemn to me. There lies the body of the man you loved and revered while living, whose doctrine hath often made your souls feel the 'Powers of the world to come.' In a dark day he was made able to sound the trumpet of Universal Grace. Opposition to the cause of free grace, in which he had engaged, was made to do it service, and all things wrought together for his success in making the theme famous.

"Having for a season traveled in the United States, and preached at many places, he came at length into New England, and visited Cape Ann, where was his first establishment. From thence he removed here, where he has closed his days.

"Since his infirmity, which closed his public services for about six years, he often appeared impatient for a passage into the World to come. Shall we who shed tears of sympathy and friendship, grieve at his release? Nay, let us rather be thankful to our Heavenly Father that he hath delivered him from the burden of the flesh.

"I would address his surviving Consort and Daughter, and say, Weep not that your Husband, your Father, is translated to heaven, freed from every care, trouble, sorrow, and all infirmities, but rejoice that you are assured that you shall, without failure, join him in the immortal inheritance.

"I would address you, his once beloved Church and congregation, under the Chief Shepherd, and say to you, Cherish ye the seed sown among you by him who is no more among the living upon earth. Let the Morning which shone forth fair in him, proceed to its high Meridian without a cloud; while ye cry out with Elisha, 'The chariots of Israel, and the horsemen thereof.' And while ye pray that a double portion of the Spirit of Truth that rested upon him may rest upon you and upon your surviving Pastor in the Lord. May his hands be strengthened, his knees confirmed, his light be abundant, and his usefulness be enlarged, to the gathering in of many to the knowledge of the Truth. May God enlarge you as Japeth, and make your numbers like Ephraim.

"Bless ye God, most cordially, for the first light which shone upon many of you, by the ministry of your now deceased pastor. Would you honour his memory, then stand ye fast in the Liberty of Christ, and be not entangled with any yoke of bondage. Learn ye by the Doctrine of Grace, which the personage you now mourn had the pleasure and honour of opening to you, to glorify God by a Christian Profession, and a Conversation becoming the Gospel of Christ.

"For all the gifts which God hath given you, bless ye God, and say ye, God gave the word, and at length great was the number of its publishers. We expect not man to be immortal upon earth. He hath only taken away what he gave; acknowledge ye his gift, 'The Lord gave,' and acquiesce ye in his doings by saying also, 'The Lord hath taken away, Blessed be the Name of the Lord. Let your minds this day, from the valley of the shadow of death, look forward to the immortal state which we expect as the free Gift of God revealed in His Son. Jesus hath triumphed over death. His glorified person is our Pledge of Immortality. Then, as death comes near us, and snatches away our friends and companions, let us fear him the less. Death is only an enemy to our feelings in flesh and blood. Death itself is ours, for we are more than Conquerors over death, through him that loved us.

"These things I have said, in a cursory way, for your edification under the present dispensation of Providence, and shall not enlarge by entering more particularly into the history of our beloved mutual friend and brother. A succinct account of his life since his removal to this country, being in manuscript written by himself, will give such information to those who may desire it.

"I shall therefore read an appropriate text on the occasion, and deliver a discourse therefrom."

The text from which Mr. Jones then preached was: "Then shall the dust return to the earth as it was, and the spirit shall return unto God who gave it."—Ecclesiastes xii : 7.

The Sermon was not written for this occasion, but had seen service before, and was subsequently used. It contained no further allusion to Mr. Murray.

The introduction to his Sermon in Boston, the Sunday following the funeral, contains little or nothing that would be new to any one who had perused the Life of Murray. About all that it offers of biographical information is also in the following preface to a Sermon preached in Gloucester the second Sunday after the funeral:

"Your Fathers, where are they? and the prophets, do they live forever?—Zechariah i : 5.

"One generation passeth away, and another generation cometh; but the earth abideth forever.—Ecclesiastes i : 4.

"My Friends, we are this day called to pay a tribute of respect to the memory of our Friend and Brother, Mr. John Murray, (now no more among the living upon earth), as the first preacher of the doctrine of Universal Salvation in America.

"In this place was his first permanent settlement as a Minister of the Gospel proclaiming glad tidings unto all people. Several yet alive in this house were taught the glad sound from his mouth. He first ministered to you in holy things. His doctrine made your souls feel the Powers of the World to come. In a dark day he was made able to sound the trumpet of Universal grace. Opposition had no success, but was generally pressed into the service of the cause of free Universal grace in which he had engaged; and all things wrought together for his success in making the theme famous.

"Since the closing of his public labours by infirmity, (which will be six years next month), he often appeared impatient for a passage into the world to come. Shall we grieve at his long-desired and earnestly prayed-for release? Nay, but let us rather be thankful to God that he hath delivered him from the burden of the flesh.

"Would you honour his memory? Then stand ye fast in the liberty of Christ, and be not entangled with any yoke of bondage; but learn ye by the doctrine of Universal free grace to glorify God by a Christian profession, and a conversation conformable to pure morality.

"Let our minds this day, from the 'valley of the shadow of death,' look forward to the immortal inheritance which we have as the free gift of God in Christ Jesus. Jesus hath triumphed over death. His glorified person is our pledge of Immortality! Then as death comes near us, and snatches away our friends and companions, let us fear him the less. Death is only an enemy to our feelings in flesh and blood. Death itself is ours in the ordained process to glory. We are more than conquerors over death, through him that loved us.

"Perhaps I cannot gratify my audience more, on this occasion, than by giving the following short sketch of our venerable Brother's life.

"Mr. John Murray was born near London, and continued in England till he was about eleven years of age, when he was taken to Ireland by an uncle [by his father], with whom he continued till he was about nineteen years of age; and then returned to England, and resided in London.

"While in Ireland, young in years, he was religiously impressed, among the followers of Mr. John Wesley, and at length spoke in select societies of that people, and then publicly for a time. After his return from Ireland to London, he was in process of time led to hear the celebrated James Relly, against whom he had once (I have heard him say) conceived the most inveterate prejudice, as a heretic of the worst kind. However, his prejudices were so far overcome, that he went to hear the reputed heretic for himself; and hearing, he inferred from the doctrine presented, the sentiment of Universal grace and salvation for all the offspring of God.

"I have heard Mr. Murray say that when he came into this country he had no thought of preaching, but only to bury himself in its hidden recesses. But peculiar events induced him to yield to pressing solicitations. He preached first in New Jersey, and afterwards at New York, Philadelphia, Virginia, New Hampshire, Massachusetts, Rhode Island, Connecticut. In this Town, being invited, he came, and first preached here Nov., 1774. Here he found a few who were in favour of Universal Grace, from reading Mr. Relly's Works, who heard him gladly, and received additional light from his preaching. In 1775 this place became his permanent home; and in 1780 the Meeting House in which we met when I first came here, was built for him, in which he preached till his removal to Boston, in the year 1793.

"That Meeting House has been succeeded by this in which we now assemble, dedicated in 1806; and since then has the Society of Universalists in Portsmouth also built a large new house; and the Society of Salem have done in like manner; and so also has a branch of the Boston Society, associated with others, built a new Meeting House in Charlestown. So that in the space of nine years, four large, elegant Churches have been built and Dedicated to God as Love, as the Saviour of all men, near enough together for the Ministers to make exchanges without much inconvenience.

"Here we may stand still and say, 'What hath God wrought' by means of the work begun by our now deceased brother!

"Against the Doctrine of Universal Grace and Salvation

prejudices at first ran high. Sincere people became alarmed at it as a dangerous heresy. Strange infatuation! that the common Grace of God towards His common offspring should be counted a heresy!

"The opposition and persecution our venerable deceased Brother met with, did not weaken his faith. He grew stronger and stronger. He traveled and preached at different Towns occasionally. Many heard him, and many felt joy and peace in believing that God is Love.

"The confinement of six years by palsy, was no small affliction, especially to him, who delighted in being about among his friends. It was a heavy and sore confinement. But to the calamity he resigned himself, as under the conduct of God, who presides over all things, and so Superintends all things as to manifest His own glory thereby, and to bring forth the ultimate good of his creature, man, therefrom.

"The greatest anxiety he manifested during his state of confinement was an ardent desire to put off this Tabernacle; to be clothed upon with Immortality, that mortality might be swallowed up of life.

"During the triumph of his long infirmity he never manifested any fear or doubt, but a full assurance of the understanding. And when he heard from time to time of the death of some of his old friends, he would exclaim in language like the following: 'O, why am not I released? Why was not I called first?'

"His easy manner of communication in his public ministration, his rich flow of appropriate language in preaching, his shrewd and pertinent remarks, fully to the point in hand, and especially the clear and bright light he threw on the Law and the Prophets, will not be forgotten by his hearers while they live upon the earth.

"His sympathy was as great as any man's. He would literally weep with those that wept, and rejoice with those that rejoiced.

"But he is no longer in the regions of mortality. He finished his course with joy, this day fortnight, at 6 in the morning. He continued stedfast in the faith of Universal Salvation; it was his theme of rejoicing while he retained his senses. Let us all who are journeying after him, glorify God in our bodies and spirits, which are God's.

"Now, my friends, I will turn your attention to the appropriate texts read on this occasion; bidding our venerable and beloved Brother Adieu, till we join him in that world where neither sickness, pains, troubles, nor death, shall be known any more forever."

APPENDIX W.

THE SUNDAY SCHOOL.

The First Universalist Sunday School was, I have no doubt, established in the Lombard street Church, Philadelphia, in 1816; and may have grown out of a system of catechizing children in the church, adopted by Rev. George Richards in 1812. Another school was organized in the same Church in 1834, the first having ceased to exist about 1826.

The next Sunday School was organized in 1817 by Rev. Paul Dean, in the First Universalist Society in Boston, of which he was then pastor. On his ceasing to be pastor, in 1823, the school died.

When the School in Gloucester was started, the New Testament was the text book employed, the scholars committing verses to memory. Moral selections were also read to the school, from the English Reader. Within a year the school began to use "The Child's Scriptural Catechism, by Hosea Ballou." And not long after this, the committing to memory of the Psalms of David, and the Hymns used by the congregation, formed part of the instruction.

The Superintendents of the school, with the dates of their commencing service, have been as follows: Dr. William Ferson, 1820; Miss Judith Millett, 1826; Dr. Ebenezer Dale, 1830; John J. Babson, 1833; Benjamin K. Hough, jr., 1836; Benjamin H. Corliss, 1840; William Babson, 1842; Thomas Baker, 1848; Henry Cummings, 1856; George W. Plumer, 1859; Francis Bennett, jr., Assistant Superintendent and acting Superintendent, 1860; James Davis, 1861 : Edward Dolliver, 1878.

APPENDIX X.

THE SEMI-CENTENNIAL.

The following is the article furnished by Rev. Paul Dean for the *Universalist Magazine:*

MESSRS. EDITORS, — At the request of the Society, and agreeable to previous notice in the public prints, a number of ministering brethren assembled at Gloucester, Mass., on the 3d instant, for the purpose of attending the semi-century commemoration of the first preaching of Universal grace and salvation in that place, fifty years from that day, by the late Rev. John Murray.

"This occasion awakened in many bosoms the most interesting and sacred recollections. The goodness and help of Divine Providence 'in the day of small things:' the faith, patience and perseverance with which some endured trials; and the peace, joy and triumphant hope in which many others had finished their earthly course, passed in review before us in the animated visions of remembrance, and reminded us of our sacred obligations of gratitude and faithfulness to Heaven for the success and prosperity of that holy faith which now causes the pulsations of joy to beat high in so many hearts, in the full assurance of universal happiness, through the grace of our Lord Jesus Christ.

"The public services of the morning were introduced by the reading of the second chapter of St. Paul to the Corinthians, first epistle; and after singing, continued by an introductory address, by Br. Thomas Whittemore, of Cambridgeport, on the importance of the occasion, the propriety of commemorating the joy with which the proclamation of God's universal salvation was at first received by the believing Gloucesterians; the sufferings and persecutions through which they had contended for the faith delivered unto them: and the success which had crowned their perseverance in the doctrine of impartial grace; after which he also offered the introductory prayer.

"A sermon was then delivered by Br. Paul Dean, of Boston, from the 7th chapter of the 1st of Sam. and the 12th verse: 'Hitherto hath the Lord helped us.' In this were noticed the good Providence and favor of God in sending to this country, his servant, the late Rev. John Murray, to preach to its since free, independent and favored inhabitants, 'the grace of God that bringeth salvation to all men;' and in the success which attended his personal labors; in the courage and constancy with which the early believers of this heavenly doctrine met, sustained and overcome the trials of excommunication, calumny and oppression, in the name and for the sake of Christian liberty; in the progress which has attended this cause in that place, and in our Commonwealth and country, notwithstanding the tide of determined opposition which set against it; and in the gift of Br. Thomas Jones as a second gift and messenger of 'good tidings from a far country,' to be the Pastor and guardian of the first Universalist Church gathered in America. The mention of some of the many signs of the final and universal prevalence of this grace, the felicity which will attend its triumph, and the duty of those who are permitted to look for its coming, finished the discourse. The concluding prayer was by Br. Zelotes Fuller, of Charlton, Mass.

"In the afternoon, the first prayer was offered by Br. Barzillia Streeter, of Troy, N. Y., and the discourse given by Br. Sebastian Streeter, of Boston, from the first of Cor. iii : 10, 'According to the grace of God, which is given unto me as a wise master-builder, I have laid the foundation, and another buildeth thereon.' In which it was ably and eloquently shown that Christ Jesus the Lord, as preached by the Apostles, John Murray, and others, is the sure and precious foundation laid in Zion for the salvation of the World. He continued by describing the support which this benignant sentiment has yielded and still yields its sincere followers in the hour of affliction and death; and concluded by ingeniously setting forth and defending the mild and happy influence, which, as it advances, it will exert upon the minds and hearts of men, and upon all the institutions of society. Br. Ezra Leonard, of Cape Ann, made the concluding prayer.

"The evening service of said day was commenced with prayer by Br. Hubbard H. Winchester, of Wilmington, Vt., and continued by an interesting sermon by Br. Hosea Ballou, 2d, of Roxbury; Text, Isaiah lx : 2, 3, 4: 'For behold, the darkness shall cover the earth, and gross darkness the people; but the Lord shall arise upon thee, and his glory shall be seen upon thee. And the Gentiles shall come to thy light, and kings to the brightness of thy rising. Lift up thine eyes round about, and see; all they gather themselves together, they come to thee; thy sons shall come from far, and thy daughters shall be nursed at thy side.' He contrasted the views of religion which prevailed in these parts fifty years ago, with those more rational and enlightened, which are entertained at the present day; and inferred from hence the speedy approach of this blessed day, when divine light and truth shall disperse the darkness, and fill the whole earth with the glory of the Lord, and bring all the sons and daughters of Adam to worship before him in the beauties of perfect holiness. These animating services were interspersed with excellent and appropriate music by the choir, attended by full and solemnly attentive audiences, and closed with a devout prayer by Br. Thomas G. Farnsworth, of Newton, Mass. After which we returned to Col. Pearce's, by whose Christian liberality and attention, in connection with others, we were entertained in a most friendly manner. By ourselves and many others, we feel assured this celebration will be long remembered, and numbered among the happiest occasions of our lives. And we cherish the hope and belief that the semi-century return of this day will be celebrated with religious gratitude and joy until Christ shall have an altar in every place, and at every altar an herald of salvation ministering to his redeemed. By order,

PAUL DEAN."

APPENDIX Y.

TITLES OF THE ORGANIZATION, AND OFFICERS OF THE CHURCH AND SOCIETY.

1779. "Free and Independent Church of Christ in Gloucester."

1785. "Independent Christian Society of Gloucester."

1788. "Christian Independent Society of Gloucester."

1792. By Act of Incorporation: "The Independent Christian Church in Gloucester."

The dates appended to the names of the following Officials designate the time of commencing service; the length of service being indicated by the appointment of successors, except in the case of the Deacons, where death alone has terminated the time of service, although in several instances, age and infirmities have necessitated the appointment of successors while the seniors were living.

CLERKS OF THE SOCIETY: John Stevens Ellery, 1785; Barnett Harkin, 1788; Benjamin K. Hough, 1795; William Saville, 1804; William Babson, 1843; William Babson, jr., 1845; Benjamin F. Somes, 1851; George L. Ford, 1865; John Corliss, 1867; Edward Dolliver, 1875; Albert P. Babson, 1879; Samuel M. Shute, 1884; Charles C. Cressy, 1890.

TREASURERS OF THE SOCIETY: Epes Sargent, 1792; John Somes, 1794; William Pearce, 1812; Benjamin K. Hough, 1813; Benjamin H. Corliss, 1853; Leonard A. Burnham, 1875; Robert R. Fears, 1881; Edward P. Ring, 1887.

CLERKS OF THE CHURCH: Rev. Thomas Jones, 1806; William Babson, 1840 to 1846; after which no records were kept till the appointment of Rev. George W. Skinner, 1863. From March, 1864, there is also a break till the election of Miss Georgiana Parsons, 1869.

TREASURERS OF THE CHURCH: Until 1840, the Deacons. 1840 to 1846, William Babson. 1846 to 1869, the Deacons.

Miss Sarah H. Corliss, 1869; Miss Lucy W. Davis, 1871; Mrs. Maria Dodge Gibson, 1876; Miss Ada E. Davis, 1880; Miss Annie H. Dolliver, 1883; Miss Carrie A. Procter, 1890.

DEACONS OF THE CHURCH: Isaac Elwell, 1808, died 1832; Payne Elwell, 1808, died 1820; Cyrus Stevens, 1820, died 1838; Richard Friend, 1832, died 1849: Samuel Friend, 1838, died 1850; George Friend, 1842, died 1872; James Davis, 1864; Theodore Lane, 1873, died 1885; John W. Brown, 1880; William Tucker, 1889. The following persons have also officiated as Deacons, by temporary appointments: William Pearce, James S. Sayward, Richard G. Stanwood, William Ferson, Benjamin K. Hough.

PARISH COMMITTEES:

1785. Capt. Winthrop Sargent, Col. Joseph Foster, John Somes.

1786, '87, '88. No record.

1789. David Plumer, Epes Sargent, William Pearce.

1790, '91. No record.

1792. Capt. Winthrop Sargent, Col. Joseph Foster, Capt. David Pearce.

1793. John Somes, Epes Sargent, Benjamin Hale.

1794. Isaac Elwell, William Card, David Plumer.

1795. David Plumer, Col. William Pearce, Caleb Norwood, jr.

1796. John S. Ellery, David Plumer, Joseph Allen, Caleb Norwood, jr.

1797. David Plumer, Col. William Pearce, Caleb Norwood, jr., Capt. Isaac Elwell.

1798. David Plumer, Capt. Isaac Elwell, Capt. Jeremiah Foster.

1799. Col. William Pearce, Capt. Joseph Foster, jr., Benjamin K. Hough, Thomas Oakes.

1800. David Plumer, Capt. Isaac Elwell, Joseph Procter, John Gott.

1801. Capt. David Pearce, David Plumer, Capt. Joseph Foster, jr., Capt. James Saville, John Gott.

1802. Maj. Ignatius Sargent, Capt. Isaac Elwell, Capt. David Pearce, Caleb Norwood, jr.

1803. Capt. Isaac Elwell, Col. William Pearce, Joseph Allen, jr., Caleb Norwood, jr.

1804. Benjamin K. Hough, Col. William Pearce, Joseph Allen, jr., Dr. John Manning.

1805. Col. William Pearce, Benj. K. Hough, Capt. I. Elwell, Dr. John Manning.

1806. Capt. Isaac Elwell, Capt. William Pearce, Jacob Hodgkins, Maj. Francis Norwood.

1807. John Mason, Robert Elwell, John Somes, jr.

1808. Capt. David P. Tarr, Capt. Samuel Calder, Eli Stacy, Ebenezer Oaks, Nathaniel Parsons.

1809. Col. William Pearce, Benj. K. Hough, Col. James Tappan.

1810. John Johnston, William Pearce, jr., Israel Trask.

1811. William W. Parrott, David P. Tarr, Addison Plumer.

1812. John Somes, jr., Joseph Procter, Cyrus Stevens.

1813. William Saville, John Somes, jr., Solomon Pool.

1814. Capt. Samuel Calder, John Somes, jr., William Babson, jr.

1815. John Somes, jr., Samuel Elwell, Robert Elwell.

1816, '17, '18, '19. John Somes, jr., William W. Parrott, Israel Trask.

1820. John Somes, William Ferson, William Babson, jr.

1821, '22. John Mason, William Babson, jr., William Pearce, jr.

1823. John Mason, Samuel Pearce, William Babson, jr.

1824. William Babson, jr., William Collins, Samuel Pearce.

1825, '26, '27. William Babson, jr., Samuel Pearce, William Stevens.

1828. Elias Davison, Abraham Sawyer, Samuel Buckley.

1829, '30. Abraham Sawyer, Dr. William Ferson, Thomas Stephenson, Esq.

1831. Abraham Sawyer, William Ferson, Richard Friend.

1832. Abraham Sawyer, Elias Davison, Richard Friend.

1833. John J. Babson, Richard Friend, Richard G. Stanwood.

1834. John J. Babson, Samuel Friend, Frederick G. Low.

1835. Samuel Friend, Epes W. Merchant, Eben H. Redding.

1836. Joseph Stacy, Epes W. Merchant, William Ferson.

1837, '38. William Ferson, Joseph Stacy, Joseph J. Procter.

1839. William Ferson, John Mason, John J. Babson.

1840. William Pearce, jr., Samuel W. Brown, Robert Fears.

1841, '42. Samuel Jones, Benjamin K. Hough, William Ferson.

1843, '44. Benjamin K. Hough, William Ferson, Richard G. Stanwood.

1845. Samuel Friend, Robert Fears, William P. Dolliver.

1846. William P. Dolliver, Samuel Friend, Robert Fears, Charles Fitz, George Friend.

1847. William P. Dolliver, Charles Fitz, Calvin Putnam, Epes W. Merchant, Samuel Jones.

1848. Eben H. Stacy, Gorham Parsons, Samuel Jones.

1849. Eben H. Stacy, George Friend, Richard G. Stanwood, jr.

1850. Benjamin H. Corliss, Edward Babson, Simeon Burnham.

1851. Epes W. Merchant, Edward Babson, James L. Bott.

1852, '53, '54. Charles Fitz, Richard G. Stanwood, jr., William P. Dolliver.

1855. William P. Dolliver, Frederick G. Low, Epes W. Merchant.

1856. Frederick G. Low, George W. Plumer, George L. Ford.

1857. Thomas J. Foster, George L. Ford, Camden C. Davis.

1858, '59. Thomas J. Foster, George L. Ford, George Friend.

1860. Gorham Parsons, Robert Fears, Epes W. Merchant.

1861. George Friend, George W. Plumer, Edward Burnham.

1862, '63. Gorham Parsons, George L. Chesbro, William P. Dolliver.

1864, '65. William P. Dolliver, Robert Fears, Charles Fitz.

1866. William P. Dolliver, Charles Fitz, Charles A. Beckford.

1867. Edward Babson, Charles A. Beckford, Robert R. Fears, William M. Winchester, Robert A. Tibbetts.

1868, '69. Edward Babson, Robert A. Tibbetts, Wm. M. Winchester, Josiah O. Friend, jr., Robert R. Fears.

1870. Josiah O. Friend, jr., Horatio Babson, jr., Thomas J. Knowles, James L. Shute, Robert R. Fears.

1871. Horatio Babson, jr., Robert R. Fears, James L. Shute.

1872, '73, '74. Horatio Babson, John Todd, William T. Merchant.

1875, '76, '77, '78. George Todd, Charles C. Cressy, Benjamin F. Cook.

1879, '80, '81. George Todd, Benjamin H. Corliss, Isaac N. Story.

1882. Benjamin H. Corliss, George Todd, Isaac N. Story, Edward P. Ring, Fitz J. Babson, jr.

1883, '84. Francis Procter, Daniel H. Wallace, Elias P. Burnham, Charles S. Tappan, Fred W. Tibbetts.

1885. Francis Procter, Daniel H. Wallace, Elias P. Burnham, Fred W. Tibbetts, Thomas J. Knowles.

1886, '87, '88, Francis Procter, Daniel H. Wallace, Fitz J. Babson, jr.

1889, '90, '91. Daniel H. Wallace, Fitz J. Babson, jr., David R. Frost.

AUXILIARY SOCIETIES.

"The Ladies' Sunday School Society," was organized in 1852, with Mrs. Francis Chesbro, President; Miss Caroline Mayo, Secretary; Miss Georgiana Parsons, Treasurer. In the nearly forty years of its existence it has raised in various ways and expended for the benefit of the various interests of the parish, over $15,000. Its present officers are: Mrs. Lucy E. Friend, President; Miss Lucy P. Burnham, Secretary; Miss Marietta Davis, Treasurer.

"The Murray Club," organized as a social and literary club, in 1881, has rendered substantial aid to the parish, having paid into its treasury about Nine Hundred Dollars. Its present officers are: Charles A. Mason, President; Miss Blanche F. Sanford, Secretary; Herman Lane, Treasurer.

IMPORTANT SPECIAL COMMITTEES.

1785. To answer a letter received from the Association organized at Oxford, and to revise the Charter of Compact: Col. Joseph Foster, David Plumer, Epes Sargent.

1788. To transact the Ceremonies at the Ordination of Rev. John Murray: Capt. Winthrop Sargent, David Plumer, Barnett Harkin.

1795. To purchase of Capt. Fitz Wm. Sargent the land the Meeting House stands on: Col. William Pearce, David Plumer.

1810. To keep the boys, and all others who disturb the Society when at Public Worship, in order: Jonathan Parsons, jr., the Sexton, John Mason, David Haraden, jr., and John Johnston.

1820. To consult about putting stoves in the Meeting House: Benjamin K. Hough, William W. Parrott, John Johnston.

1824. To arrange for the observance of the Semi-Centennial Anniversary of Rev. John Murray's First Preaching in Gloucester: Col. William Pearce, and the Pastor, with the Parish Committee.

1826. To obtain consent of members of the Society to be

taxed for the purchase of an Organ: William Ferson, Aaron Parsons, Samuel Bulkley.

1826. To lay out the Burial Ground into proper sections: Eli Stacy, John Mason, William Saville.

1837. To wait upon the Rev. Mr. Jones, and ascertain his views on the settlement of a Colleague: Benjamin K. Hough, Richard Friend, Capt. William Pearce, jr.

1838. To obtain consent of Pew Owners to contemplated alterations in Pulpit and pews: Samuel Friend, John P. Ober.

1838. To apprize the Pews preparatory to alterations: Moses H. Shaw, William Babson, Benjamin K. Hough, John J. Babson, Thomas J. Foster, Joseph Shepherd.

1838. To superintend the alterations of Pulpit and Pews: Richard G. Stanwood, jr., Frederick G. Low, John J. Babson.

1839. To make alterations of the Gallery Pews: John Mason, Benjamin K. Hough, jr., Richard Friend, jr.

1841. To arrange with Rev. Mr. Jones for his release from Pastoral duty: Benjamin K. Hough, William Collins, Charles Fitz.

1844. To seek an adjustment with the Independent Universalist Society: Robert Fears, Epes W. Merchant, Gorham Parsons, William P. Dolliver, Samuel Friend.

1844. To circulate a Bond for extinguishing the debt of the Society: Benjamin K. Hough, George Friend, Richard G. Stanwood.

1861. To assist the Parish Committee in making alterations in Galleries and Vestibule: Eben H. Stacy, Edward Babson.

1868. To carry into effect the vote of the Society in respect to raising the Church, furnishing a Vestry under it, remodelling the pews, putting the Organ and Singers behind the pulpit, etc.: William P. Dolliver, Robert Fears, Wm. M. Winchester, Josiah O. Friend, jr., Fitz J. Babson, James L. Shute.

1870. To act in conjunction with the Parish Committee in making suitable arrangements for the reception of the Centenary Convention: Benjamin H. Corliss, Wm. P. Dolliver, James Davis, David W. Low, John Todd. Charles W. Dennison, Leonard A. Burnham, Wm. M. Winchester, Eli F. Stacy, George Friend, jr., Benj. F. Cook.

1874. To arrange for the Celebration of the Centennial Anniversary of Rev. John Murray's First Sermon in Gloucester: the Parish Committee and the Pastor.

ORGANISTS.

Ann Ross, 1826; Charles G. Millett, 1829; Miss Clarissa Hayes, 1830; Charles G. Millett, 1831; Samuel F. Bulkley, 1833; Miss Clarissa Hayes, 1837; Miss Serena P. Dale, 1843; Edwin Bruce, 1846; Franklin K. Woodbury, 1847; Miss Caroline E. Hays, 1850; Miss Georgiana Parsons, 1851; George B. Blake, 1856; Miss Clara M. Loring, 1858; Miss Carrie M. Presson, 1864; Miss R. L. Tuckerman, 1880; Everett Steele, 1882; Miss Grace Caswell, 1884; George B. Stevens, 1888.

SEXTONS.

John Burnham, 1788; Benjamin Lufkin, 1790; Gideon Challis, 1793; David Day, 1794: James S. Sayward, 1806; Jonathan Parsons, 1808; Benjamin Newman, 1814; Jonathan Parsons, 4th, 1815; William Tucker, 1819; John and Denmark Procter, 1822; William Long, 1829; James S. Sayward, 1835; Henry Staten, 1839; Peter J. Hazel, 1850; John Davis, 1858; Daniel Plumer, 1861; Charles H. Brown, 1879; William Tucker, 1885; Isaac P. Morse, 1888.

APPENDIX Z.

ADDENDA.

In the immediately preceding pages, the list of Officials in the Parish, Church and Sunday School has been brought down to the close of the year 1891, and it has been deemed advisable to complete, in brief words, the history of the Parish to this latter date. As in the Historical Discourse, this will be done here without the recital of details, but merely in the way of general statement in regard to the pastors and the status of the vital interests of the church at the time of putting these pages to press.

The pastorate of Mr. Eddy closed in September, 1877.[75] In January, 1879, Rev. Costello Weston, then of Bath, Me., was called. He served the parish acceptably until his resignation, taking effect May 1, 1883. During his pastorate, a heavy debt, which had long been a burden to the parish, was reduced by the payment of $7,700 thereon. The one hundredth anniversary of the Dedication of the first House of Worship occurred during Mr. Weston's pastorate, and was appropriately observed, Sunday, December 26, 1880.[76]

In August, 1883, Rev. William H. Rider, then pastor of the Universalist Church in Cincinnati, Ohio, was invited to be pastor. Accepting the invitation, Mr. Rider was installed October 3d, of that year. The sermon was by E. C. Bolles, D. D., of Salem. Hymns for the occasion were written by Deacon James Davis and Miss Georgie Parsons, Clerk of the Church.[77]

---

[75] His subsequent settlements have been in Akron, Ohio; Melrose, Mass; Providence and Georgiaville, R. I.

[76] After leaving Gloucester, Mr. Weston resided on his farm in Mt. Vernon, Me., supplying vacant pulpits as opportunity offered, till the Spring of 1888, when he became the Missionary Agent of the West Fund Trustees, at Halifax, N. S. In September, 1890, he became pastor of the parish at Charlton, Mass.

[77] Other portions of the service were: Introductory Sentences and Invocation,

During Mr. Rider's pastorate, which continues to the present, prosperity has attended the parish in all its interests, and the church property has been greatly improved and beautified by alterations securing increased accommodations in the vestry, repairs of the spire, and frescoing the ceiling and walls of the auditorium, involving an expenditure of about $4,200. The parish is now wholly free from debt. The church numbers seventy-four members, and the Sunday School four hundred and fifty members.

In 1876, "The Society of the Lanesville Universalist Parish," representing thirty-five families, was organized. A church edifice was erected in 1878, costing $5,000. Its first pastor was Rev. B. G. Russell. Subsequently Rev. George Procter had charge; and since 1889, Rev. George W. Penniman, also in charge at Annisquam, has been the pastor.

In 1884, a parish representing thirty-four families was organized at East Gloucester; also a Sunday School of one hundred and twenty-four members. Two years later, a church of fifteen members was organized, and a church edifice costing $7,000 was erected. Heretofore its pulpit has mainly been supplied by the pastor of the old parish and by non-resident preachers; but in December, 1891, Rev. E. Fitzgerald became resident pastor.

At the present time there are five Universalist parishes in the territory covered by the city of Gloucester, all having church edifices and settled pastors. Including Rockport and Pigeon Cove, which were originally in the town of Gloucester, there are now seven Universalist parishes, all owning church edifices and having settled pastors, in the territory from which John Murray gathered his congregation in 1774. In a population of less than thirty thousand, this fact is without a parallel in the history of the Universalist Church.

Rev. W. S. Preble, of Beverly; Scripture Reading, Rev. J. S. Thompson (Unitarian), of Gloucester; Prayer of Installation, Prest. E. H. Capen, D. D., of Tufts College; Right Hand of Fellowship, Rev. J. Coleman Adams, of Lynn; Address to the Society, R. Eddy, D. D., of Melrose; Welcome Address, Benj. H. Corliss, Esq.

INDEX.

Abel, Rev. Townsend P., 62
Act of Incorporation, 31, 198
Adams, Rev. John Coleman, 233
—Rev. John G., 62
—& Chapin's Hymn Book, 49
Addenda, 232
Agreement to be taxed for Support of Mr. Murray, 194
Allen, Jacob, 110
—John, 187, 195, 198
—Joseph, 226
—Joseph, jr., 198, 226, 227
—Winthrop, 130, 156, 194, 198
Andrews, William Tarr, 195
Annisquam Parish, 50, 51, 57, 233
"Answer to An Appeal," 26, 157
"Anti-Universalist, The," 57
"Appeal, An," 26, 133
Appendix, 105-233
Arnold, Rev. A. C. L., 39
"Articles of Association," 19, 154
—of Faith, 209, 215
Association at Oxford, 27
Atkinson, Rev. Joseph P., 56, 98
Austin, Rev. John M., 59
Auxilliary Societies, 229

Babbitt, Thomas, 187, 195

Babson, Albert P., 225
—Anne, 19, 111
—David, 202
—Edward, 228, 230
—Fitz J., 230
—Fitz J., jr., 228, 229
—Horatio, jr., 228
—James, 130, 188
—John, 106
—John J., 15, 132, 221, 227, 230
—Joseph, 203
—Rebekah, 156
—Solomon, 130, 156, 195, 198
—William, jr., 54, 225, 227, 230
—William, [son of William, jr.] 221, 225
Baker, Joseph, 188, 198, 202
—Thomas, 221
Ball, Hannah, 156, 211
—Isaac, 130, 156
Ballou, Rev. Hosea, 34, 35, 59, 62, 121, 189, 221
—Rev. Hosea, 2d., 49, 54, 59, 224
Barns, Lucy, 123
—Rev. Thomas, 34, 35, 121
Bartlett, Rev. Joseph A., 52
Baty, William, 198
Beckford, Charles A., 228
Beecher, Lyman, D. D., 79
Belding, Rev. Henry, 56
Bell, Long Service of, 47
Bennett, Francis, jr., 221

Bennett, Isaac, 130, 156
—Moses, 156
—Nathaniel, 187
Benton, Rev. F. A., 52
Bill of Rights, 22, 152
Blake, George B., 231
—James, 187, 195
Bolles, E. C., D. D., 232
Boston Society requests services of Mr. Murray, 195
—Society, Mr. Murray settled over, 33
—Sunday-school, 221
Bott, James L., 228
Boys, provision for keeping them in order in church, 46
Bradbury, Hon. Theophilus, 24
Brimblecome, Rev. Samuel, 59
Broadside published by Mr. Murray, 26, 177
Brooks, Rev. E. G., 62
Broom, James, 130
Brown, Abraham, 187
—Charles H., 231
—Ephraim, 195
—John W., 226
—Jonathan, 187, 195
—Jonathan, 3d, 202
—Samuel W., 227
—Stephen, 195, 202
Bruce, Edwin, 231
Buckley, Samuel, 227
—Samuel F., 231
Bulkley, Samuel, 230
Burial Ground, 40
Burnham, Edward, 228
—Elias P., 228

Burnham, John, 231
—Leonard A., 225, 230
—Lucy P., 229
—Simeon, 228

Calder, Samuel, 202, 227
Candles used for lighting the Meeting House, 48
Capen, Rev. Elmer H., 68, 69, 97, 233
Card, William, 106, 130, 188, 195, 198, 226
Caswell, Grace, 231
Centennial Celebration in 1870, 70, 230
—Celebration in 1874, 230
—Celebration in 1880, 232
Challis, Gideon, 188, 195, 231
Chambré, Rev. A. St. John, 68, 69
Chandeliers, 48
Chandler, Rev. Samuel, 12, 159, 178
Chapin, Rev. E. H., 62
—Rev. J. H. 69
Charter of Compact, 27, 185
Chesbro, Mrs. Francis 229
—George L., 228
Children, Mr. Jones' Sermons to, 53
Church Organization, 49, 208-215, 225, 233
Clark, Rev. Benjamin H., 52
—Rev. C. C., 79
Clerks of the Society, 225
—of the Church, 225
Cleveland, Rev. John, 16
Clock, when placed in the Church, 47
Close, John, 202

Coas, William, 110
Coffin, Rev. E. W., 52
—Rev. Michael, 35, 126
—Peter, 110
Collins, Daniel, 203
—Eben H., 203
—William, 54, 227, 230
Columbia Centinal's account of Dedication of New Meeting House, 45
Committee of Safety, 17
Convention, General, session of in 1870, 70
Cook, Benjamin F., 228, 230
—Jemima, 19, 111, 156
Corliss, Benjamin H., 99, 221, 225, 228, 230, 233
—John, 204, 225
—Sarah H., 226
Creighton, George, 106, 156
Cressy, Charles C., 225, 228
Crossman, Edward, 156
Crosswell, Rev. Andrew, 12
Cummings, Henry, 221
Cushing, Zenas, 203

Dale, Dr. Eben, 221
—Serena P., 231
Dalton, Gloster, 188
Dana, Hon. Francis, 24, 26
Davis, Ada E., 226
—Camden C., 228
—Elias, 203
—James, vi, 221, 226, 230, 232
—John, 106
—John, 231
—Lucy W., 226
—Marietta, 229
Davison, Elias, 227

Day, David, 211, 231
—Lucy, 211
Deacons of the Church, 50, 212
Dean, Rev. Paul, 54, 55, 221, 222
Dedication of Children, 49, 205
—of First Meeting House, 20
—of Second Meeting House, 44, 69
Dennis, John, 202
Dennison, Charles W., 230
Dexter, William, 202
Divine Revelation, Society in Defence of, 72
Dodge, Benjamin, 203
—Jonathan, 202
Dolliver, Abigail, 156, 211
—Annie H., 226
—Edward, 221, 225
—Peter, 130, 188
—William, 130, 156, 194, 202, 203, 208
—William P., 228, 230
Doyle, William, 187
Duley, Sarah G., viii

East Gloucester Parish, 233
Eddy, Rev. Richard, 70, 232, 233
Ellery, Esther, 156
—John Stevens, 106, 130, 156, 188, 194, 198, 225, 226
—Nathaniel, 106
—William, 110
Elwell, Isaac, 20, 187, 194, 198, 202, 203, 208, 211, 212, 226, 227
—Isaac, jr., 130, 202

Elwell, Payne, 50, 208, 212, 226
—Robert, 227
—Samuel, 227
—Tammy, 211
Everden, Joseph, 156, 187, 195, 202
Everett, Rev. L. S., 62
Evidences of Christianity, Lectures on, 72
Expenses of Exchanges paid by the Parish, 197

Farnsworth, Rev. Thomas G., 54, 80, 224
Fears, Robert, 227, 228, 230
—Robert R., 225, 228
Ferson, Dr. William, 53, 203, 221, 226, 227, 229
First Parish, 13, 15, 21, 23, 24, 130
—Parish Church, 19, 111, 116
Fitz, Charles, 228, 230
—Moses, 198
Fitz Gerald, Rev. E., 233
Flagg, Rev. Joshua, 35, 128
Folsom, Sarah, 211
Fobes, Rev. Perez, 50
Forbes, Rev. Eli, 15, 105, 111
Ford, George L., 225, 228
Foster, Jeremiah, 187, 195, 226
—Rev. John, 35, 126
—Joseph, 21, 40, 131, 156, 188, 194, 198, 202, 203, 226, 229
—Joseph, jr., 188, 194, 226
—Lydia, 156
—Nathaniel, 130
—Thomas, 187, 194, 198
—Thomas J., 228, 230
Friend, George, 226, 228, 230

Friend, George, jr., 230
—Joseph, 61
—Josiah O., jr., 228, 230
—Mrs. Lucy E., 229
—Richard, 58, 226, 227, 230
—Richard, jr., 61, 230
—Samuel, 48, 226, 227, 228, 230
Frost, David R., 229
Fuller, Rev. Daniel, 55
—Rev. Zelotes, 54, 223

Gaffney, Michael, 187, 202
Galaca, Rev. Charles, 56
Galleries, Provisions for keeping boys and girls still in, 46, 229
Gammage, Joshua, 187
Gardner, Rev. Calvin, 55
—Coas, 188, 195
Gates, Lemuel, 198
Gee, William, 188, 195, 198
Gibson, Maria Dodge, 226
Giddings, Daniel, 130
—Mr. [Quaker], 132
"Gleaner, The," 190
Gleason, Benjamin, 36, 128
Gloucester, 10, 11, 14, 18
—Wealth of Universalists in, in 1793, 33
Gott, Ebenezer, 187, 198
—John, 187, 198, 226
Greene, Gen. Nathaniel, 18
Griswold, Right Rev. Bp. A. V., 72
Gunnison, Rev. N., 52

Hale, Benjamin, 188, 195, 198, 226
—John, 110

INDEX.

Hales, Samuel, 21
—William, 188, 195
Hall, Aaron, 198
Haraden, David, 202, 211
—David, jr., 202, 229
—Hannah, 211
Harkin, Barnett, 29, 188, 195, 198, 225, 229
—Hannah, 211
Harriman, Rev. John, 52
Harris, James, 187
Haskell, Elizabeth, 156
—Henry C. L., vii
—Deacon Hubbard, 110
—Deacon Nathaniel, 110
—Philemon, 21, 106, 130, 156, 188, 194
Hays, Caroline E., 231
Hayes, Clarissa, 231
Hazel, Peter J., 231
Henderson, Joseph, 203
Herrick, Joseph, 130, 194, 198
—Josiah, 203
Historical Discourse, 9-78
Hodgkins, Jacob, 202, 227
Hooper, Rev. William, 52, 56
Hough, Ann, 211
—Benjamin K., 53, 58, 99, 191, 195, 198, 202, 203, 215, 225, 226, 227, 229, 230
—Benjamin K., jr., 221
—Ebenezer, 136, 195
—Mary, 136
Hubbard, John R., 203
Hutchins, William, 195
Hymn Books used by the Society, 21, 49, 204

Important Special Committees, 229

Independent Church of Christ, Articles of Association, 154
—Christian Church, Act of Incorporation, 198
—Christian Church [Communicants] 49, 208-215
—Universalist Society, 60, 61
Ingersol, Hannah, 211
—Rebekah, 136
Instrumental Music, First Use of in New Meeting House, 48
Ireland, Thomas, 48

Johnston, John, 202, 227, 229
Jones, Rev. Thomas, 36, 37, 38, 42, 44, 49, 50, 52, 53, 56, 58, 59, 61, 62, 64, 71, 74, 196, 197, 200, 203, 208-215, 225
—Samuel, 227, 228
—Sophia, 48, 61, 211
Jordan, James, 106, 130
—Jerusha, 156

Killam, Rev. Robert L., 56
King, Hon. Rufus, 24
—Rev. Thomas F., 59
Kingman, William, 203
Knight, Job, 187
Knowles, Thomas J., 228, 229

Ladies Sunday School Society, 229
Lane, Herman, 229
—Isaac, 130
—Samuel, 188, 195
—Susanna, 156
—Theodore, 226

Lane, Theophilus, 130
Lanesville Parish, 233
Lathe, Rev. Zephaniah, 34, 35, 124
Leach, Rev. George C., 52
Lee, Downing, 187
Leonard, Rev. Charles H., 69
—Rev. Ezra, 50, 51, 54, 56, 223
—Rev. Henry C., 56, 58, 59
Liberal Institute, 59
Liberty Hall, 56
Lincoln, Ebed, 203
Long, William, 231
Loring, Clara M., 231
Low, David W., 230
—Elizabeth, 211
—Francis, 187, 194, 198
—Frederick G., 227, 228, 230
—John, 110, 202
—John, 3d, 187, 194, 198
—Jonathan, 187, 195, 198, 202, 203
Lufkin, Aaron, 130, 156, 187, 195
—Benjamin, 156, 187, 195, 198, 231
—Joseph, 156, 187
—Joseph, jr., 195
—Samuel, 195
—Sarah, 156
—Zebulon, 130

Mace, Rev. Fayette, 39
Mackay, Andrew, 202
Manning, Dr. John, 227
Mansfield, Rev. Isaac, 34, 124
—James, 202
Marchant, Daniel, jr., 198
Marshall, Benjamin, 198

Marshall, Samuel, 188
Mason, Charles A., 229
—John, 202, 227, 229, 230
—Thomas, 187, 195
—Triphene, 211
Mayo, Rev. Amory D., 56, 63, 64, 65, 66, 88
—Miss Caroline, 229
—Mrs. S. C. E., 56, 64
McKean, John, 106
Mellen, Rev. W. R. G., 66, 67, 95
Mellings, Susanna, 156
Meeting House built in 1780, 20, 35, 42
—House built in 1805-6, 39, 40, 42, 44, 45, 48, 59, 69
Merchant, Epes W., 227, 228
—William T., 228
Millen, James, 130
Millett, Charles G., 231
—James, 111
—Judith, 221
Miner, A. A., D. D., 68
Ministerial Helpers of the Society, 20, 118
Minot, Christopher, 195
Missionary Society Agent attacks Universalism, 57, 58
Mitchell, Rev. James Ure, 101
Moore, Joseph, 188, 202, 211
—Hannah, 211
—Thomas, 195
Morgan, Samuel, 187, 195
—William, 106
Morhead, Samuel, 188, 195
Morse, Humphrey, 188, 195
—Isaac P., 231
—Lydia, 211

INDEX.

Murphy, William, 21, 187, 194, 198
Murray Club, 229
—Institute, 59
—Rev. B. B., 39
—Rev. John, 10-19, 23, 24, 26, 28, 29, 30-37, 44, 49, 53, 107, 156, 177, 191, 200, 205, 215
—Mrs. Judith, 29, 156, 189
—Rev. Noah, 36, 128

Newell, Rev. Maxcy B., 52, 62
Newman, Benjamin, 231
Norwood, Rev. Abraham, 51
—Caleb, 187, 195, 198, 211
—Mrs. Caleb, 211
—Caleb, jr., 187, 195, 226
—Francis, 187, 198, 227
—John, 187, 195, 198
—Stephen, 187, 195

Oakes, Ebenezer, 227
—Thomas, 195, 226
Ober, John P., 230
Odell, James, 106
Officers of the Society and Church, 225
Ollive, Ann, 156
Ordination and Reordination of Mr. Murray, 28, 29
Organs used by the Society, 21, 35, 48
Organists, 231
Oxford Association, 27

Page, John, 196
Paige, Rev. Lucius R., 39
Paine, Rev. Ebenezer, 35, 127

Palfrey, Nabby, 156
Parish Committees, 226-229
Park, Nathan, 203, 227
Parker, Rev. Noah, 20, 120
Parrott, William W., 227, 229
Parsons, Aaron, 230
—Ebenezer, 19, 106, 130
—Georgiana, 225, 229, 231, 232
—Gorham, 228, 230
—Jacob, 110
—Jemima, 19, 111, 156
—Jonathan, jr., 229
—Jonathan, 4th, 231
—Lydia, 156
—Nathaniel, 227
—Phebe, 112
—Philemon, 106
—Rebecca, 19, 156
—Theophilus, Esq., 24
Partridge, Rev. Emmons, 52
Patrick, James, 202
Pearce, Clara Sargent, 49
—David, 19, 21, 23, 31, 106, 111, 130, 131, 156, 188, 198, 208, 211, 226
—Elizabeth, 211
—Samuel, 54, 227
—Thomazine, 211
—William, 21, 23, 39, 40, 41, 42, 53, 156, 187, 195, 198, 202, 203, 204, 208, 211, 212, 224, 225, 226, 227, 229
—William, jr., 49, 58, 202, 203, 227, 230
Penniman, Rev. George W., 233
Pew, Richard, 188
—William, 195
Pew-seats, Noise made by, 46

242   INDEX.

Phelps, Henry, 198
Philadelphia Convention in 1790, 31
— First Sunday-school organized in, 221
— Church makes a liberal offer to Mr. Murray, 34
Plumb, Rev. David H., 61
Plumer, Addison, 227
— Daniel, 231
— David, 20, 29, 130, 156, 188, 195, 198, 226, 229
— Eben, 202
— Elizabeth, 156
— George W., 221, 228
— Joshua, 131
— Mary, 202
— Samuel, 110
Pool, Caleb, 187, 195, 198
— David, 187, 195
— Ebenezer, 187, 195, 198
— Francis, 187, 195
— John, 188
— Nathan, 187, 198
— Solomon, 227
Porter, Rev. Charles S., 79
— James, 110
Portsmouth, N. H., Society in, solicits services of Rev. Mr. Jones, 196
Powers, Rev. J. F., 68
Preble, Rev. W. S., 233
Prentiss, James, 156
— James [of Boston], 196
— [or Prentice], Lydia, 19, 111, 156, 211
Presson, Carrie M., 231
— William, jr., 203
Proctor, Carrie A., 226
— Daniel E., 198, 202

Proctor, Elizabeth, 211
— Denmark, 48, 231
— Francis, 228
— Rev. George, 233
— John, 48, 231
— Joseph, 195, 198, 202, 226, 227
— Joseph J., 227
Putnam, Calvin, 228

Record, Rev. Lewis L., 52
Redding, Eben H., 227
Relly, Rev. James, 12
— Rev. Messrs. James and John, Hymn Book of, 21 129
Rhode Island Brigade, Rev. John Murray Chaplain of, 14
Richards, Rev. George, 35, 37, 126, 196, 221
Rider, Rev. William H., 232
Ring, Edward P., 225, 228
Roberts, Ephraim, 187
Rockport, See Sandy Bay.
Rogers, Charles, 203
— Daniel, jr., 202, 203
— John, 203
— William, 202, 203
Root, Rev. Isaac, 36, 128
Ross, Ann, 231
Row, Abraham, 110, 187
Russ, Rev. Benjamin K., 68
Russell, Rev. B. G., 233
Rust, Sarah, 211

Salary to Mr. Murray, 30
Sanders, Anna, 156
— Bradbury, 21, 106, 130, 156
— Nancy, 130

INDEX.

Sandy Bay, Universalists at, 38, 39
Sanford, Blanche F., 229
Sanger, Rev. George J., 61
Sargent, Aaron, 198
—Catharine, 19, 111, 156
—Daniel, 130
—David, 187, 195, 198
—Epes, 19, 21, 23, 26, 106, 111, 130, 188, 194, 198, 225, 226, 229
—Fitz William, 202
—Ignatius, 226
—John Osborne, 194
—Judith. See Murray, Mrs. Judith
—Mary, 156
—Nathaniel, 187, 194
—William, 106, 130, 229
—Winthrop, 12, 13, 19, 20, 23, 29, 31, 32, 106, 110, 111, 130, 131, 156, 188, 194, 198, 226, 229
—Winthrop, jr., 130
Saunders, James, 188, 195
—Joseph, 188, 195
—Nancy, 19, 111, 130
Saville, James, 226
—Jesse, 188
—William, 49, 202, 204, 225, 227, 230
Sawyer, Abraham, 21, 106, 130, 156, 188, 195, 198, 208, 211, 227
—Mrs. Abraham, 211
—Abraham, Jr., 21, 187, 195, 198, 202
—James, 198
—James, 3d, 188, 195
Sayward, Henry, 202

Sayward, James S., 202, 226, 231
—Samuel, 21, 106, 130, 156, 187
—Susa, 136
School Street Choir, Boston, Concert by, 48
Second Parish, 55
Semi-Centennial Anniversary, 53-55, 222
Sewall, Hon. David, 24
Sextons, 231
Shaw, Moses H., 230
Shepherd, Joseph, 230
Shute, James L., 228, 230
—Samuel M., 225
Skinner, Rev. George W., 67, 68, 225
—Rev. Otis A., 59, 62
Smith, Rev. Daniel D., 58, 59, 60, 215
—Rev. Gibson, 39
—Jacob, 42, 202, 203
—John, 110
—Rebecca, 19, 111, 156
—Rev. Matthew Hale, 58
Snelling, Josiah, 196
Somes, Benjamin F., 225
—John, 21, 39, 41, 130, 131, 156, 188, 194, 198, 202, 208, 225, 226, 227
—John, jr., 202, 227
—John, 3d, 202
Soule, Rev. Henry B., 63
Sparling, Thomas, 156
Spear, Rev. Charles, 39, 59
—Rev. John M., 56
Stacy, Benjamin, 46
—Eben H., 228, 230
—Eli, 202, 203, 227, 230

244 INDEX.

Stacy, Eli F., 230
—John, 202
—Joseph, 227
Stanwood, Richard G., 226, 227, 228, 230
—Richard G., jr., 228, 230
—Susannah, 211
Staten, Henry, 231
Steele, Everett, 231
—James, 188
—Mary, 156
—Rev. Joel, 79
Stephenson, Thomas, 227
Stevens, Cyrus, 202, 226, 227
—George B., 231
—John, 110, 130
—John, jr., 106, 156, 188, 189
—Mrs. Judith. See Murray, Mrs. Judith
—William, 227
—Zach., 203
Stickney, Rev. William A., 56
Stiles, Ezra, D. D., 16, 162, 181
Stoddet, Jonathan, 196
Story, Isaac N., 228
Stoves, First use of in the Meeting House, 47
Streeter, Rev. Adams, 20, 120
—Rev. Barzillia, 54, 223
—Rev. Sebastian, 54, 223
Strickland, Rev. Geo. G., 56
Sullivan, Hon. James, 24
Sumner, Hon. Increase, 24
Sunday School, 53, 221, 233

Tappan, Charles S., 228
—James, 202, 227
Tarbox, Benjamin, 195, 198

Tarbox, Sally, 202
Tarr, Benjamin, jr., 187, 195
—Benjamin, 4th, 203
—David P., 202, 227
—Robert, 203
Thayer, Rev. Frederic F., 62 63, 82
—Rev. Thomas B., 62
Theodosia, English barque, Wreck of, 42
Thompson, Rev. J. S., 233
Third Parish, 50
Tibbetts, Fred W., 228
—Robert A., 228
Titles of the Organization, 225
Thurston, Daniel, 110
Todd, George, 228
—John, 228, 230
Townsend, Shippie, 20, 119, 196
Tracy, John, 26
Trask, Abigail, 156, 211
—Isaac, 187
—Israel, 40, 156, 187, 202, 227
—Jonathan, 130, 156, 188, 195
Treasurers of the Society, 225
—of the Church, 225
Trees in Church Yard, 41
Trew, Daniel, 195
Trull, Rev. Elbridge, 52
Tucker, Hannah, 19, 111, 156, 211
—John, 42, 203
—William, 226, 231
Tuckerman, R. L., 231
Tudor, William, Esq., 24
Tuller, Rev. J. H., 52

Turner, Rev. Edward, 35, 36, 127
Tyler, Rev. John, 20, 118
Tyrian Lodge, F. A. M., 42, 203

Universalists of Gloucester, Their Secret, 132
Universalist Societies in Gloucester, 50, 55, 60, 233
Usher, Rev. James M., 56

Vacations provided for by the Parish, 197
Vestry, Old, Original Size and Uses, 47
—New, in Murray Institute, 59
—Made by Raising the Meeting House, 69

Wallace, Daniel H., 228, 229
War of 1812, Effects of, on the Society, 52
Warner, Nath'l, 203
Watson, Robert, 195

Webber, Benjamin, 106
—Mrs. Harriett, 36
Webster, Joshua, 188
West Parish, 55, 56
Weston, Rev. Costello, 232
—Robert, 156
Whipple, Job, 188
Whittemore, Samuel, 110
—Rev. Thomas, 54, 222
Wier, H., 188
Williams, Abraham, 202
Willis, Rev. John H., 52, 68
Wilson, Jesse, 203
Winchester, Rev. Elhanan, 20, 120
—Rev. Hubbard H., 54, 223
—Rev. Moses, 20, 121
—William M., 228, 230
Wonson, Samuel, 198
—Samuel, jr., 198
Woodberry, Joshua, 203
Woodbury, Franklin K., 231
Wright, Rev. Matthew, 20, 34, 118
Worth, Ignatius, senior, 106

www.ingramcontent.com/pod-product-compliance
Lightning Source LLC
Chambersburg PA
CBHW032004230426
43672CB00010B/2249